T0068315

"Brilliant . . . a book that at times burns slow and hot with outrage and at other times proceeds at the ecstatic pace of a thriller."

—*The New York Times Book Review*

"Only a very good writer could turn a story about chickens, hogs and cattle into a thriller, and Leonard is that. He brings his characters to life. . . . The book is a scary portrait of capitalism run amok."

—Bethany McLean, *The Washington Post*

"Gripping . . . *The Meat Racket* is a riveting book, and the picture Mr. Leonard paints is a disturbing one."

—*The Wall Street Journal*

"Leonard's book argues that a handful of companies, led by Tyson, control our meat industry in ways that raise concerns about the impact on animals and humans alike, while tearing at the fabric of rural America."

—Nicholas Kristof, *The New York Times*

"One of the best books of investigative reporting that I've seen in quite a while . . . if you think muckraking is dead or even on its last legs, *The Meat Racket* is proof positive that it's very much alive. The big question is whether or not there are any reformers and regulators left who have the will and the strength to pick up the ball and run with it."

—*Strategy + Business*

"A fascinating look at what has happened in the past decades to the meat business as huge companies essentially staged a takeover while no one, except struggling farmers, paid mind."

—*New York Daily News*

"An engrossing report on the industrialized American meat business . . . a richly detailed examination of factory farming, which has reshaped small-town life for the worse. . . . An authoritative look at a ruthlessly efficient system."

—*Kirkus Reviews* (starred review)

"A minor miracle of reporting. Tyson isn't the sort of company that likes to show reporters around its operations. . . . Leonard managed to penetrate that secrecy, and has painted an intimate picture of the company and the people who made it."

—Grist

"In his eye-opener to the inner workings of the corporations that control and manipulate the nation's meat supply, journalist Leonard reveals how these vertically integrated behemoths operate to the detriment of both farmers, who do the hard and risky work of raising animals, and consumers, who have actually fewer true choices when shopping in the grocery store or ordering at the local fast-food franchise."

—Booklist

"Cruelty, greed, and monopoly power—that is what Christopher Leonard has found at the heart of America's meat packing industry. This book offers a devastating portrait of an industry's irresponsible behavior."

—Eric Schlosser, author of Fast Food Nation

"Leonard's primary concern is the grim and gripping story of how American meat went industrial. But he also spins a nuanced tale of how the family farm was America's first small business—and what we've lost by letting it go. A fascinating read."

—Tracie McMillan, author of The American Way of Eating

"A meticulous exposé of the meat industry . . . also telling a broader story about American business, consumerism, and—most of all—greed. . . . What makes *The Meat Racket* stand out is Leonard's superb storytelling and his clear passion for the topic. . . . He is a man on a mission—and that is clearly the best kind of reporter to write a book like this."

—Jessica Valenti, Bookforum

The MEAT RACKET

The Secret Takeover of
America's Food Business

CHRISTOPHER LEONARD

Simon & Schuster Paperbacks

NEW YORK · LONDON · TORONTO · SYDNEY · NEW DELHI

Simon & Schuster Paperbacks
A Division of Simon & Schuster, Inc.
1230 Avenue of the Americas
New York, NY 10020

Copyright © 2014 by Christopher Leonard

All rights reserved, including the right to reproduce this book
or portions thereof in any form whatsoever. For information address
Simon & Schuster Paperbacks Subsidiary Rights Department,
1230 Avenue of the Americas, New York, NY 10020.

First Simon & Schuster trade paperback edition February 2015

SIMON & SCHUSTER PAPERBACKS and colophon
are registered trademarks of Simon & Schuster, Inc.

For information about special discounts for bulk purchases, please contact
Simon & Schuster Special Sales at 1-866-506-1949
or business@simonandschuster.com.

The Simon & Schuster Speakers Bureau can bring authors to your
live event. For more information or to book an event, contact the
Simon & Schuster Speakers Bureau at 1-866-248-3049
or visit our website at www.simonspeakers.com.

Interior design by Paul Dippolito

Manufactured in the United States of America

7   9   10   8   6

The Library of Congress has cataloged the hardcover edition as follows:
Leonard, Christopher.
The meat racket : the secret takeover of America's food
business / Christopher Leonard.—1st ed.
p.   cm.
Includes bibliographical references.
Meat industry and trade—United States.   2. Tyson (Firm)
3. Investigative reporting.   I. Title.
HD9415.L46 2014
338.7'636500973—dc23
2013040588

ISBN 978-1-4516-4581-1
ISBN 978-1-4516-4583-5 (pbk)
ISBN 978-1-4516-4584-2 (ebook)

This book is for my father, George Edward Leonard,
the finest man whom I have ever known. As they used to say
back in the day, Dad: Come now, let us argue it out.

CONTENTS

AUTHOR'S NOTE

Only quotations that can be confirmed through the author's own notes and observations, or through direct transcripts of an event, are contained within quotation marks. Quotations and dialogue that are re-created from the memory of one or more sources are set aside by a hyphen rather than quotation marks. One name has been changed to protect a source: "Perry Edwards" is a pseudonym for a source who requested to remain anonymous for fear of retaliation.

"*Agriculture is our wisest pursuit, because it will in the end contribute most to real wealth, good morals and happiness.*"

THOMAS JEFFERSON, 1787

"*Just keep it simple. Kill the chickens, sell 'em, and make some money.*"

DON TYSON, 2009

"*If a (poultry) industry of many firms could only look forward to chronic instability, there might be good reason to accept some concentration. But concentration exacts its price. It has its own consequences. In any honest assessment of the future . . . those consequences must be taken into account.*"

HAROLD BREIMYER, 1965

"*They're doomed.*"

JERRY YANDELL, 2008, COMMENTING
ON HIS NEIGHBORS

The Hidden King

N OBODY EVER visits the stranded little community of Waldron, Arkansas. But even if they did, a tourist would never see the place for what it really is. Most outsiders would be fooled into thinking it was an actual small town.

On any given morning, the residents awaken and begin their routines along Main Street. Old men park their pickup trucks by the curb in front of the Rock Café, which opens early for breakfast. As the café's booths and tables fill up, a congregation of old-timers in cowboy hats gathers in a loose ring of aluminum chairs out front, smoking and talking and stubbing out their cigarette butts in a bucket full of sand. Later in the morning, Chambers Bank on the south end of town opens up and the tellers cheerfully greet customers by name. On Thursday at noon, the livestock auction opens in a cavernous barn on the north side of town, drawing crowds of ranchers who haul steel trailers behind their trucks, with cows staring out between the horizontal slats. In the late afternoon, teenagers park their cars by the gazebo south of the auction barn, proudly displaying their Mustangs and Broncos like big game trophies.

These events have a rhythm of their own, the clockwork functioning of a small-town economy. But it's just window dressing. All of it could cease to exist in a moment and have no impact whatsoever on the true Waldron, or its true economic reason for being. The real tempo of the town's economic pulse is measured by the coming and going of semitrucks that roll down Main Street at periodic intervals, twenty-four hours a day, seven days a week. In the middle of the night tanker trucks full of animal feed rumble past the empty stores and out onto country roads that lead into the hilly terrain that surrounds town. At dawn, other trucks trundle in from the hills, heaped high with battered metal crates full of chickens that exude clouds of white feathers along the highway. The tempo can be measured in the regular arrival of train cars full of grains and oilseeds that dump their loads at a feed mill that clanks and hums and churns all night, and in the parade of refrigerated trucks that pull up to a slaughterhouse near the feed mill and get loaded with pallets of frozen meat. This is the real functioning of Waldron, Arkansas, and its true reason for being. This is the heartbeat of Tyson Foods, the nation's biggest meat company.

The Tyson plant on the north end of Waldron is the only thing that keeps the town on the map. Appropriately, many residents simply refer to it as "the complex." That's because the Tyson plant isn't just a factory; it's more like an entire small-town economy consolidated into one property. The complex contains its own feed mill and hatchery, its own trucking line and a slaughterhouse that covers several acres of land and processes about one million dead chickens a week. The complex is like an economic dark star that has drawn into itself all the independent businesses that used to define a small town like Waldron, the kinds of businesses that were once the economic pillars of rural America.

Of course, tourists to Waldron would never see the Tyson plant, and not just because it sits on the northern fringe of town and away from Main Street. Visitors are stopped at its front gate and forbidden from exploring the grounds. So a tourist would have to be content to stroll along the sidewalks downtown, observing the fake Main Street, the deceptive array of little businesses that make it seem like a community.

This illusory appearance cloaks Tyson's existence all the way from its roots in rural America to the grocery store shelves and restaurant menus where its products finally reach consumers. The average shopper is usually fooled when he or she peruses the meat aisle, seeing what appears to be an abundance of choices and products. The Tyson brand name wouldn't necessarily stand out, with its logo gracing just a handful of products. But the rotisserie chicken slowly turning in its oven, the Bonici brand pepperoni, the Lady Aster brand chicken cordon bleu, the frozen chicken pot pie and the Wright Brand bacon all come from the same company: Tyson. And then there is all the unlabeled meat that Tyson floods into the U.S. food system every day: the meat served in cafeterias, nursing homes, fast-food restaurants, and suburban eateries where more and more Americans eat their meals. There is a very good chance any of the meat purchased in these places was made by Tyson. Even if Tyson did not produce a given piece of meat, the consumer is really only picking between different versions of the same commoditized beef, chicken, and pork that is produced through a system Tyson pioneered. Tyson's few competitors have resorted to imitating the company's business model just to survive.

This book aims to explore the vast, hidden territory between the remote farms and towns like Waldron where Tyson raises millions of animals, and the final point of contact where consumers buy the company's meat. Unseen between these two poles is a hidden power structure that has quietly reshaped U.S. rural economies while gaining unprecedented control over the nation's meat supply. Just a handful of companies produce nearly all the meat consumed in the United States, and Tyson is the king among them. The company sits atop a powerful oligarchy of corporations that determines how animals are raised, how much farmers get paid, and how meat is processed, all while reaping massive profits and remaining almost entirely opaque to the consumer. Because Tyson and its imitators are based in the geographic and economic fringes of America, in forgotten places like Waldron, the company has managed to escape the scrutiny it deserves.

While Tyson's operations are remote, the company's business practices affect virtually everyone. About 95 percent of Americans eat chicken, which means they almost certainly eat chicken produced by Tyson. Because of this, American consumers are using their money to support a system that keeps farmers in a state of indebted servitude, living like modern-day sharecroppers on the ragged edge of bankruptcy. The system extracts its costs from consumers as well. There is so little competition in the meat industry today that companies like Tyson can virtually raise the price of meat at will. And these companies have been raising prices more and more in recent years, even as the wages of U.S. households have stagnated.

This situation is nothing new. When companies gain power over a market, they use it. Back in the early 1900s, a similar oligarchy of meat companies controlled the industry and earned the nickname the Meat Trust. These companies depressed the prices they paid farmers for meat, while raising the prices they charged consumers—just like Tyson Foods is doing today. But unlike the last time around, the modern Meat Trust isn't facing significant resistance from government officials. There is no Teddy Roosevelt in sight, no president willing to fight corporate power on behalf of consumers and farmers. The Obama administration launched a halting attempt to reform the industry in 2010, and its failure to do anything meaningful only entrenched the power of Tyson and its allies. If change is to come, it will have to originate with the people who buy meat and those who raise it.

The first barrier to change is the fact that everything about Tyson Foods seems hidden, from its industrial farms behind locked gates to the company's pristine headquarters in Springdale, Arkansas. Until very recently the only way to get to the company's main offices was to drive down a winding country highway, past dilapidated old chicken farms and feed mills until the road crested a hill, suddenly bringing into view a pristine campus of black steel-and-glass buildings. Even in its splendor, Tyson seeks obscurity. Examining the company is all the more difficult because of the apparent code of silence of its employees, and fear of retaliation on the part of virtually anyone who works with it.

But there is no way to better understand the way our food is produced than to understand Tyson Foods. Tyson hasn't just insinuated itself into virtually every corner of the modern food system; Tyson helped invent the very system itself. The company was founded in the depths of the Great Depression, just as American agriculture was undergoing the greatest upheaval in its history. The company helped redraw the new system that emerged. By doing so, it wrote the blueprint for modern meat production.

At the core of Tyson's strategy is an economic principle called vertical integration. In a nutshell, this refers to the way companies buy up the outside firms that supply them (picture what would happen if Apple Inc. bought the company that sold it microchips). When a company becomes vertically integrated, it takes under its control and ownership all the independent businesses that once supported it. In Tyson's case, the company has swallowed up all the businesses that used to make up a small-town economy. It owns the feed mill, the slaughterhouse, and the hatchery. It owns the trucking line and the food-processing plant where raw meat is packaged and cooked into ready-to-eat meals. While Tyson doesn't directly own most of the farms that supply it with animals, it controls them through the use of restrictive contracts. It's as if the broad-based network of small businesses that were once the backbone of rural America had been sucked into a single, towering silo called Tyson Foods. The company controls and owns everything that happens inside it. There is no competition among the various entities, no free market to determine the price at which baby chicks are sold to farmers or at what price grown chickens are sold back to a slaughterhouse. It all happens within the walls of Tyson's corporate structure.

Tyson first pioneered this model in the poultry business. Then the company expanded into raising hogs. Within two short decades America's independent hog industry was wiped out and replaced with a vertically integrated, corporate-controlled model. Ninety percent of all hog farms disappeared. The amount of money spent at grocery stores went up, but the amount of money farmers received went down. Companies like Tyson keep much of the difference. The cattle industry is the last holdout against vertical integration, but even the cowboys are starting to buckle under the pressure to surrender their independence. Tyson and three other companies so dominate the beef industry that they have been able to short-circuit the once vibrant cash market for buying cattle in the United States, giving them power to control the nation's ranches and feedlots even if they can't own them outright.

From the 1960s through the 1990s, this industrial meat machine provided tremendous benefit to American consumers. By industrializing animal production, Tyson's system rewrote the stubborn biological equations that once constrained the meat industry. Between 1955 and 1982, the amount of time it took to raise a full-grown chicken fell from 73 days to 52 days. And the chickens got bigger during that time, expanding from an average 3.1 pounds to 4 pounds. Perhaps most impressive of all, it took less and less chicken feed each year to accomplish this feat. In 1955 it took about 285 pounds of feed to grow 100 pounds of chicken. By 1982 it took less than 208 pounds. A similar trend held for pigs and, to a lesser degree, cattle during that time.

The benefits of this transformation were passed from the farms to the consumers as Tyson aggressively competed to win a bigger share of the U.S. market. People didn't see the radical transformation that was taking place on American farms, but the benefit invisibly accrued to their food budgets with each pound of Tyson chicken, beef, and pork they brought home. But this benefit wasn't free. Consumers got savings up front, but they paid for it over time. Essentially, consumers traded away the U.S. farming system in order to get the up-front savings from industrial meat. Each new Tyson farm, and each new Tyson meat factory, ate away at the fabric of a profitable sector of Middle America's economy.

Ironically, just as consumers traded away control over the way meat is produced, the meteoric production gains of industrialized animal production started to fade away. After realizing the huge boost of savings that came from raising animals in factories, the growth curve started to flatten in the 1990s. It seems that the genetics of the poor chicken have been pushed about as far as they can go. Today, no matter what Tyson or its competitors do, they seem to have run up against a wall of just how cheaply you can raise a bird on a given amount of food. The same thing is happening with the hog and the cow, who appear to be getting as fat as the laws of biology will allow on their given rations of feed.

The cost-savings from factory farming are slowing down, but Tyson's control over the marketplace has not loosened. Once the broad-based meat industry was traded away for a vertically integrated one, the deal could not be easily undone. The economies of scale now make it almost impossible for new competitors to enter the field and compete head-to-head with Tyson and its imitators. The tallest ramparts that protect Tyson's rule are its network of meat factories in places like Waldron. To compete against those facilities, a new company would need to invest hundreds of millions of dollars up front, before the first day of business. It would need animals, of course, and Tyson has much of that supply locked down with its contracts. And a competitor would surely know that even if it built a plant and secured supplies of chickens or hogs, Tyson and its few competitors have the ability to flood the market with product and make prices collapse in the short term, a hardship they could surely endure while an upstart struggled. The competitor would need to surmount these obstacles for the relatively lousy promise of just a one to three percent profit margin. Needless to say, upstarts are hard to find.

This makes the oligarchy of meat companies virtually impregnable, and as a result they don't have to compete too fiercely with one another on price. That's another key reason why the economic gains of the industrial meat machine's early years have disappeared. Since the mid-1980s, when consolidation among Tyson and its peers really began, the price of meat has risen steadily, even as farmers have been getting paid less out of every dollar spent on food. In translation, that means companies like Tyson are extracting savings from the farmer without passing them on to the consumer. In 2008, food prices jumped 6.4 percent. After falling during the Great Recession, prices are climbing once again, and only the tepid competition between Tyson and two or three other companies can be expected to bring them down.

Not only does Tyson have control over how meat is priced, it also sets the rules for how meat is produced. To take just one example: At the feedlots where cattle are raised for Tyson's slaughterhouses, Tyson was among the first companies to aggressively use a little-known growth drug called Zilmax. The drug causes cattle to put on weight much faster than they would naturally, but it reduces the quality of beef. Because Tyson tightly controls production at vast feedlots, it can use such drugs on an industrial scale without most consumers ever knowing about it. Other companies started using Zilmax to keep up with Tyson, and the drug quietly became the industry standard. Tyson Foods has similar discretion in deciding how much antibiotic drugs called ionophores it will feed to its chickens, or what kind of chemicals it will spray on chicken carcasses at its slaughterhouses to fight food-borne illness.

The standards Tyson uses to raise one out of every five chickens eaten in the United States are its proprietary secret. Consumers can't cast a vote at the grocery store, choosing chicken with a lighter or heavier dose of antibiotics in its feed, for example, because the recipe for producing that chicken remains entirely hidden to them. Consumers would not even know if Tyson itself raised the bird because most of the company's meat is unlabeled.

For all its power over the meat supply, Tyson escapes the news coverage it deserves because from a Wall Street–centric perspective, Tyson looks pretty boring. There's no such thing as a day when Tyson Foods delivers an earnings surprise and moves the markets. No one is waiting for the company to introduce the next iPad, or make some sort of stunning merger or acquisition (itself a sad testament to the fact that Tyson has no one left to buy). Tyson is a Fortune 100 company that feeds most families, but that's the single thing that it does day after day, in a quite predictable fashion. There's nothing especially innovative happening, and no expectation that there ever will be. The company's stock ticker symbol, TSN, just slowly crawls around and around each day at the bottom ring of everyone's circle of concern. It hovers near the same level where it's been for years, with a value that neatly mirrors the nexus between the price of corn and the price of wholesale meat at the butcher shop.

But the view of Tyson looks different when you're at the bottom, looking up. And that view provides the more accurate picture. Because Tyson doesn't really exist on Wall Street. It doesn't exist in the studios of CNBC or even at Tyson's own headquarters in Springdale. Tyson exists within its footprint of slaughterhouses, feed mills, and farms. It lives in the widely dispersed network of industrial fortresses, like the Tyson complex in Waldron and other isolated towns like Berryville, Arkansas; Dexter, Missouri, and Broken Bow, Oklahoma. In these places, Tyson is the center of economic gravity. In these places, it is revered and feared. It provides the jobs. It provides the tax base. If Tyson ever closed up shop, the town itself would evaporate.

This is power, very real power, and it can be felt only by visiting the far-flung places Tyson calls home. The power is etched into the fretful face of men like Edwin, who once tended to the industrial-sized flocks of birds that Tyson owns. Edwin is a polite man, a country man, and so was willing to sit on a bench in his front yard and entertain questions from a reporter. But Edwin was too scared to give his name, too scared to share his phone number. And that was back in 2004, when things were good for Edwin and his wife and kids, well before the fainting spells that Edwin blamed on the fumes in the chicken houses where he worked every day. Well before Edwin lost his farm and got divorced. This was before all that, when Edwin's life was about as stable as it was going to be. Edwin was willing to talk anonymously about the diseased birds Tyson gave him to try and raise, and how they died en masse and left him losing money with each new flock. But he was mortified at the thought that his story might end up in a newspaper.

Tyson's power could be felt several miles down winding country roads from Edwin's farm, at a small house where an elderly woman answered the door. She was also polite, and she stood out on her front porch to entertain questions. But her face zipped closed when Tyson's name was brought up. Her son worked at the Tyson plant. She didn't want to talk about the company. There wasn't anything around but green hillsides and fresh country air, not a person to overhear what she might say. But it was as if a Tyson field technician were sitting right there on her porch, in his trademark khaki uniform. She'd talk about anything in town except Tyson, insistently fending off any questions about the company until the painful encounter was over and she went back inside.

When a reporter knocked on the door of a Tyson field veterinarian in a small town in rural Missouri in 2009, the man came outside to talk. His wife joined him, then his children. The reporter might as well have been a federal agent in the age of Prohibition, poking around rural enclaves and asking residents how they made their money. The message was clear, from both the field tech and frigid stares of his family: Go away. Get off this property. Stop asking questions.

At its heart, Tyson's power is economic, and it has used this power to redraw the laws of wealth and income in rural America. The way the company is structured has done more than revolutionize how meat is produced. It has also fundamentally altered the way money is distributed in America's Heartland. This fact is difficult to discern by simply visiting the towns where Tyson operates. The run-down streets of Waldron and the shabby farms in surrounding rural Scott County help perpetuate a peculiar American stereotype about farming: that it is a hardscrabble business defined by thin profits and economic volatility. The financial decline of farming towns has become an accepted fact of American life, and the economic plight of farmers (who seem to complain incessantly about their low prices, high debt, and the ever-present threat of bad weather) is now considered a kind of inescapable destiny. The American farm and the small towns it once supported, the thinking goes, have died over the last fifty years because there's no money to be made in a largely backward-looking business.

This would be a sad thing, if it was in any way true, but it is not. Farming is immensely profitable. The agriculture sector is one of the richest, most productive moneymaking machines in American life. After all, a lot of the business simply involves sitting around and letting plants grow and letting animals get fat. Mother Nature does the heavy lifting. Then the farmer harvests the plants, kills the animals, and watches the money roll in. In 2010 alone Tyson Foods sold $28.43 billion worth of meat and cleared $780 million in pure profit. And that was during a tough year, when consumers were dining out less and scrimping on steaks and the precooked meals that are Tyson's real moneymakers. Other agriculture companies did just as well.

The critical question isn't whether there is money in agriculture, but rather where the money goes. It certainly doesn't go to places like Waldron. On Saturday night, Waldron's Main Street is quiet to the point of abandonment. The new strip mall at the southern end of downtown is vacant, with lumpy black garbage bags peppering its empty parking lot. The sole locus of activity is the renovated Scott County Movie Theater, which draws a crowd for its single screening of the night. A young woman named Frankie Watson takes tickets, chatting with the clientele. Watson takes cash from a young couple, no older than teenagers, and the shy blond girl mutters something toward the window.

"What?" Frankie asks.

"I found out I'm pregnant," the blond girl says louder, no note of particular urgency in her face. The boy with her smiles faintly.

"I knew it!" Frankie exclaims.

"I didn't know it," the girl says over her shoulder as she walks inside the theater. Moments like this have kept Watson and her husband in Waldron, even though they probably should have done the sensible thing and moved out of town to find a job, as many of her grade-school friends have done. Instead, they renovated the city's theater, gutting the moldy insides that had been empty for years. The weekend shows make enough money to pay the bills. The Watsons thought of Waldron as home, and so they wanted to stay there, even if it meant earning far less than they could easily find just an hour north in Fort Smith. The people are so poor in Waldron, Watson said, that the Great Recession of 2007 and 2008 largely passed them over, unnoticed.

If the money isn't circulating in places like Waldron, if it isn't in the hands of Frankie Watson or the teenagers who visit her theater, then where is it?

The money is riding on a one-way current. It is generated in the churning machinery of Tyson's slaughterhouse: Cash is minted along the conveyor belts carrying chicken carcasses and in the industrial ovens where chicken patties are cooked and breaded. But the money exists for only a moment or two within Waldron City limits. Almost as soon as it's created, it rides a current north to Springdale, to the treasury of Tyson Foods. It stops there temporarily and some of it is doled out to workers in the black steel-and-glass office buildings. Then the current carries the cash to Wall Street, which acts as a post office address for Tyson's owners. These owners are mostly big institutions and shareholders, and Tyson's profits stay with them.

Tyson's structure, and its dominance over all aspects of the rural economy, has delinked the corporation's well-being from the fortunes of the towns in which it operates. The average per capita income in Waldron and surrounding Scott County has stagnated in Tyson's shadow, growing just 1.4 percent over the last decade, to about $22,000. During that time, Tyson's annual income rose 245 percent. The same pattern is writ large across other communities where the company operates. While Tyson profits, rural America treads water and consumers pay more for their food.

Tyson's power has become entrenched over decades, as Democratic and Republican administrations traded places in Washington. But the economic malaise of rural America caught the attention of a young presidential candidate named Barack Obama as he spent months campaigning in Iowa during 2007 and 2008. In towns like Council Bluffs and Storm Lake, Tyson's economic power is a fierce and partisan political issue, a fact that did not escape the Harvard-trained lawyer from Chicago. When Obama was elected, he named Iowa's governor, Tom Vilsack, to the post of secretary of agriculture, and he told Vilsack to take action on the concentration of power among a few giant agribusiness companies. Unlike a parade of agriculture secretaries before him, Vilsack actually took up the challenge. The U.S. Department of Agriculture proposed the toughest antitrust rules over meat companies since the Great Depression. The USDA has held a series of workshops with the U.S. Department of Justice, with Vilsack and Attorney General Eric Holder traveling to places like Normal, Alabama, and Ankeny, Iowa, to learn more about Tyson's power. The workshops were the biggest effort in decades to find a legislative prescription for the ills of highly concentrated corporate power over the U.S. food supply.

In retrospect, the Obama administration seems almost naive in the way it attempted to reform the meat industry. The series of workshops were launched with soaring rhetoric about the creation of a new food system and new rural economy. What the administration did not seem to anticipate was the organized resistance it would face from Tyson Foods and other multinational meat corporations. The companies were not enthralled by the promises of change. Instead, the corporations marshaled millions of dollars and teams of lobbyists to help turn back the biggest effort to reform the meat industry since the 1930s.

The system that Tyson pioneered is now entrenched in the American economy and American way of life. Tyson's corporate culture became small-town America's corporate culture while no one was paying attention. There have been benefits to this but also deep costs. If America's consumers and farmers cannot rid themselves of the system that Tyson has imposed on them, they are at least entitled to understand the company, and to see it from the inside.

PART 1

"THINGS ARE BORN. THINGS DIE."

CHAPTER 1

How Jerry Yandell
Lost the Farm*

(2003–2004)

K ANITA YANDELL was waiting for the men to come and clean out the carcasses so her family's farm could die in peace. And the men showed up, eventually, arriving in a caravan of trucks emblazoned with the red oval TYSON logo. The men got out and milled around next to the long chicken houses that had been emptied out earlier. Kanita didn't become afraid until she saw them donning the blue plastic suits: big, baggy plastic suits with bulging helmets that swallowed their heads. They were dressed like men who handle nuclear waste. And they did this to enter the chicken houses where Kanita had worked with her sons just days before, laboring long hours shuttling in and out with wheelbarrows and buckets full of rotting chickens. Days and days her family had worked in there, breathing the air, grabbing the piles of hot dead birds and gathering them up to take outside.

When Kanita saw the men wearing blue moon suits, she returned to her house to grab her camera, and she photographed the men as they worked.

---

* "Farm" being an antiquated and misleading term often used to describe the heavily indebted industrial footprint of four loosely regulated factories under Jerry Yandell's control, with each factory housing flocks of 75,000 chickens at a time, grown under the exacting specifications of Tyson Foods, the nation's largest meat company.

The chicken houses sat side by side on a grassy plateau, just east of Waldron, Arkansas. The Ouachita Mountains rose up behind them like a green wall. The houses were long and squat and their walls were studded at regular intervals with round silver fans that ventilated them during the summer months. At the back end of each house was a big bay door that could slide open like a loading dock. These doors were where the men in blue moon suits entered and left.

Kanita had called the Tyson plant again and again, for months, begging them to come, demanding help, asking for explanations. She and her husband, Jerry, had been raising chickens for two decades, since they were teenagers, and they'd never been through anything like the last six months. It was a strange disease, or an industrial accident, or both. It was something gone wrong on a grand scale, something that got worse and worse, and something they didn't understand and couldn't stop. The birds were simply dying. Dying just hours after they arrived by the hundreds, and not from some ordinary flu. It seemed like they had started rotting even while they were still alive. She and Jerry worked ten-hour days, seven days a week, and even enlisted their sons to help. Their labor seemed to do nothing but dig them deeper and deeper into debt. But the Yandells had no choice but to continue working. Their home, their farm, and their livelihood depended on whether the birds lived or not.

About every eight weeks, a Tyson truck delivered birds to the Yandell farm. A crew of men unloaded crates of baby chicks, each worker filing into the barn and dumping the birds in neat rows on a fresh bed of litter. Jerry's and Kanita's job was to raise the tens of thousands of birds, keeping them fed and watered and warm and fattening them up until Tyson returned six weeks later to collect them for slaughter. It was a routine the couple knew well, one that defined the rhythm of their twenty-six-year marriage and the lives of their three boys.

It was a routine that collapsed in the fall of 2003, when the birds started dying overnight in great piles. Jerry and Kanita hadn't seen anything like it. Tyson field technicians visited the farm and looked inside the plastic freezers full of limp white carcasses. They told the Yandells to turn up the heat, turn on the fans, and give the birds more water.

Kanita walked through the houses and picked the rotten birds off each other. Their bodies were like soft, purple balloons by the time she gathered them. They fell apart to the touch, legs sloughing off the body when she tried to pick them up. It was like they were unraveling from the inside at a heated speed. She walked along the floors of the cavernous barns and put the gelatinous pieces of the dead chickens into buckets, looking at the pink featherless chests that were blooming with the colors of a violent bruise, like fruit in the sun. She started wearing gloves, and she made her sons wear masks. She kept calling the Tyson field men, asking them to come and inspect the buckets full of liquefying birds.

But the Tyson men never had answers, only more instructions. Turn up the fans; keep the heat higher. Salt the ground between flocks and clean out the litter. It's got to be a problem with your chicken houses, they said. But Kanita knew different. Rumors spread in town; she heard secondhand from other farmers that they were seeing the same strange disease in their own chicken houses. The birds all came from the same Tyson hatchery, so there must be a problem there, the neighbors speculated. But the field techs would never say.

Around Christmas, Kanita and Jerry realized it didn't matter. Whatever it was that burned through the chickens, it had eaten their livelihood as well. They had taken on more than $260,000 in debt to build the chicken houses and they had borrowed thousands more to buy propane to heat them this winter. Still, the sickness wiped out the birds. And the dead birds wiped out their paycheck. This would be the last flock and the end of their farm. The end of their home.

So the crew of Tyson men came to gather the last flock. They only picked up the birds that were still alive, birds that Kanita knew would be dead in a few hours anyway. They loaded them onto the truck to ship to the slaughterhouse where they'd be quickly transformed into chicken nuggets and frozen breasts. But the crew left a litter of carcasses behind, and freezers still stuffed with dead birds. So Kanita called the plant and demanded they come clean out the houses. She was still naive enough then to hope that she and Jerry might be able to stave off bankruptcy and sell the farm. So she wanted the chicken houses to be clean.

And that's when the men in blue suits arrived and terrified her. She and her sons had worn gloves, and many times facemasks, when they were cleaning out the houses. But not always. The hours were too long; the work was hot and sweaty. Sometimes they'd slipped off the masks, dropped the gloves, and kept working. Now she wondered what they had been breathing, and what they'd held in their hands.

The Tyson field men had told her it was safe. They told her it was nothing to worry about.*

And now here they were in plastic suits, as if fending off a plague.

The struggles on Jerry Yandell's farm could be observed on blinking computer screens inside the offices of Tyson Foods. Employees inside Tyson can look at operations on the farms that supply the company as if with an X-ray. Tyson can measure the profitability of every square foot of space under a farmer's control, gauging how much weight the birds gained given the precisely measured amount of feed, water, and medicine Tyson provided. Tyson employees create graphs of each farm's profitability to see in real time how efficiently the farmer transforms feed into fatter chickens. The information is aggregated on computer servers at Tyson Foods' headquarters in Springdale, Arkansas, where engineers search through the vital statistics from farms stretching through Georgia to Delaware to Arkansas. Tyson's headquarters is the real seat of power in the new, vertically integrated meat industry.

To understand how vertical integration works, and how it controls the livelihoods of people like Jerry and Kanita Yandell, it is helpful to

---

* Tyson Foods refused to comment in detail on its relationship with the Yandells or the problems on their farm. The company provided a broad statement in response to a list of dozens of detailed questions sent to the company after this book was completed. That statement is printed in full at the beginning of the Notes, and readers are encouraged to read it.

tour the wide expanse of concrete on the north side of town in Waldron, Arkansas. This concrete plain is the Tyson Foods plant. It is the heart of the city, its economic lifeblood and the reason for Waldron's existence.

The Tyson plant is a self-contained rural economy. Within its fenced confines are a slaughterhouse, a feed mill, a food-processing factory, a trucking lot and maintenance shop, administrative offices, a railroad spur, and a sewage plant. Decades ago, a big meat-producing town like Waldron—which pumps out millions of pounds of chicken products each week—might have contained a small network of businesses that supported and thrived from the local meat industry. There might have been several hatcheries that provided baby chicks to farmers, one or two slaughterhouses to kill the birds when they were grown. Feed mills would have mixed raw grains into chicken food to sell to local farmers, and local trucking companies would have hauled the feed and the birds between factories and the scattered farms where chickens were raised.

Under Tyson, all these businesses have been drawn onto one property. The company controls every step of meat production, with each aspect being centrally directed from the company's headquarters in Springdale. The company's control spans the lifetime of the animals it raises. Before there is a chicken or an egg, there is Tyson. The company's geneticists select which kinds of birds will be grown. They breed and crossbreed the avian bloodlines to engineer meaty breasts and rapid metabolism in the same way automobiles are first cut from clay, then engineered on a drafting board before they're built. The birds begin their brief life at the Tyson plant, within the heated hive of its industrial hatchery. The company produces more than two billion eggs a year, but none of them are sold to consumers. They are all hatched inside the company's buildings and the chicks are transported in Tyson trucks to Tyson farms. The Tyson trucks retrieve the birds six weeks later, bringing them back to the plant, where the chickens are funneled into chutes in the side of the slaughterhouses and hung upside down on hooks and decapitated before they travel down a disassembly line, where workers in hairnets and white aprons cut them apart by hand. The meat is battered, cooked, and frozen, then sealed inside airtight bags and piled in vast freezing rooms. The bags are loaded onto Tyson trucks and taken to grocery stores, cafeterias, hospitals, and restaurants around the country. From its conception until its consumption, the bird never travels outside of Tyson's ownership and control. The company collects every penny of profit to be made along the way because it owns every step in the process. The feed dealer or local trucker or slaughterhouse owner doesn't complain about the arrangement because he simply doesn't exist anymore. The money stays inside the system, with the surplus handed over to the company's shareholders.

There is one link in the chain that Tyson has decided not to own, one part of the rural economy that the company has pushed far outside the limits of its property. While most businesses are drawn steadily into the integrator's body, the force of gravity has been reversed when it comes to the farms. The farms are exiled, shoved away, and dumped from the balance sheet.

The reason for this is simple, even if it has been kept secret from people like Jerry Yandell. During the 1960s, Tyson Foods realized that chicken farming was a losing game. When Tyson executives examined operations at the company, they saw that farming was the least profitable, and most risky, side of the business. When they looked to invest in the future, they decided not to invest in farms. One of the people privy to those discussions was Jim Blair, who for decades was one of the company's top attorneys.

"You need to allocate whatever capital you have where it produces the most return on your investment. Owning the land itself wasn't in that category," Blair explained. The company was more interested in the new equipment being developed for slaughterhouses. Buying just one of the big steel machines could cut out the need for hundreds of hours of labor. Other contraptions could automatically turn raw chicken meat into sliced and breaded chicken tenders, which magically doubled or tripled the product's profit margin.

"That isn't true, of course, in a four-hundred-by-forty-foot-wide chicken house. You can't crowd the chickens in. [When] there's too much chickens you create disease and you lose efficiency. You can't keep a curve on the growth of production in the chicken house," Blair recalled.

The economics of chicken farming was stubborn, and new technology wasn't changing it. Companies were inventing new ventilation systems, new vaccines, new feed lines that whirred automatically to deliver food around the clock. But this was just an incremental boost of efficiency and profitability.

"There were never any huge leaps," Blair said.

So Tyson plowed its capital into the slaughterhouses, where new dollars bought new machines that cut production time and fattened profit margins. The least profitable part of the business was left to the contract chicken farmers, who quickly learn how much of their money it takes to do the job.

Modern chicken houses are the length of several football fields and as wide across as a gymnasium. They are wired with automatic feeders, ventilation systems, watering lines, and thermostats, all of them controlled from a centralized computer system and command room off the side of the chicken house. Each house costs hundreds of thousands of dollars to build, and acres of property are needed to dispose of the waste they produce each month. Between the industrial barns and the land, a single complex can cost north of two million dollars to build. And hundreds of complexes must be in continual operation to support a single Tyson plant.

Farmers take out bank loans to finance the operations, and rural banks have become proficient at helping the farmers become indebted. The banks have learned to break down a farmer's debt payments into a schedule that perfectly coincides with the life cycle of a flock of chickens. The farmer pays the bank every six weeks or so, just when his paycheck arrives from Tyson. In many cases Tyson cooperates with the bank and draws the loan payment from the farmer's pay, directly depositing it into the bank. So with every flock, the farmer is racing against his debt, hoping the birds Tyson delivers will gain enough weight to earn a payment that will cover the mortgage and bills for electricity, heating fuel, and water.

Tyson has offloaded ownership to the farms, but it maintains control. The company always owns the chickens, even after it drops them off at the farm; it doesn't sell baby chicks to the farmer and buy them back when they're grown. So the farmer never owns his business's most important asset. Tyson also owns the feed the birds eat, which is mixed at the Tyson plant according to the company's recipe and then delivered to the farm on Tyson's trucks according to a schedule that Tyson dictates. Farmers are accustomed to the big white feed trucks with the TYSON logo on their side arriving unannounced to refill the steel feed tanks that jut from the top of the houses like blunt horns. Tyson dictates which medicine the birds receive to stave off disease and gain weight, and Tyson field veterinarians travel from farm to farm to check the birds' health.

Tyson also sets the prices for its birds. When the chickens arrive at the slaughterhouse, Tyson weighs them and tallies up how much it owes the farmer on a per-pound basis. When that price is determined, Tyson subtracts the value of the feed it delivered to grow the birds. This determines a rough payment for the farmer. But the farmer isn't paid this flat fee. Instead, final payment is based on a ranking system, which farmers call the "tournament." Tyson compares how well each farmer was able to fatten the chickens, compared to his neighbors who also delivered chickens that week.

The terms and conditions of Tyson's relationship with its farmers are laid out in a contract the farmer signs with Tyson. This contract is the single most important document for a farmer's livelihood. It ensures the steady flow of birds a farmer needs to pay off utility bills and bank debt. But for all their importance, the contracts are usually short and simple documents. While a farmer's debt is measured in decades, the contracts are often viable for a matter of weeks and signed on a flock-to-flock basis. Farmers certainly have the right to negotiate terms when the contract is laid out on the hood of a Tyson truck that has arrived to deliver birds, but most often they do not. They accept the terms and sign. The contracts reserve Tyson's right to cancel the arrangement at any time.

Farmers like Jerry Yandell, who are only called "farmers" for lack of a better word, don't usually pay attention to the fine print of their contracts. They know it doesn't matter anyway. The power arrangement is set by Tyson, and the farmer learns the rules quickly enough, whatever the documents might say. Vertical integration gives companies like Tyson the kind of power that feudal lords once held. The company can cancel a farmer's contract and put him out of business. And with its control over all aspects of farming, Tyson Foods can ensure that it gets as much profit as possible out of the process, squeezing farmers who know they can't fight back.

Jerry Yandell knew how to work.

He grew up in the wooded hills of Scott County, Arkansas, outside the town of Waldron, where daily life was directed by the hungry task of finding work. Men found jobs in town when they could, or out in the countryside, where they hauled timber or raised cattle or grew whatever crops they could in the sparse red soil. Jerry's dad made a living hopscotching from one job to the next. Mostly he hewed raw timber from the endless acres of the Ouachita national forest surrounding their small home. The Yandell family had a small sawmill on their property. It almost paid the bills.

Jerry Yandell spent his childhood summers as a migrant farm worker, traveling to Oregon with his family to work in the orchards there. His mom and dad rigged a tarp over the rust-pocked flatbed of his father's pickup truck, and Jerry and his seven siblings crawled beneath it, finding a seat among the packed baggage as the family drove west. The trip took at least five days. The Yandells went to the same fruit orchard every summer, where the family worked six days a week picking fruit—mostly strawberries. They lived in small cabins with other families who came looking for work, families with big broods of kids from small towns like Waldron, out-of-the-way places in the woods where kids knew how to split wood and prayed at the supper table. After work, Jerry Yandell played with the other kids in the dirt-packed yard outside the barracks. They slept on the floor. When he got back home and enrolled in Waldron Elementary School, his hands were as tough and gnarly as fresh-dug potatoes. His dad returned to the daily pursuit of a paycheck, logging in the national forestland or hewing timber in the mill behind their home.

One year his dad built a big long barn with wooden beams and a tin-looking roof. He grew chickens there for a new slaughterhouse in town. The birds yielded just about as much cash as the pulpy softwood tree trunks.

Jerry Yandell's life was a chain of long days spent at labor, in the hope of good pay, with little concern about cheap pleasures or entertainment. That was life in Scott County. He grew up into a thin and rangy man, with eyes set deep in his face, who doesn't talk for fun. He parts with his words slowly, as if they were saved-up coins.

Jerry bought his first chicken house from his father, just after he graduated high school. The birds didn't yield much money, but the pay was steady. Jerry married a slight and pretty girl named Kanita who lived a few miles down the road. Just after his wedding, Jerry brought Kanita home to live with him and help with the new chicken house. She was almost seventeen years old. After the couple was married, it wasn't unusual for Jerry to leave the house before dawn and start the long drive out to the chicken houses he owned.

The chicken business in Waldron picked up in the mid-1980s when Tyson Foods bought the local processing plant. Tyson was big, one of the biggest in the business, and it started to pump money into every corner of Scott County. Bankers were hot to extend loans on poultry houses. Tyson field men visited local ranchers and landowners with brochures and cash-flow sheets, enticing them to borrow outsized mortgages that could have financed mansions no one in Waldron had ever dreamed of owning. Jerry and Kanita signed contracts with Tyson, took on loans with the local Chambers Bank, and built more chicken houses. By 1997 the Yandells had seven houses spread around on plots of land within a few miles of their home, with clusters of the barns hidden up by a bend in Lick Skillet Road and a few more on wide, flat pastureland near the lonely hutch of homes called Hale Town. Jerry and Kanita had three sons, and by the time they were teenagers, each boy had his own truck and helped out in the chicken houses after school. Jerry thought he had given his boys a prosperous and stable life he had never known.

The Yandells received their first flock of diseased chickens in the winter of 2003. Shortly after the birds were delivered, Jerry opened a small door in the side of the chicken house and entered the dim space inside, making his way through the floating feathers and the heavy stink of ammonia. Big round steel lamps hung from the ceiling, suspended just a few feet above the carpet of wood chips where piles of white chicks clustered together. The brooding lamps hissed and emitted blue discs of propane flame that gave the young chicks their warmth.

When Jerry looked at the floor his stomach went cold. The birds were piled on top of each other in white mounds. They were sick, feverish, climbing on each other to survive. Jerry had been running the heat lamps full bore, pouring propane into the houses to keep the birds warm. But they had huddled there in piles and died overnight. He got the wheelbarrow and pushed it through the flock of birds, shooing them away from each other and trying to break up the piles where they smothered. But they just waved their wings listlessly as he passed. He dug into the piles of dead birds, where they were rotting like hot fruit. He tried to pull them away and their legs slipped off the body.

He started another hard day of work, piling the birds and parts into a wheelbarrow, taking it out to an overflowing freezer unit full of carcasses, and wondering how he was going to keep his family from going broke.

By the time the Tyson trucks arrived at Jerry Yandell's farm to pick up the first flock of sick chickens, just about half of the birds were still alive. The chickens were dropping dead in the hours before they were gathered up for slaughter. That's the sorriest flock of birds I ever seen, Jerry told the Tyson field man as he watched the birds get loaded onto Tyson's truck. He was promised the next batch would be better.

Later that fall, the Tyson trucks arrived with the new flock, and they were unloaded as always. The truck pulled up to the open doors of his barn, where a fresh bed of litter was laid for the birds to rest on. A long row of brooding lamps hanging low from the ceiling glowed orange as they burned off propane. It was near a hundred degrees inside the house. Men unloaded crates of chicks from the trucks and walked down the row of hot lamps, flipping the crates upside down to dump the loads of downy yellow chicks on the fresh litter. The chicks sat stunned for a moment, then began flapping their wings, skittering around in startled circles. The birds looked healthy enough then. The next day, Jerry drove between his chicken houses, monitoring the new chicks, keeping the lamps hot and ensuring there was ample water.

As the birds were unloaded, Jerry had probed the truck driver for clues.

— I hope these are good, Jerry said.

— We don't know nothing about them, the driver replied.

On the second day after Jerry's newest flock was delivered, the birds began to form rings around the brooding lamps. It was a hundred degrees beneath the lamps, so the birds were scalded when they drew too close. But still they pressed in as tightly as they could. Even then, they seemed to be freezing. They piled on top of one another and died and began to rot. Jerry walked along the row of lamps and used a rake to pull them away from each other and spread them apart. But as soon as he walked past, the birds recircled and pressed into the heat. Within hours they were bloated and black like little balloons. He spent the days wheeling pile after pile of dead birds out of his chicken houses and into the overstuffed freezers outside. It had only been a couple of months since the first batch of sick birds arrived, but Jerry knew his farm was already sinking dangerously into debt.

He called the field techs, trying to control the anger in his voice. He drove between his properties and when he got home at night he sometimes found the reports the field men had delivered while he was gone.

Temperature: adequate. Water level: adequate. Feed system: adequate.

He called the field techs on their cell phones and they gave him the same suggestions as before. He kept his heat high. He scattered the birds with rakes. He carted the dead away.

Jerry kept calling the field techs and telling them what he saw. And he kept hoping that during one of those calls, a field tech might actually give him some answers.

One of Jerry Yandell's field technicians over the years was a man named Tommy Brown. Brown didn't work with Yandell during the time when Yandell's flocks were dying, so Brown couldn't help him understand what was happening. But because Brown worked on the inside of Tyson's system, with the managers rather than the farmers, he understood deeper truths about how things worked. He knew about fundamental problems on the Yandell farm that had nothing to do with sick birds.

On any given workday, Brown had roughly one million chickens under his watch. As a Tyson field veterinarian, Brown spent most of his day driving a truck down winding back roads in the Ouachita Mountains, traveling to the secluded farms in his territory, some as far as eighty-five miles away from his home in Waldron. Brown was a babysitter of sorts, checking on the flocks of chickens that Tyson placed in its network of farms. He was part of the fleet of Tyson trucks that busily pass each other on the country roads outside Waldron, the red TYSON logo on their doors carrying the air of absolute authority that ends conversations when they arrive on a farm.

Brown knew the farms on his route well. He knew the setup of the houses and knew the owners. When he stopped at a farm, he donned tall rubber boots that prevented him from spreading disease as he went from barn to barn. He always entered barns by the same door. It was the door where the farmer kept his mortality chart, the worn paper showing daily hatch-marks that counted dead chickens. Ten a day wasn't bad. More than that, and Brown started asking questions.

After counting the dead, Brown would sometimes walk through the barn, looking over the downy white floor of birds with practiced eyes. The chickens seemed as delicate as a crop of indoor snow being grown in the Ozark summer. With just the slightest glitch, a broken fan or feed line or dirty water tank, the birds would expire fast as melting ice.

More than anything, he thought, it took vigilance to raise chickens. This is what he preached to farmers. This was his solution when he entered a barn and saw that the feeder was broken and the birds were pecking each other to death. Vigilance, above all.

In many cases, that is about all the farmers could offer: attention. Most didn't know a thing about the business when they got into it. They borrowed the money to build or buy the houses and entered a contract with a huge corporation that could cut them off at any moment, all without ever having even fed a single chicken in their lives. They did it to hold on to a way of life, most of them, to stay in the countryside where they were born and make a living that paid slightly more than cutting timber or digging ditches.

Even Brown didn't know that much about birds when he became a field veterinarian in the 1970s. He was a truck driver at the time, and his brother worked at the feed mill. He heard the company needed field men, so he applied. He learned everything he knew by following another field man from farm to farm.

And so he told the farmers what he could: how to arrange fans and keep water lines clean, or how to open the side vents of a barn during certain hours to cool the birds.

But he also knew what farmers didn't: that no matter what they did, no matter how many hours they worked or what new equipment they bought or innovations they tried, it wouldn't affect their profitability at the end of the day. That profitability was determined before the loads of baby chicks were placed on the bed of fresh litter. It depended on how healthy the birds were at birth, and whether Tyson delivered good feed or the dregs from the bottom of the feed mill silos. That was it. Good chicks. Good feed. Good profit. The dice were loaded from the minute the baby chicks and feed were delivered.

Just before he retired in the early 1990s, Brown attended a meeting that changed Waldron's economic destiny.

A memo arrived from Springdale. The field techs were told that the Waldron plant was going to be put to a new use. It was part of a new strategy that the bosses in Springdale were pushing. Each plant would concentrate on making and selling specialty products rather than providing standardized birds for the grocery store. Waldron was going to sell smaller chickens to be used by fast-food restaurants like Wendy's and Kentucky Fried Chicken. The idea was to sell a three-and-a-half-pound bird rather than a four-and-a-half-pound bird. The chickens would yield smaller breast patties that were ideal for fast-food consumption. The change would be immediate and easy to implement. The field techs would schedule the chickens to get picked up earlier than usual, giving them less time to grow.

Brown was uncomfortable. He knew that growing smaller birds would mean less money for the farmers, and all of the farmers had fixed mortgages to pay on the chicken houses. The farmers paid a fixed cost to raise each flock, and they needed to sell as many pounds as possible to cover their bills. Cutting down the size of the bird was a pay cut for all of them.

Brown raised his hand during the meeting.

— When are we going to tell the farmers about the change? he asked.

— We're not going to, he was told.

The field techs seemed uneasy at the answer.

— Don't worry, the manager said, the farmers will figure it out. They'll notice that you're there two weeks early to pick up the birds.

And so the new regime was put into place. The Waldron plant would serve up smaller chickens for fast-food restaurants. Farmers might or might not figure it out, depending on how closely they watched the calendar of their bird deliveries and pickups.

For farmers around Waldron, it was the beginning of a fifteen-year bleed on their bank accounts. Each flock that was taken away was smaller, and so was the paycheck, if only slightly. But the mortgage payments continued at the same level. So each flock chipped away, payment after payment, at the profit and equity farmers had invested in their farms.

Brown often visited Jerry Yandell. They didn't have too many disagreements. Jerry was all right in Brown's book. Jerry was willing to work hard, he didn't gripe any more than most. He was willing to try new things and knew the chicken business like someone who had done it his whole life, which, of course, he had. Yandell was willing to put in the seven-day workweek required for chicken farming. Brown chatted with him on the farm and walked with him through the chicken houses. But Brown knew that with each new flock, Yandell was working hard to put himself just one step farther behind.

By December of 2003, Jerry and Kanita Yandell were sinking into a financial hole. The couple was behind on paying their farm loan and gas and electric bills. This was in the middle of raising the second flock of sick birds. Day after day, they hauled loads of chicken carcasses out of the houses and stuffed them into the plastic freezers provided by Tyson. Kanita called Tyson. The field techs came to the farm and emptied the freezers, then they returned a few days later to do it again.

The Tyson field technicians suggested the Yandells circulate the air more to cool the chicks. So Kanita and Jerry spent three thousand dollars on new industrial fans. They hauled the fans into the houses and stood on ladders and drilled them into the ceiling. The fans roared to life and kept the warm air circulating. The money they borrowed to install them would surely make this flock a loss.

The birds kept dying. The field men suggested that Jerry turn on the fans on the side of the house to vent the air outside. This was an extraordinary, and seemingly stupid, thing to do in December. The side fans were meant to run in spring and summer to push hot air out of the barns. But the field men said it might help, so Jerry did it. He turned on the side vents and blew out the air he was paying to heat and circulate with new ceiling fans.

The Yandells' son Jeremy lived on one of their farm properties with his wife. He spent his days in the houses, helping his parents haul out the dead birds. Kanita and Jeremy wore facemasks and gloves as they walked the long length of the barns, trying to gather the dead birds before the survivors began to pick away at them for food.

Perry Edwards arrived for work before dawn. He drove north from downtown Waldron on a side road that leads to the Tyson plant's front gate. He arrived when the sky was still dark and the town still sleeping. Edwards drove over a set of railroad tracks and onto a broad parking lot near the base of the towering feed mill. Trains brought loads of grain to the mill, where it was mixed with vitamins and medicine and funneled into a waiting line of Tyson feed trucks that hauled it to farms throughout the countryside. Just beyond the feed mill was the slaughterhouse, a short, broad building with smokestacks that sent up white wisps of steam in the morning. Tyson's "live haul" trucks came into the gate, their beds piled high with steel crates full of white chickens. These trucks rolled onto metal platforms that recorded the weight of the birds they carried. Then they drove alongside the building where their live cargo was loaded into the slaughtering line inside.

Edwards had an office job in the complex, where he had a view into the vortex of paperwork that spun between the trucks being loaded with feed and trucks hauling birds to the slaughterhouse.

This paper trail was critical for the office at the Tyson Plant that was alternately called the Live Grow Division, or simply the Broiler Office. This was the nerve center of the network of farms around Waldron, where the daily functions of an ecosystem of a million growing birds is coordinated. It's where the flow charts were printed that determined the number of eggs to be hatched in a given week, and where the schedule was written for the trucks to haul new chicks out to farms. It's where the weight of the birds at slaughter was tallied and scored against the amount of feed delivered to a farm. This office determined the farmer's payment, based on Tyson's ranking system.

During Edwards's tenure at Tyson, the Broiler Office was run by Gary Roper, an affable Texan who moved to Waldron for the job with Tyson. Roper was not well known in town. He was a young and good-looking man with a trim physique and short brown hair. The farmers knew Roper was in good with the big wheels at Tyson headquarters in Springdale. He had no problem dispatching orders and dismissing complaints. He had a remarkably easy feel for authority. Gary Roper called the shots, but he rarely visited the farmers. There were multiple layers of power between his office and the farms, leagues of field technicians, truck drivers, office clerks, and managers insulating him from people like Jerry Yandell. Roper commanded the fleet of Tyson trucks that perpetually crisscrossed Waldron and surrounding Scott County: the beige pickup trucks with the TYSON emblem on their door that the field techs drove, and the big white feed tankers with TYSON printed on their side that arrived in the middle of the night to refill feed bins. The farmers talked to the men in these trucks and asked that they pass the comments on to Roper.

Edwards knew the power that Roper had, seemed to know it even better than Roper himself. Edwards had grown up around the chicken industry in Waldron. In the 1970s, the money was good. But by 2000, chicken farmers weren't getting paid much more than they earned three decades earlier. And the cost of fuel and electricity and all the other necessities had risen so much that there was little or no profit left over for shopping or nice houses. Rather than go into farming, Edwards got a job at the Tyson plant in town. He was making a decent hourly wage, and he had health insurance. Not a fortune maybe, but it was steady.

When Edwards arrived at the office, trucks were rolling into the plant with live birds and others were leaving empty. Other trucks sat scattered in a parking lot, still heaped with crates of chickens after being weighed and waiting for their turn to unload. Edwards sometimes noticed mistakes on the trucking logs. That was to be expected, considering that about forty or fifty trucks came through the plant during a full shift. Tyson Foods kept track of which farms the trucks had visited so the company could credit the weight of the chickens back to the right farmer. But as Edwards looked through the logs left over from the night shift, he noticed the numbers didn't always add up. Truck number 549, for example, was recorded in the logs to have delivered chickens from a certain farm just west of town. But a separate log said chickens hadn't even been picked up yet from that farm, and empty trucks were just now heading there to get a load. That meant that a load of chickens had been weighed and credited to the wrong farm.

It was a small mistake, but Edwards knew what that kind of error meant to farmers. It meant a farmer had been assigned a completely arbitrary weight for the chickens he just spent six weeks raising, a discrepancy that would directly affect how much he got paid. Correcting the mistake meant calling busy truckers as they sat parked on farms with crews of workers piling crates of squawking birds onto their flatbeds, and asking them to retrace their steps and recite the other farms they visited. Some office workers wouldn't bother with such corrections because they were too much of a hassle. They would have to correct the weigh-in tickets and fix the logs, even as more trucks rolled in with chickens and others were loaded with feed for delivery, piling up yet more paper on their desk.* When the mistakes were pointed out to Tyson managers, the response might be just a shrug. To Edwards, it did not seem anyone was too worried about financial damages for the farmers.

Edwards often answered the phone when farmers called with questions. They called after getting their paychecks and weigh-in receipts, wondering how the average weight of their birds could have possibly been three pounds when the farmer himself had seen the birds were no smaller than three and a half pounds when they were picked up. Farmers like Bill Bethel could hardly control the anger in their voice.

Bethel was an older farmer who'd been in the business for decades. So he'd seen the industry's good times come and go. He had too much historical perspective on the business, and he seemed perpetually upset that he hadn't gotten a pay raise in twenty years, even though Tyson was bigger and more profitable than ever. He quibbled over the weights, and he argued about the volume of feed Tyson claimed to have delivered. He railed on the phone when he was convinced there had been a mistake on his weigh-in ticket. Edwards listened, but he always came to the same conclusion: There was nothing Edwards could do. The scales didn't lie, he would say. So Bethel would ask him to put a plant manager on the phone; he wanted to talk to someone who *could* do something about it.

One afternoon, Edwards heard the dispatchers talking back and forth after a trucker tipped over his load of feed out on a country high-

---

* Tyson Foods said it has a computerized system with "safeguards in place" to make sure farmers are not credited with the wrong batch of birds, but the company refused to describe those safeguards.

way. After hours of cleanup, they managed to get the feed into the trailer and the truck up and running again. But the trucker called to say the feed was filled with gravel and asphalt and dirt from the road. It was a total loss, and it would have been insane to pour the feed into a bin on a farm and expect it to run properly through the automated feed lines into a chicken house. It was even crazier to think birds would eat it. The driver asked what to do and where he should dump it.

Edwards heard a plant manager give the reply.

— Send it to Bill Bethel.

The incident gave Perry Edwards a queasy feeling that stuck with him for years. He knew that what was happening at the Tyson plant wasn't right.*

Over the years, Edwards made it a habit to look over Tyson's delivery logs, tracking which baby chicks were delivered to which farms.

It was an open secret that any Tyson hatchery would produce a certain number of chicks that were unhealthy. As industrialized as the whole farming process had become, that simple fact remained unchanged. Some of the birds were good. Some were bad. And it was clear, almost from the moment they were hatched, which birds were which. Whole batches of yellow chicks rolled off the line at the hatchery and were deemed "culls," too weak and spindly to ever gain weight at a healthy pace. But even these birds must be delivered to farms because the pace of the machine could never slow. There was never a time-out available to Tyson, when a day's worth of production could be omitted and the plant shut down because a flock or two of birds was sub-optimal. So the culls went out, the farms stayed full, and the slaughterhouse kept running at full capacity.

---

* Bethel said that on more than one occasion he received the wrong kind of chicken feed from Tyson Foods, a mistake that hurt production on his egg-laying farm. Bethel sometimes found bolts, screws, and even a wrench inside his feed bins. Bethel said he was not aware that Tyson sent him feed contaminated with gravel, but that it would not surprise him. His farm was close to the plant, and he assumed the company considered it a convenient spot to "dump" unwanted or leftover feed.

Tyson could roughly predict which chicks would be healthy based on the age of the hens that laid the eggs. Older hens produced weaker chicks, while younger hens laid more vigorous broods. Edwards noticed that some farmers were consistently receiving chicks produced by the healthiest, youngest hens. Whoever was setting up the deliveries in the Broiler Office was giving these farmers the cream off the top. And he noticed something else: Other farmers were consistently getting the batches of culls.

As Perry Edwards pored over the shipping logs, he saw that the pattern was the same. When there were bad batches of birds, they went to the same group of farms. And the healthiest birds also went to a select group of farms that, not coincidentally, always ranked as the highest paid farms in the network.

Tyson Foods insists that such accusations are the stuff of "urban myth." The company says that plant managers cannot determine which baby chicks are likely to be healthy and which are not, because so many chicks are born at each hatchery—875,000 a week in the case of Waldron's hatchery. But Edwards's observations seem to be validated by sworn testimony in a 2010 lawsuit. In that case, Tyson Foods employee Geraldine Henson testified to observing what Perry Edwards had seen. Henson had been secretly taped by two Tyson Foods chicken farmers who had been trying to form an organization for poultry growers. The farmers confronted Henson at her home, and she told them that Tyson Foods had been giving the farmers chicks from older hens. She told the farmers she had seen paperwork showing the ages of the hens. She stood by the story under oath in court. Cynthia Johnson, an attorney who has represented chicken farmers for decades, said that depositions in many lawsuits against poultry companies show that plant managers can determine the health of baby chicks based on the age of the hens that lay them, a metric that most companies track to a great level of detail.

The pattern Perry Edwards saw at the Waldron plant looked unmistakable to him, and so was the reason behind it. As he looked through the figures, Edwards wasn't surprised to see which farmers were at the bottom of the ladder and which consistently got delivered bad chicks.

The latter were the Bill Bethels of the world. The complainers. It was understood within the office that those who complained would be marked. And it was as obvious as a list of names on a bulletin board who was who. Some farmers went with the program and ensured the system ran smoothly. And others, he believed, posed a threat by complaining, calling the office, or demanding more money.

Edwards did not see any evidence that Tyson Foods delivered sick birds to Jerry and Kanita Yandell to retaliate against them for any perceived bad behavior. But what he observed was that the company had the ability to do so if it wanted to. Farmers around Waldron did not have the front-row view of this power that Edwards was afforded. But they knew it existed. They felt it. They perpetually feared it. And for that reason, they often stifled their complaints and took what Tyson gave them.

After New Year's Day of 2004, Jerry Yandell sat in the office at Chambers Bank in downtown Waldron. He was speaking with a loan officer who had driven an hour down from Fort Smith to visit the bank's small branch and talk over Jerry's troubling debt of $260,000. The bankers had started calling Jerry that winter. He'd been able to make only half of his mortgage payment each month and was barely keeping up with the interest on his loan. When the bankers called, he explained what was happening clear and simple. They hung up, only to call back a few days later to ask if he possibly had extra money he could put toward the note. He didn't.

According to the Yandells, by January they had received three batches of sick birds from Tyson, and they'd lost money with each flock. So there Jerry sat in the glassed-in office just off the bank lobby by the front door. Customers who filed in and out of the lobby saw him sitting there, speaking with the well-dressed banker on the other side of the desk. It must have been obvious to everyone that Jerry Yandell was a man on the edge of ruin.

Jerry and the banker went over the math of Jerry's life. And it wasn't complicated.

He owed the bank about $3,500 for every batch of chickens he grew.

On good batches, Jerry got paid a total of $6,500 for his six weeks of labor. After paying his mortgage, he usually owed $1,500 for propane to heat the houses (when the chicks were very young they needed to feel like they were inside a brooder) and $250 for electricity. That left him $1,250 at the end of a batch. Which meant he made $208 a week, or $5.20 an hour. On good batches, he might make $9.16 an hour.

In just a few months time, the farming operation the Yandells had built over twenty-six years had been pulled so far under it appeared unsalvageable.

He had been paid roughly $4,000 for each batch of the sick birds, leaving him nothing at the end of six weeks. The disease hit during the winter months, when propane costs were $3,000 a batch or more. The field techs had told him to superheat the houses, and on their advice he was also venting the heated air outside.

The second batch had been the same, with Jerry getting paid less money than it cost to pay his mortgage and bills. He expected the third batch would be even worse, when all was said and done. By the time he met with his banker, Jerry owed the fuel company $7,000.

Accepting another batch of chicks from Tyson would mean borrowing more money from the fuel company, getting further behind on his mortgage, and working seven days a week to do it. The banker advised him to declare bankruptcy. If Jerry put up his house and ten acres of land, he could probably cover most of the debt for the chicken houses.

Jerry asked the banker if he had any pull with the men at Tyson. If Jerry could just get one batch of good birds, maybe then he could start to dig his way out of this.

Kanita photographed the men in blue suits as they emptied the remaining chicken carcasses from her houses and loaded them into freezers that were already overflowing with dead birds.

She approached the field techs by the truck and asked what they knew and why they were dressed in biohazard suits. They told her the suits were a precaution, nothing to worry about.

— I'll be ruined by this, she said. I'll lose my farm.

— I'm sorry, the field man said. He shrugged at his powerlessness to do anything about it.

— You look at my boys and you tell them how sorry you are about it, she said.

In March 2004, Jerry and Kanita sat in an office with their attorney and signed paper after paper that cemented their bankruptcy. They had never defaulted on a dollar of debt in their lives together. Jerry suspected they'd never be able to borrow a dime again, and he was right. The Yandells listed all their assets to be counted against their debt. A court date was set for that summer in Fort Smith, where a federal judge would dispense with the matter and determine which creditor got what.

Shortly after signing the papers, Kanita took out an advertisement in the *Waldron News*, the local paper that was printed from an office on Main Street.

Bold letters across the top declared:

AUCTION

PERSONAL PROPERTY

SATURDAY, MARCH 20, 2004

The ad listed items that would be for sale that day. It was an inventory of the Yandells' home: Dell computer; porch swing; Rainbow vacuum; one hay fork; small freezer; two dressers; one Lincoln Welder; oak dining table and six chairs. Down the center of the ad there were crudely drawn clip-art pictures of a dresser, a hammer and nails, and a riding lawn mower. The ad was a catalog of middle-class life in rural Arkansas.

The Saturday auction was busy. By the end of it, the Yandells' home was empty.

In the spring of 2004, Jerry walked the trails on a blasted hillside. The ground was covered in soot, the burned tree trunks stood aloft and stinking of cinders after the fire passed through. Jerry was part of a work crew that walked through the ruined wilderness. The hills had been swept by wildfire, and Jerry's crew built dump sites in the woods where they set up heavy equipment to dispose of big brush piles the forestry crews left behind as they cleared the woods. All day, Jerry chipped the piles of burned brush, his arms and face covered in black ash, before moving on to the next dump site. He made $150 a day when he could get work.

Jerry had gotten the job with the crew after hearing that FEMA was looking for help in California. Fires had swept through the hills and devoured subdivisions, and men were needed to clear out the burned brush left behind. Jerry had taken his son's truck and driven out west looking for work, just as he'd done as a child when his parents took him to the orchards. But this time he was alone in the cab of the truck.

He found a small apartment to rent near San Bernardino and shared it with a man he knew from Scott County. During the day they followed the loggers and found their brush piles and fed the blackened limbs into the chipper. They passed gutted houses and cul-de-sacs covered in ash. All of it ruined.

At night he lay awake, with fear gnawing at him. He thought about the papers he and Kanita had signed to declare bankruptcy, about their debts for the propane and the mortgage on their chicken houses. Everything was on the line to cover it: their house, their land, and their cars. It had been just four months, just sixteen weeks or so, since the first batch of sick birds arrived.

He let himself toy with hope. Maybe he could earn enough money on the brush crew to finance one more flock—just one flock to make a little cash, maybe break even. That's all he would need. Maybe then he could pay down the debt he'd taken on over the winter, the debt that had swallowed his life. He had borrowed money against his house and land to finance the farm. The house where his sons were raised. The stable home they knew and the trucks they drove. All of it was bound up in the debt. Lawyers were deciding somewhere right now how it would be divvied up and what the Yandells would be able to have in the end.

Jerry didn't sleep at night, and during the day his mind stayed numb and tired as he pushed burned branches into a wood chipper. More than twenty-five years of chicken farming had brought him here.

About a month before his bankruptcy hearing, Jerry Yandell moved back to Arkansas. He woke up in his old bedroom. The floor and walls were bare, and the room was empty. He lay on a borrowed bed with Kanita, who was still asleep. The house was very quiet. He had returned from California the week before, after getting news that Kanita's father had just had a heart attack. He needed to be back home, in Waldron, to help her family. So he quit his job with FEMA and went home.

The Yandells' home was left vacant while the couple waited for the bankruptcy case to be settled. So they decided to live there, in the empty house, until their court date. Jerry didn't quite know if he or the bank owned the house. But he still had the keys, and no one had shown up to run him out yet. So each night he and Kanita slept there like squatters.

They set up a hot plate and small microwave in the kitchen. The water was still running, so they washed the few dishes they had in the sink.

Jerry had built this house, five years earlier. He had poured the concrete foundation and framed out the walls and put the roof on with his son Jeremy. He had paid outright for the materials and owned all the land around it. Back then he was flush with cash, having sold off two chicken houses a few miles away.

Jerry's three sons knew a life then that he'd barely dreamed of living when he was a child. Jerry and Kanita bought each of their sons a four-wheeler that they rode over the pastures and along the wooded hillsides around the house. Their boys got their own trucks when they were teenagers, and the family went on vacation each summer. They saw Mount Rushmore and traveled to Florida. They stayed in hotels and didn't worry about the cost.

Jerry had gotten comfortable in this home. He thought it was a new plateau for his family, a place he'd reached after climbing for many years. His house, its concrete foundation, was the bedrock of their middle-class life. It was something he and Kanita thought they would build on over the years, handing it over to their sons when they passed away. He was proud on those summer vacations, proud of what he could give the boys and Kanita. It was a horizon that his father had worked toward all his life but never reached.

Now Jerry walked through the empty rooms into the kitchen to microwave his breakfast. He could see out the windows and look at the grass outside. It was a nice view, and Jerry savored it while he could. Before too long, he wouldn't be allowed on this property.

This house was the high-water mark of the Yandells' affluence. It was an empty monument for a dream. In just a few weeks he would be back where his father had been: harvesting lumber, taking odd jobs in town, working construction when jobs were available. Maybe his mistake had been expecting something more out of life.

News of the Yandells' ruin spread fast around Waldron. Jerry ran into friends and neighbors at the gas station, and they were polite about everything. Many people didn't bring it up at all. He never called the Tyson plant, and they didn't call him. Jerry let the bankruptcy lawyer handle all of that. Yandell never had any evidence that Tyson Foods intentionally delivered sick birds to his farm to target him, and the company later refused to answer questions about the incident. Regardless, the damage was done.

Jerry Yandell wasn't the only farmer to receive batches of sick birds, and as he was heading to bankruptcy court his neighbors began to compare notes. Doug Elmore, who also grew chickens outside of Waldron but had never met Jerry Yandell (though their farms were ranked against one another), heard about Yandell's trouble. Elmore was having the same problem. Flocks of birds were dying mysteriously, in spite of his best efforts to save them. Elmore had tried to get his birds tested at a laboratory to find out what was making them die, but a lawyer told him he couldn't do that because Tyson technically owned the birds. Elmore asked Tyson to test some of the dead chickens. The company told Elmore that, according to its tests, a high level of ammonia appeared to have sickened the birds. That meant, in essence, it was Elmore's fault.

Edwin, who lived just a few miles down Highway 80 from the Yandells' house, heard the same stories and began to understand why his own flocks had been dying out. He too had labored for weeks carrying the birds out to the freezer, thinking he must have gotten a batch with the flu or some other disease. He'd wondered whether his old houses were to blame. Even Jerry Yandell's sister Carry Owens, who knew what was happening at her brother's place, began seeing her own flocks die.

Up and down the valleys, the stories spread from farm to farm. The Elmores and Owenses and Edwins began putting hard questions to their field techs. What was the matter with the birds? If it was just a problem with the heating and ventilation, then why were birds dying on other farms, in newer houses? The field techs relayed their questions to Gary Roper, and soon the field techs began delivering the same answer to their isolated clients on the farm. The company initially speculated that something might be wrong with the baby chicks' digestion, causing them to die off. But eventually the company blamed the farmers, noting that ammonia levels were high inside the chicken houses where some of the birds died. Outside experts said Tyson's hatchery was a key suspect as a possible cause for the high mortality. Tyson Foods never publicly revealed if anything went wrong inside its hatchery that caused birds to sicken and die around Waldron.

Even years later, many farmers affected by the problem still had no idea what had happened. Tyson Foods eventually fixed the problem, whatever might have been the cause, but not soon enough to save the Yandells' farm. Eventually, Jerry and Kanita drove up to the federal courthouse in Fort Smith. They waited in line outside a courtroom for their name to be called. Then they went inside and sat at a table with a judge and several lawyers circled around it. Assets and debts were discussed, and it was decided all their assets would be sold or conveyed to the creditors to pay down the debt. Even after losing their home and their land, the Yandells still owed money. Their future paychecks would be garnished to pay it off over the years.

As he made his rulings, the judge was friendly toward Jerry and Kanita. Toward the end of the meeting, he turned and addressed Jerry, who was seated just a few feet away.

— Chicken farming is not too good, is it?

— No, it's not, Jerry replied.

— I understand, the judge replied.

Jerry Yandell never fought back. He never filed a lawsuit and never filed a case with the U.S. Department of Agriculture division that was created specifically to protect farmers like him. After losing his farm, Yandell took the kind of odd jobs that had supported his family growing up. He eventually got a job working on a road crew around Waldron. Yandell's bankruptcy went mostly unnoticed outside the small network of his friends and relatives.

When the Yandells went out of business, they were followed by many of their neighbors. The profits were being drained from their farms, and many felt they had no choice but to leave the business. As they quit, they took down the red aluminum signs by their driveways that once advertised their Tyson farms. All along the highways outside Waldron the signs came down, erasing the landmarks that once carried names like Yandell, Forrest, and Kelly.

The collapse of these farms did not appear to harm the Tyson plant in Waldron, nor even slow down its production. The company found a new crop of farmers who were willing to sign new contracts. The old farm signs were replaced with new ones, this time emblazoned with names like Phouthavong and Sengkhamyong and Vongsyprasom. These signs were erected by Laotian immigrants who had moved to Arkansas and bought ruined farms from local families. Stories about chicken farming had been spreading through the tightly knit networks of Asian immigrants who worked in factories and fast-food franchises in cities like Chicago and Minneapolis. Chicken farming looked great on paper, with a farm of three houses generating $300,000 in cash a year. And the cost of living in small-town Arkansas and Oklahoma was just a fraction of what the immigrants paid in cities up north.

And so immigrants like Cecil Phrasounonh moved to Waldron. Cecil bought a Tyson farm from a man who was desperate to leave the business. The farm had two chicken houses and a small shed that Cecil moved into. He installed a potbellied stove for warmth, slept on a mattress on the floor, and used a primitive outhouse for his bathroom.

Cecil and his brethren were the farmers of the future. Their arrival was inevitable, because it was what Tyson dictated. Just as longtime local workers left their jobs inside Tyson's slaughterhouses and were replaced by Hispanic workers, local farmers dropped their contracts and left their farms and were replaced by men and women like Cecil. They were obeying a mathematical formula that exerted a downward pressure on all things it touched. It pushed down costs and living standards and expectations. The pressure drove men and women down until they couldn't take it. Then it drove them out and found new men and women to take their place. The pressure never ended, and it was exerted on every farm where Tyson operated. It was an old pressure and impossible to stop.

The roots of this pressure went deep, went back decades, all the way to the birth of Tyson Foods. To really understand how the company came to be and how it obtained the power that it has in modern times, it helps to start at the beginning, back before the Great Depression. That's when a young farmer named John Tyson came upon hard times.

CHAPTER 2

The Eden Crash

(1929–1958)

IN 1930, a twenty-five-year-old man named John Tyson was exiled from his family's farm in Missouri. His inheritance was one working truck and one half bale of hay to sell on the open market.

A college student studying agriculture at Kansas State University, Tyson was preparing to walk in his father's footsteps and inherit the family farm outside Kansas City, the type of small operation where kids like John Tyson helped raise cattle, hogs, and corn. But just a year before, the world had been upended by speculators and bankers on Wall Street who had somehow inflated the stock market to ludicrous heights through lies, self-delusions, and drunken speculation. It wasn't at all clear to farmers like Tyson just what exactly had gone wrong in New York, but it was clear that the stock market crash had brought to an end a decade of prosperity and national dreams of grandeur.

Midwesterners felt the shock wave of the collapse in their bones. Prices for produce, grain, and livestock collapsed, rendering a summer's labor worthless in the snap of time it took for a telegraph to arrive from the East Coast. It was hard to find work in the big cities, near impossible in the small towns.

Before the crash, John Tyson would have had every expectation that his family's farm would be able to support him and his wife as they began their life together. But after 1929, the farm's meager income could hardly keep his father afloat. So John got all he would ever get from the farm: the truck, the hay to raise a little cash, and his father's best wishes to have a good life. John and his young wife made the long car trip south through Missouri and into Arkansas, toward Fort Smith, where he'd heard there were jobs.

The few photographs that capture John Tyson in his youth show him as a lanky man with a narrow face and pinched expression that reflected the hard times he'd known. Those who knew him said he had little time for sentimentality. As he turned his back on the farm where he was raised, and the stable life it had promised, it seems likely John Tyson didn't take much time to feel sorry for himself. He wouldn't have had time for reflection anyway. He ran out of money well before he ever reached Fort Smith and its promised jobs and found himself marooned in the small town of Springdale, planted in the middle of the wide-open green plains of the Ozark Plateau in northwestern Arkansas.

The people of Springdale were known as hill folks, remote and backward, disconnected from the world. The rocky red soil around town wasn't good for growing row crops like corn, soybeans, or cotton, leaving the area poor and separated from the rest of the state's plantation economy. But there was some money to be made from the richer soils west of town, where orchards were plentiful and landowners cultivated wide, neat rows of peaches, grapes, and strawberries during the long summers.

John Tyson rented a house in town with his wife and used his inheritance, in the form of one rickety truck, to start making a living. He hauled fruit to markets in Kansas City and Saint Louis—deliveries that kept him away from home for days at a time. But with each trip he brought home enough money to pay rent and buy food, relative luxuries in those days. John hired local men to drive overnight trips with him for no more payment than a single meal. Over time he developed a steady business and got to know the farmers and orchard keepers west of Springdale. He worked every day, any hours he was awake, without question. It's what he needed to do to survive.

And by 1931, he needed all the work he could get. He had a new baby boy depending on him, named Don.

The ruination of a family farm was more than just a business failure in the 1930s. It represented the collapse of a political and economic system that sustained a fifth of the American population and provided a foundation for the middle class. Seventy years later, the decimation of the family farm is an accepted fact of American life and is mourned only in sentimental terms. But as it cascaded through the nation, the wave of farm failures during the Great Depression was an unprecedented calamity. Families weren't just losing their livelihoods; they were also losing their homes and their birthrights. It would be as if the banks of today foreclosed on entire Manhattan neighborhoods at once, evicting the residents and emptying block after block of apartment buildings, leaving families adrift without the benefit of a public safety net to help pay the bills.

For more than a hundred and fifty years before the Depression, the family farm was the basic economic and social building block of the country. Thomas Jefferson wrote paeans to independent farmers, not just because he thought that farming was a pretty and virtuous thing, but because it represented the keystone of a democratic society at the time. For centuries, a citizen's relationship with land had been at the center of a society's power structure. In the European Dark Ages, the feudal system of land ownership had divided citizens into broad classes of lords and serfs, creating a system of centralized power, parceled out by access to land. The lords owned everything, and serfs owned nothing but their labor, which they exchanged for a plot of land on which to live and grow food at the lord's behest and whimsy.

If Thomas Jefferson had been writing a play, the feudal lords would have been his villains in black, and the system they created the dark nightmare from which humankind was trying to escape. So along came America, where citizens threw off the mantle of colonial power (which was an outgrowth of Europe's dark feudal history) and were given the right to control their government through voting.* Initially, only land-

---

* In Jefferson's time, citizenship was afforded only to white men, of course. But that combustible idea of inalienable rights to land and voting would later be redefined to include a broader portion of the citizenry.

owners could vote in America, so farming was deeply entwined with citizenship. In the minds of thinkers like Jefferson, the relationship between agriculture and citizenship ran deep — Jefferson realized the power to vote alone wasn't a sufficient guarantee of liberty and sovereignty. For that, citizens needed land. They needed to own land and have access to the resources that could nourish them and grant them economic independence. So Jefferson became history's best-known advocate of the system of agrarian democracy, whereby a patchwork of independent farmers—all of them economically self-sufficient but also connected through the open market for their goods—sprawled across the vast new land that was the ever-increasing United States of America.

And it worked, for the first time in history, really, because there was this ultra-rare historical window during which a young country was rapidly gaining new land on which to settle.*

From Jefferson's seminal era in the late 1700s until John Tyson's father had established a successful farm years later, a new system of land-owning, self-sufficient, democratically empowered citizens emerged. And the farms established a new culture in the United States, one of self-reliance and democratic power. That historical fact is probably at the root of our vague sentimental mourning for the family farm and all we lost along with it. Even in 2012, there is a sense that somehow, without small towns and rural communities, America has lost a piece of itself, even though most people today would never want to actually live on a farm or in a rural community.

For John Tyson's generation, the farm crisis was an injury still new and raw. The loss of the farm was a profound eviction. It was the loss of a system and the breaking of a promise. Young families found themselves nomadic, needing to escape the collapse of market prices and the blasting environmental scourge of the Dust Bowl. They migrated toward the coasts. They picked fruit or built roads as government

---

* Again, this was largely restricted to white citizens, making it more like an agrarian-democratic country club. Suffice it to say, the system worked for those who had access to it.

workers. They searched for factory jobs. They became beggars and, in some cases, alcoholics.

They fled an economic system that was collapsing.

But in the rarest of cases, such as John Tyson's, these refugees created an economic system that was altogether new to America.

In 1931 Springdale was a tiny crosshatch of streets populated by modest houses and small stores. Even eighty years later, the architecture of Springdale is utilitarian, and it speaks to a meager past where the greatest economic ambition was to put food on the table and little else. Today, the tallest buildings downtown are the grain silos, and the commercial strip downtown is a squat reef of one- and two-story rectangular buildings that look as though they were designed by architects who felt that tilting their heads upward was overly presumptuous. A building was as tall as it must be to fulfill its designated function and no taller.

It was the economic badlands, and John Tyson was stranded there with a wife, a one-year-old son, and a truck. Yet he had insinuated himself into the orchard economy west of town, becoming a regular produce shipper who ran routes to city markets up north.

Don's earliest memories were of strange men sleeping in a room in the back of his house between trips with his father. John paid the men a dollar a day, or in some cases simply gave them a hamburger and a cup of coffee to rent their company on an overnight haul to Kansas City. Sometimes Don's mother accompanied John, and they left the boy with a neighbor. Don was raised in a commercial house, where visitors were poor men desperate for work, and the rhythm of family life revolved around John Tyson's shipping schedule.

Don was an observant child. He took it all in.

The orchards outside Springdale had been profitable for decades, but in the early 1930s the fruit business began to slowly collapse. Dry summers and hard winter freezes drove many apple growers to failure. The hot winds from Oklahoma brought new pests: worms and mites and fungi that ate away at the peaches and berries. This happened just a few unlucky decades before the Green Revolution, when the invention of pesticides made it possible to grow homogenized crops on thousands of contiguous acres. In the 1930s, however, the pests spread unrestrained through the orchards. Fewer and fewer farmers needed John Tyson to ship their crops up north.

But John Tyson noticed a new opportunity growing in the shadow of the orchards. More farmers were increasing their investment in chickens, which used to be a kind of agricultural side bet they'd long used to generate a little cash in the winter months or after a weak harvest.

There had always been chickens roaming the grass and dirt lots around farmhouses and barns, but more farmers were experimenting with building big houses in which to raise them, growing enough to kill dozens and pack them in ice for a trip up to urban markets. Chicken was a delicacy in cities like Chicago and St. Louis, where housewives bought them whole and took them home to clean and cook for special occasions and Sunday dinners. For farmers, the trick was growing enough chickens at one time to make it worth their efforts. A wild profusion of oversize chicken coops sprang up along the edges of orchards to serve this purpose. Wooden sheds with tarpaper roofs and coal heaters in the bottom appeared, some built on wooden skids so they could be moved from spot to spot in order to have fresh grass beneath them. The chicken houses had all manner of tubes and vents installed to give the birds air and to blow out the noxious ammonia from their droppings. The hardest part was heating the houses to keep baby chicks alive. Kerosene lamps and coal stoves were used, and accidental fires were common.

As the fruit business declined, John Tyson began to haul more chickens. It was profitable but tricky. The chickens would stop eating as they jostled up rutted roads during trips that took several days, losing the precious weight that determined John Tyson's profit margin. So Tyson built a truck with a metal trough that ran between the chicken crates. He filled it with a mushy paste of water and food. The chickens pecked at it enough to keep the weight on during their trip. Soon John was hauling nothing but chickens.

Within a few years of arriving in Springdale, John Tyson was running a steady pipeline of live chickens from Arkansas to northern cities as far away as Chicago, Detroit, and Saint Louis.

The price disparities between those urban markets and the farms outside Springdale was so wide he made $250 from a single haul. He used the money to buy more birds and developed a regular coterie of farmers who built more, and larger, chicken houses to supply him. The chicken-house fires became rare as farmers figured out better ways to ventilate the big sheds, and the University of Arkansas extension system taught them which breeds grew biggest and fastest.

John divorced and remarried, bringing Helen Tyson into the family home when Don was still a child. Over the years, as his small shipping company grew, John Tyson became a respected businessman in Springdale. But the income wasn't dependable. Chicken prices swung fast, depending on the vagaries of big-city markets. Sometimes the profit on a load of chickens was wiped out in the time it took to deliver them. And John Tyson saw a steadier business in the local feed mills. A number of feed dealers had sprung up around Springdale to supply the growing number of chicken farms. Feed was the most expensive ingredient for chicken farming, and the profit margins were fat. Tyson signed a contract with Ralston Purina and became the company's local dealer. When Ralston later canceled his contract, he started buying grain and mixing it with vitamins to make his own brand of feed. He sold it to farmers and picked up their birds to ship north, making money on both ends of the deal.

By the time Don was ten years old, he was pressed into service at his father's business. It wasn't a question of wanting to join. He simply did what he was told. But the boy was quick to learn and eager to help. He helped his dad at the new feed business, using a shovel to mix piles of tawny grain in an empty warehouse. He and his dad packed crates of chickens in the back of Helen's car and shipped them across town. John built some chicken houses behind his company's small office, and Don spent his afternoons after school cleaning the coops and feeding the birds.

At night, Don Tyson sat at the family dinner table with John and Helen, listening to them talk back and forth about the family business. Soon he and his dad would spend long evenings engaged in their own discussions as Helen kept the books, entering the day's accounts in neat script.

Business was good but volatile. Farmers were discovering the unique economy of growing chickens, which was riskier than selling crops or raising cattle. One rooster with six hens could produce enough chickens to fill a chicken house in weeks, and the birds grew to maturity in a matter of a few months, rather than the two years it took to raise a cow or the season it took for cotton and corn. That meant the chicken population fluctuated with the frenzy of a stock market.

This made John Tyson's business almost entirely unpredictable. One day he might have too many birds to ship and need to hire extra drivers. Another day, after the price crashed and farmers cut back, he would have nothing. He needed a way to steady his income, since it was seemingly impossible to steady the market.

For Tyson, controlling the chicken farms was paramount to his success. What he needed more than anything in the early 1940s was a steady supply of birds. He had more demand than ever from customers up north. World War II was making big demands on resources and the government had rationed beef and pork but not chicken. Grocery stores wanted to buy all the chicken that Tyson could sell them to help fill up their meat counters. But if he came up empty-handed, the grocery chains would look to other suppliers to meet their needs.

Left on their own, farmers couldn't be counted on to supply Tyson enough chickens. They overproduced when prices were up, then grew gun-shy and refused to raise new flocks when prices were low. As orchards disappeared they were being replaced with casino-like poultry farms.

To solve the problem of undependable farmers, Tyson simply needed to look east, toward the scrubby Ozark Mountains and the marshy delta region beyond.

Farmers in the Ozark hill country were long on labor and short on capital.

In the 1930s and 1940s, they worked a thin layer of soil on the rocky bones of mountains, and after just a few generations of farming they had usually depleted the ground until it yielded very little. Big families had returned to hunting and foraging for some of their food, barely scratching a living out of a few hogs and cash crops. Cotton was the crop of choice: green, reedy rows planted in the most fertile soil along riverbeds in the valleys. The crops were reachable only by narrow, steep footpaths, inaccessible to farm machinery. They were a desperate man's imitation of a cash crop, and everyone knew cotton production was not a way to get rich.

For John Tyson, the lesson wasn't in the crops or the soil. It was in the financing. Cash-poor farmers rented land, and their landowners arranged a credit system that financed crops up front for the farmers who were broke. So the landowner provided the money, the farmer provided the labor, and they split the money when the crop came to fruition. The system spread throughout the South, carried on the back of poverty, allowing wealthy landowners and bankers to raise crops without working the land, while forcing farmers to grow crops they would never truly own.

In shorthand, it was called tenant farming.

The method slowly migrated to Springdale, where John Tyson and other feed dealers were trying to ensure a steady supply of chicken. The feed dealers started providing their product up front for farmers, collecting their payment when the chickens were sold. Then they started fronting the money to buy chickens as well.

John Tyson took it a step further. He bought the chickens himself from a hatchery, then he essentially loaned them to farmers who agreed to raise the birds and get paid a fixed price on delivery. The farmer didn't take any risk on prices because he never owned the birds, and Tyson got his steady flow of chickens to deliver to customers up north.

The system worked well, but that still left Tyson dependent on a hatchery for his birds. He got so frustrated depending on other companies for baby chicks that he eventually bought a hatchery of his own.

John Tyson consolidated his network of chicken farms, the feed mill, and the hatchery. It was like a deep well that gushed more profits with each day. He had effectively purchased every point in the chain of production where someone else might have made a profit, or inconveniently increased his cost of business. He made the feed. He hatched the birds. He paid farmers to raise them. And he shipped them north. In 1947 he incorporated his company, Tyson Feed and Hatchery.

Don Tyson watched. He listened to his father talk at night over the dinner table. And Don saw his father fire workers with all the sentimentality of a farmer flicking the head off a rooster with a sharp hatchet. It was simple: Do what John said. Or you were fired.

Don did what his father said.

When Don was a teenager, his father sent him to the University of Missouri to take a course in testing birds for disease. He spent long hours in the hatchery, drawing blood from hens, mixing it with an antigen in a petri dish and ensuring the health of the flock. By the time he was sixteen, he was driving trucks and shipping birds outside of the state when drivers weren't available.

There is a photo of John Tyson, somewhere during this time, perhaps in the early 1950s, standing in front of a wood-slatted chicken house and holding a white chicken in his hands. His face looks as drawn and stern as the times in which he was raised. His wan smile looks as utilitarian as a farm hat. He holds the bird with all the affection of a shovel. He was a man who never forgot the dark cloud of poverty from which he ran until the day he died. Each day at work, each nightly conversation at the table with his son, was a long campaign to survive and to ensure the family's future.

And no matter how hard they worked, or how much money they made, it would never be enough to ease John Tyson's hunger to make more.

As Tyson's company slowly grew in Arkansas, a new agricultural economy was developing in the United States. Like Tyson's endeavor, this new economic structure could be traced back to the early 1930s, when the fabric of the rural Midwest was coming unraveled. During the Great Depression, farmers raised bountiful crops but couldn't sell them for enough money to pay their rent or their bank loans or to buy food for their family. In states like Iowa, banks that tried to auction off foreclosed properties were met by groups of farmers toting guns. The armed men stood at the public auction and ensured that the original owner of the farm could buy it back for a bid of one dollar. The "dollar auctions" became common as small towns fought for their survival.

In response, politicians in Washington passed a series of bailouts and emergency programs to help the middle class.

A federal law called the Agricultural Adjustment Act let the government set the volume and the price of the nation's biggest crops. Passed in 1933, the act created a new bureaucracy in which economists figured out how many acres of wheat or cotton farmers could raise in order to fix prices at a profitable level. The government set edicts for crops after the economists finished their calculations. To eliminate surpluses, farmers plowed under acres of cotton plants and slaughtered millions of baby hogs so they would never reach the market. The idea was to keep prices high enough to throw the middle class a lifeline and iron out the volatility of the market. Critics of the plan said it would lead to a dangerous level of government control over the economy, but they were answered with a simple response: The laws were temporary.

They were emergency actions that would be repealed once farm prices stabilized.

In Arkansas, the new edicts all but wiped out the cotton farmers who scratched a living from the Ozark soil, creating a willing crop of farmers to build chicken coops and buy chicks on contract from John Tyson. It wasn't the first gift that John Tyson would get from government intervention. The emergency measures would not only stay in place over the next seventy-five years, they would expand and evolve, and deliver to Tyson exactly what he needed most: cheap, reliable supplies of grain.

When he was twenty-three years old, in 1953, Don Tyson took a trip to the local bank while his father, John, was on vacation. He knew it was the only chance he'd have, sitting in a chair at a bank, talking with a loan officer and seeing just how much money he could get away with borrowing.

He had plenty to borrow against. His father's company was growing and it now had an office in downtown Springdale. Regular shipments of chickens were sent north and sold, and batch after batch of chicks rolled out of Tyson's hatchery. The company was hauling the chicks, as well as tons of feed, to a growing network of farms that were being built on the flat plains around Springdale and on the denuded hillsides in the Ozarks. The company was generating the kind of cash John Tyson never would have dreamed of possessing when he left his family farm nearly twenty-five years before. And in a way, he didn't possess it. Every penny and every dime was instantly plowed back into more production: more feed to mix, more chicks to deliver, and more trucks and drivers to ship north.

Don could see the profits just over the horizon, and he wanted to borrow money to make them happen. But John refused to borrow. He had seen the farms around his father's take on loans during the 1920s, when crop prices were good and people wanted to believe the good times would last forever. What happened in 1929 didn't teach John Tyson a lesson so much as it permanently scarred his appetite for risk and debt.

So Don simply waited for his father to go on vacation before he visited the bank.

When the loan officer asked Don how much he wanted to borrow, Don simply asked how much he could have. The banker said the maximum loan they could extend was $80,000.

— Well, that's how much I want then, Don said.

He wired the money to Michigan, where a hatchery was selling cheap birds. The hatchery had badly misread the market and hatched a flock of chicks just as prices fell through the floor. The hatchery was unloading the chicks for the bargain price of three cents each. It cost Don Tyson about ten cents to hatch a bird on his own. So buying the birds at such a steep discount gave Tyson a huge cost advantage, and fatter profit margins. Don Tyson sunk the entire $80,000 into the deal. He bought the cheap chicks, paid farmers to raise them, and sold them at a profitable enough price to pay back the loan and invest a profit in Tyson's accounts.

Don told his father what he had done. For a while John Tyson was quiet.

— You done good, he finally said.

Don became a field veterinarian, traveling from farm to farm and checking on the health of the flocks. He learned much of what he knew at the University of Arkansas, where he studied animal nutrition and economics. He did well at the university but never graduated, as there was too much work to be done at the company.

Don knew chickens like some men knew complicated farm machinery. He knew when the birds were sick or when they were just overheated and needed more air. He knew when they needed more food and when they needed less. And when a Tyson truck delivered chicks from the Tyson hatchery and feed from the Tyson feed mill, Don showed up at the farm to tell the farmer how to grow the chicks.

Every night he and his father talked business: what was going wrong, where they needed to cut, and what they needed to expand. They noticed that more companies were opening slaughterhouses around Missouri and Arkansas built especially to process chickens. Tyson had a growing customer base with supermarkets in Kansas City and Saint Louis, and the markets wanted the birds feathered and gutted so the butchers could easily quarter them and display the parts for weekend specials.

If there was a slaughterhouse in Springdale, the Tysons could cut their shipping costs and wring more profit from the system. Don started meeting with men from the Springdale chamber of commerce, trying to convince them to lure a plant into town. He told them about the good jobs it would bring, stable factory jobs that were rare in Springdale in the mid-1950s.

The chamber and the Tysons pooled their money and bought twenty acres north of town. A company out of Kansas City said it was interested in locating there, and Don thought he had them on the hook. But the company backed out, opting to build in Missouri and leaving the twenty acres sitting like an empty promise.

— We should build a plant there, Don told his father.

If they owned a plant, he reasoned, they could kill the chickens themselves and sell directly to the markets. John asked him how much money it would cost, and Don came up with the best sales pitch he could think of: He lied. It could easily cost close to $100,000, but Don said he could do it for $75,000. So John Tyson fronted his son the money, and construction began.

Don visited other plants to see how they worked. He lined up the purchase of new machinery built just to process chickens. He bought big vats of scalding water into which chickens were dipped to remove the feathers and long assembly lines where rows of workers used sharp blades to unzip the birds' breasts and scoop out their organs. He bought crates of ice to place at the end of an assembly line where the fresh carcasses were stacked for shipment. He bought the innards of his first slaughterhouse, piece by piece, and learned the process as he went. Then he ran out of money.

Don had spent the full $75,000 and the slaughterhouse was still skeletal, weeks from completion. Workers were already anticipating the jobs there, which were promised to pay seventy-five cents an hour, a full dime above minimum wage. Don went to his father and said he needed just a little more money to finish the job. John Tyson said no. The price tag was $75,000, and he'd already paid it. Don went to investors in town and lined up $10,000 from one and $5,000 from another.

When the first Tyson slaughterhouse was completed in 1958, there wasn't enough money left to paint it. The parking lot was a bare patch of dirt because they didn't have the gravel to cover it. Still, more than a hundred employees showed up the first day, and trucks delivered hundreds of live chickens to the bay door. The disassembly line of workers came to life. The vats boiled. The tubs filled with entrails. The ice-laden crates filled with chickens.

And Don oversaw it all.

At the end of the first day, they'd slaughtered and cleaned three thousand birds. Birds they'd hatched. Birds they'd fed. Birds they'd hauled to the killing floor. With the slaughterhouse in place, Tyson stood to make a profit from every link in the long chain.

Then a government inspector looked over the bounty, and, box by box, all the chicken was condemned. The birds were covered in grease slicks and scraps of metal from the new machinery.

The workers stood idly by and watched as their harvest was deemed to be trash. They helped haul the icy carcasses to the landfill.

John Tyson got a certain look in his eye before he fired people. His employees said that at such moments "Mr. John was in orbit." And when he was in orbit, he fired workers like he was pulling weeds. As he stood in the slaughterhouse listening to his son explain that the first day's chickens had been wasted, John Tyson went into orbit. He had sunk a fortune into this slaughterhouse and invested weeks of farm work and tons of feed into raising the chickens. And it was all for nothing.

— I can throw three thousand chickens away. You don't have to process them to do that, John Tyson told his son.

Everyone stood far from John Tyson and left Don there to talk to him. Because they all knew there was only one person in the company whom John Tyson could not fire.

By the end of 1958, Don Tyson had mastered the art of running an industrial slaughterhouse. His team of employees learned how to run the machines efficiently while avoiding mishaps that could ruin the meat. Eventually, the slaughterhouse was running smoothly and at full capacity. Don was still the manager there, though he was not yet thirty years old. His father worked in the office downtown. Every day they met for lunch at a spot halfway between their workplaces, a meat-and-potatoes place called Neal's Café. Mounted deer and boar heads hung on the walls, and the lunch prices were reasonable. Don and John sat alone in a booth and talked business.

From start to finish, they owned the chicken industry: from the breeding houses to the bloodlines of the best hens, from the hatchery eggs to the feed mill, and from the slaughterhouse to the shipping line. They even set the rules on the farms where the birds were grown, and they found more and more farmers willing to give away their control in return for a steady paycheck.

The machine was growing. The more money it generated, the stronger it grew. And as Don and John sat talking in Neal's, below the trophies of other men's hunting trips, they realized something: There was a whole world of consumers out there who rarely ate chicken but who would eat it when they realized how cheap it could be. Chicken was selling out at every grocery store that the Tysons took on as a customer. It seemed like the demand was bottomless, and now the Tysons had the means to deliver.

Making this machine wasn't the end of the process. It was just the beginning.

CHAPTER 3

Expand or Expire

(1960–1967)

HASKELL JACKSON, a college-trained accountant, was dressed like a factory worker when he showed up for his first day on the job at Tyson Feed and Hatchery. This was a curious turn of events for Haskell, who had spent the last four years of his life wearing a coat and tie to work every day as an accountant with the Phillips Petroleum Company in Bartlesville, Oklahoma. Jackson's new job with Tyson was certainly a step up professionally. But there he stood on August 20, 1960, on the sidewalk outside a two-story redbrick building dressed in matching khaki pants and shirt, with his name stitched across the shirt's front pocket in red lettering, like he was a janitor or slaughterhouse worker. This uniform, he had been told in no uncertain terms, was the standard dress code at Tyson. And the dress code even applied to him, the company's new office manager and chief accountant.

The khaki uniform was the eccentricity of the company's young president, Don Tyson, who ran the company with his dad, John. Don also wore the khaki uniform, dressing identically to the employees who worked in the hatchery and slaughterhouse he owned.

The Tyson Feed and Hatchery offices were located in a nondescript building on the east end of Emma Street, the strip of shops and offices that ran through downtown Springdale. The building was at the tail end of the town's main drag, down by the railroad tracks and away from the center of town. That was probably for the best, because the company's hatchery was located directly behind its offices, and the hatchery exuded the kind of stench of which the chamber of commerce would not approve. It was an odd place for Jackson to end up

63

as an accountant, but he felt like it was his best option at the time. He had grown up in Arkansas, and his wife had been after him for years to move back home to his home state. Finally, his mother-in-law had told him about the job opening at the hatchery in Springdale, and he had interviewed there just to keep the peace in his family.

The interviews had gone well and eventually he met Don Tyson, who quizzed him about his accounting experience. Jackson asked Don just what exactly his job description would be if he moved to Arkansas.

— Hell, I don't know. My accountant just tells me I need a full-time accountant, Don said.

Don's "accountant" at the time was a full-time auditor out of Little Rock who kept the company's books. After years of rapid growth, the auditor, Harry Erwin, told Don that if he was going to keep expanding the company as he wanted to, Don would need an in-house accountant to keep up with the books.

Jackson walked into the office on his first day and went upstairs to the bookkeeping department. As he stood in the little office toward the front of the building, he started to have his doubts. The room was a busy mess of bookkeepers and piles of paper, and his desk was out in the open, in the middle of the chaos. The days of having an office to himself were over. All around him, a team of ten clerks was busy tallying the company's receipts and invoices to farmers. Jackson realized the company's books hadn't been reconciled since April 30, four months before, and the end of the fiscal year was at the end of September. That meant he had just a little more than a month to straighten out the paperwork and figure out if Tyson was losing or making money. So he settled into a routine of twelve-hour workdays and long weekends at the office straightening out the company's paper trail.

Jackson was accustomed to hard work. The oldest of four children, he'd been raised by his parents in a three-room wooden house with no running water or electricity on a hillside homestead in rural Madison County, just east of Springdale. Jackson's father called the place a "farm," though it was little more than a patch of soil and a shack. Jackson's dad tried his hand at growing different cash crops, but he preferred heavy drinking to hard labor and none of his farming ventures ever yielded much money. Jackson moved away young and earned his accounting degree from the University of Arkansas in nearby Fayetteville. Jackson's linear mind took naturally to the profession, the orderly arrangement of numbers and the reconciliation of expenses and income. He also had a remarkable memory for dates, numbers, and facts, which made him a natural at tracking the various moving pieces of a large business.

As he settled into work at Tyson, Jackson discovered the definition of organized chaos. There weren't even generally accepted procedures for accounting in the poultry industry. As Jackson researched the industry, he found only one slim pamphlet that discussed how to account for operations at a vertically integrated chicken company. The business was simply too new to have well-defined practices. Like everyone else at Tyson, Jackson found himself making up new rules as he went along and building the foundation for a new industry in his wake. As luck would have it, the new industry was arising at the perfect moment in history. American dining habits were fundamentally shifting, opening the door to a new era of poultry production.

By the early 1960s, Americans were in a hurry. Women were entering the workforce in ever-larger numbers, and families were starting to redefine the way they ate. The family dinner as they knew it was quickly becoming a relic of the past, with a set table and roasted chicken increasingly relegated to the nostalgic paintings of Norman Rockwell. For the first time, Americans began to demand two things from their food: that it be cheap, and quick to prepare. A bird that used to be reserved for Sunday dinners was getting so inexpensive that it began to be used as lunch meat. With every passing year, Americans traded other foods for chicken, eating more of it rather than spending money on beef or taking time to make a salad. The economics of chicken made the trade-off all but inevitable.

Don Tyson saw the changes clearly and exploited them quickly. He spent his time cultivating relationships with the big grocery chains that sold more chicken than ever over their butcher counters. He figured out that he could cut the birds up in his slaughterhouses into prepared breasts and drumsticks, and sell the packaged parts, reducing the grocery store's cost of paying a butcher to do it on site. Don Tyson's young company benefited from being a new kind of animal altogether. It was both a farm and a manufacturer. It was a biological system and an industrial machine. This hybrid quality allowed it to dodge taxes and evade regulations that constrained the power of other meat companies, like beef meatpackers.

As the Tyson Feed and Hatchery business grew, Don and John Tyson earned a kind of prestige and respect in Springdale. After arriving in town destitute and desperate, John Tyson had become one of the town's biggest employers. A portrait from the time shows him sitting behind his desk in a dark suit and tie, a little more corpulent than in the early days when he slung crates of fruit into the back of his truck. His arm is draped casually across the back of his chair, and he is gazing off into the distance with a look of contentment on his face, like a man who is savoring his power.

While John Tyson carried a veneer of aristocracy about him, the memory of dire poverty never seemed to have left Don Tyson. He might as well have still been penniless in the family living room in the earliest days of the company. Don realized, perhaps more than anyone, that the success of his family's company was transitory. He learned that even as the chicken business grew by an order of magnitude, it remained as volatile as in the earliest days. He watched the big competitors get torn down overnight, and he learned that even a mountain of profit wasn't enough to keep a company alive. No matter how rich he got, or how much cash came in the door of Tyson Feed and Hatchery, Don Tyson knew that collapse could be around the corner. It was knowledge that shaped him, and his company, for decades to come. Don was more willing than his father was to take risks and borrow money, but the knowledge that his business was always vulnerable never left him. The chicken business would forever be defined by waves of boom and bust that pitted the biggest companies against each other. When the decade began, there was a frontier quality to the chicken industry, with countless start-up companies entering the fray to cash in on the growing market. The ensuing years would be pitiless to these companies, winnowing them down into a smaller group of competitors who fought each other for survival.

The companies that outlasted the rest, Don learned, were those that could exert the most control over their operations and their farmers. The survivors were the companies that relentlessly controlled their costs, pushing every possible penny of waste out of their system, even when they were turning a profit. Tyson's evolution during the 1960s unfolded quietly, beyond the notice of most Americans, who were concerned with the Vietnam War and rise of its youthful counterculture. But the agricultural revolution that took place in far-flung southern towns set the stage for a modern industry dominated by a few titanic companies.

The lessons Don Tyson learned during those years were etched into Tyson's corporate DNA and therefore began to shape the future of America's rural economy.

Don Tyson spent a lot of time with bankers. After secretly borrowing $80,000, he had finally convinced his father that taking credit from bankers wouldn't bring doom to the company. As John grew more comfortable with borrowing, Don traveled throughout Missouri and Arkansas, building relationships with bankers who were increasingly interested in investing in the new business of poultry production.

Don discovered a new source of credit that had been overlooked by many of his competitors, in the form of a sleepy federal agency called the Farm Credit Administration. The Farm Credit Administration was established to loan money to farmers who got turned away by banks. There was more to the program than just ensuring a steady food supply. The 1961 Agriculture Act, which extended cheap credit to farmers, carried language that would have made Thomas Jefferson smile. The idea was to further subsidize the family farm, which Congress called the most efficient way to produce food, and a bedrock economic base for towns and cities in rural America. To support family farmers, the Farm Credit Administration gave them cheap loans to build barns or buy wheat threshers. If the farmer defaulted, the tax-payers would cover the cost.

The agency wasn't heavily involved in the poultry business, but Don Tyson helped change that. Tyson met with Farm Credit agents and explained to them the new business of industrial chicken farming. The system evened out the wild risks that had characterized the early days of the poultry industry. A farmer growing birds for Tyson could show the Farm Credit Administration a reliable long-range prediction of cash flow and sales, regardless of the season. Perhaps most important, Tyson provided a letter of intent to the lenders, assuring them it would deliver a steady flow of chickens to make the farm profitable. Production wasn't tied to weather events or the grain markets. It was tied only to Tyson marketing arrangements and contracts. The predictability made it a safe haven for the taxpayer's money.

The Farm Credit Administration was convinced. The agency extended more government-backed loans to farmers entering the business to grow birds under contract with Tyson. Those government loans, in turn, helped assure private banks that chicken farming was a safe proposition for lending.

Loan after loan was extended to a new generation of contract farmers as Don Tyson made the circuit of banks and extolled his new business. A new breed of indentured farmer was born.

As Haskell Jackson was organizing Tyson's financial ledgers, a steady parade of train cars hauled loads of lumber into northwestern Arkansas. Wooden beams were cut to specific dimensions and stacked neatly in the train cars. Upon arrival they were moved to trucks and shipped out to the hillsides and green meadows around Springdale, where the skeletal frames of new chicken houses were being erected.

A young Tyson employee named Donald Wray visited these farms as construction got under way. Wray was a congenial man, freshly dropped out of the master's program in agriculture at the University of Arkansas. He was a country boy from Magnolia, Arkansas, and everyone called him by his nickname, Buddy. It was Don Tyson who had talked him into leaving school in 1961. Don instantly put him to work as a field technician for the company's farmers. It was a job Don himself had done as a young man, and it was fast becoming a job that was critical to the company's success.

Wray helped build a network of giant chicken farms at a time when the very definition of the American farm was transforming. Just a decade before, the American farm was still an enterprise owned and run by middle-class families. Farming was still seen as the quintessential small business, the basic economic unit for a society that prized individual ownership and wealth. But that started to change in the 1950s. Rather than being an economic foundation for families, farms were becoming rural factories that provided as much food as possible for an increasingly large and complicated food system.

Scientists made a number of breakthroughs that forever changed the economics of farming. Chemists figured out how to turn petrochemicals into nitrogen fertilizers that made soil more fertile. New pesticides wiped out insects that for centuries had made it impossible to grow thousands of acres of the same crop at one time. Farmers weren't so much dependent on the rain or sun as they were on their relationship with their local chemical dealers.

Buddy Wray was the face of this new mode of farming. He helped farmers do the two things necessary for modernization: get big and get specialized. They raised huge volumes of one crop—in this case chicken—and they did it with increasingly high costs and sophisticated equipment.

Getting big and getting specialized made farmers more dependent on outside corporations like Tyson. In 1940 farmers bought only about 34 percent of the inputs like fuel and feed that they needed to run their farm. They produced the rest themselves. By the time Buddy Wray was knocking on doors and visiting farmers in the early 1960s, farmers bought about 63 percent of their inputs. As farms became more dependent on the outside economy, they also became more productive. Aggregate farm output rose by 54 percent between 1940 and 1962, even as farm inputs rose by just 4 percent.

As farmers grew more food, prices went down and their profit margins got thinner. So they raised more crops or livestock to stay afloat, thereby increasing supply and driving down prices even more. It began a race toward bigness that still hasn't stopped, and which has driven the vast majority of farmers out of business.

Buddy Wray was offering farmers a deal that was perfectly suited to the era. Tyson arranged for farmers to build new chicken houses, helped them get the loans to do it, and provided them specially bred birds to raise. Tyson emphasized that contract farming was a way to reduce risk. The farmer was insulated from the most dangerous part of the business, which was selling birds in a wholesale market where prices could fall by half in a day.

Buddy Wray was good at his job. He is a naturally affable man, with his tall stature, close-cropped black hair, and square jaw. He has the look of someone who could naturally be trusted. His country boy mannerisms from Magnolia made him seem entirely too simple, and entirely too good, to be pitching a business deal anything less than completely honest.

In the early 1960s, Don Tyson, still hadn't figured out the best way to get his farmers to grow huge numbers of chickens as quickly and cheaply as possible. When he needed to chew over such a problem, he often turned to one of his old friends, Joe Fred Starr. The two of them had met in college, and both had a penchant for carousing. As a teenager Starr had lost most of his right hand in a shooting accident, and he had only his index finger left. While the deformity might have made other men self-conscious, it only seemed to stoke Starr's brash self-regard. Like Don Tyson, Starr was a salesman with a deep hunger for making money. The men remained fast friends for decades.

Don and Joe Fred hashed out the problem of Tyson's farms. The company had largely settled on the model of contract farming, but this had its drawbacks. The houses were getting bigger, the feed mixes more complicated, and the knowledge necessary to medicate the birds for disease was becoming more technical. In short, it took a college degree to be a chicken farmer. But the company couldn't find college-educated people willing to do the grimy, seven-day-a-week job of raising chickens.

Tyson experimented with the model of owning farms outright and staffing them with well-trained workers. This seemed like a natural fit for Tyson, because it left the farm within the company's control. But the limitations showed up quickly. It was hard to motivate hired hands to do the work, which involved hauling loads of dead chickens out of a barn where the ammonia fumes were so strong they burned the eyes. Hired hands just didn't raise the best birds, no matter how much you paid them or what kind of incentives you provided. They didn't have skin in the game.

Owning farms also had another downside: Chicken houses were a terrible investment of the company's money. The buildings served only one purpose, and they lost their value quickly as they wore out. A quick set of calculations revealed that Tyson Feed and Hatchery would never have the kind of capital it would need to buy all the land and build all the houses required to supply itself with chickens.

To counter these problems, Tyson settled on the model of using independent contract farmers. A farmer who owned his chicken houses was deeply motivated to care for the birds. He had a mortgage and debt from the chicken houses hanging over his head. It made a man get up early in the morning, and it kept him going until late at night.

Tyson provided the necessary college-educated labor on the farm by hiring a team of technicians like Buddy Wray, who visited each farm several times a week. A formula was settled upon that lasted for decades: The farmer provided the labor, and the company provided the brains.

Haskell Jackson had just barely gotten Tyson Feed and Hatchery's books under control when he was told he had a second big task: convince the Internal Revenue Service that Tyson should pay taxes as if it were a family farm.

Harry Erwin, Tyson's auditor in Little Rock, broke the news. It wasn't going to be enough for Jackson to get Tyson's books in order. He was also going to have to keep two sets of them. One set of numbers would be the figures that Tyson gave to its bankers and investors, showing how profitable the company had become. The second set of books was for the IRS, and these would show the federal tax agents how much money Tyson was losing.

The task was possible because Erwin had discovered a profitable loophole in the U.S. tax code. Unlike most U.S. businesses, family farms were allowed to use an outdated form of bookkeeping called "cash-basis" accounting. Virtually every other company had to use a different kind, called "accrual" accounting, which better reflected the true profitability of complex corporations.

Cash-basis accounting is simple. A company records its expenses only when it pays out the actual cash for them. And it only books income when the actual cash comes in the door. By contrast, companies using accrual accounting methods record their expenses when they sign a contract to pay someone, even if the cash hasn't actually left their account yet.

Farmers were allowed to use cash-basis accounting because it was simpler, and Congress didn't think small farms had the money to hire accountants for complicated recordkeeping. So a farmer would only record his expenses for seed when he paid for it, and he only booked his income for grain when he cashed the check. Erwin realized the cash-basis tax provision might apply to Tyson Feed and Hatchery. The company employed nearly four hundred people, many of them working in factory conditions in the slaughterhouse, and it invested millions of dollars in industrial plants for the feed mill, hatchery, and fleet of trucks. But Tyson's sole purpose was producing meat. Don and John Tyson maintained a majority ownership, and they were certainly family. So under U.S. tax code, their multimillion-dollar corporation was a family farm.

Jackson set up a dummy corporation called Poultry Growers Inc., a wholly-owned subsidiary of Tyson's that operated the company's network of chicken farms. Using cash-basis accounting, Jackson could easily make it look like the corporation suffered massive losses each year. Poultry Growers Inc. paid up front for its feed, fuel, and other farm expenses. Because Tyson sold its birds with long-term contracts to grocery stores and restaurant chains, it could delay reporting its income into the next tax period, when cash from the contracts rolled in. Hypothetically, the company could kick the can of taxable income down the road for years.*

While Tyson couldn't escape paying taxes altogether, it could reduce its payments substantially. In Jackson's view, the income tax ploy basically let Tyson take an interest-free loan from taxpayers. By putting off its tax payments, Tyson could put its money to work by investing it in new equipment or more workers.

The plan worked, but it was hell on Jackson. After carefully orchestrating Tyson's cost codes and accounting for all the company's transactions, Jackson had to translate all the numbers into a different accounting basis. When it came time to pay taxes, he submitted these books to the IRS. When Tyson went to banks to borrow more money, Jackson had the other books on hand, the ones that used accrual-basis accounting. Presumably, all of this was legal.

By 1985, Tyson's Foods had avoided paying $26.5 million in annual taxes through the cash-basis loophole, according to a report written by two economists with the U.S. General Accounting Office.

The morality of the ploy didn't seem to be a matter of much debate inside Tyson. When the company saw a loophole and a chance to make a profit, Tyson took it, a strategy that became part of the company's culture for decades to come. If the feds had a problem with it, it would be up to them to broach the issue. Eventually, that happened with cash-basis accounting. In 1986 Tyson was forced to quit using the scheme when the Tax Reform Act closed the loophole for farms with more

---

* Another big advantage of cash-basis accounting is that companies don't have to count their inventory as an asset on the books. So all of Tyson's chicken, being inventory, could be counted as worthless on the books, making losses look even bigger as it spent money on feed and fuel.

than $25 million a year in gross receipts. Poultry Growers Inc. was merged into Tyson Foods, Inc. in 1989.

It was a good time to be a family farm.

On Monday mornings at six o'clock, Haskell Jackson, Buddy Wray and Joe Fred Starr arrived at Tyson's offices downtown for the weekly managers' meeting. In the winter months it was still dark when they parked their cars in the lots and walked into work. They had all been raised as farm boys, so the early hours didn't bother them. But Jackson had to admit he was still groggy during the morning sessions, and he never really got used to talking business strategy before he was fully awake.

The men filed into a tiny room that had been cleared out in the back of the office, the closest thing Tyson had to a meeting room. They sat in cheap metal chairs around three small, square tables that had been set end to end to make a kind of formal meeting table. Three glass ashtrays sat along the center of the tables, and the men were quick to light up their first smoke of the day as they sat down and tried to get their brains going. The small room was hazy with smoke as the meeting got into full swing.

There wasn't much friendly banter, but Jackson felt at home with the men around the table. They were mostly college-educated farm boys like him. Leland Tollett, for example, had a PhD in agriculture from the University of Arkansas. Leland had been pals with Buddy Wray at the university, and Leland vouched for Wray when Don Tyson hired him.

Don and John Tyson sat at one end of the table, side by side. The meeting began after the men passed around a memo that laid out the day's agenda. Jackson acted as the dutiful secretary for the meetings, taking notes on everything that was said.

Don Tyson typically drove the discussion. He liked to talk about the events of the week before. He asked each manager to go over any mistakes or obstacles they'd come across so they could chart a better course for the week ahead. Some of the matters were mundane. Each man would give an update on his division, so everyone knew what was going on throughout the company.

Although the topics changed from week to week, Don Tyson consistently hammered one point home: The company needed to grow. In a business with tiny profit margins, Don Tyson thought the only way they could prosper was to get bigger, and to do it as fast as possible.

— I don't want to be the biggest or the best. I want to be the best of the biggest, he told his managers.

Wray noticed that Don Tyson was usually the voice of expansion. He wanted to push and push. He wanted more and he wanted it now. If a banker was willing to loan the company money, Don wanted to take them up on it. But John Tyson sat next to his son like a living reminder of the Depression and the hard lessons it wrought on the country. He was always skeptical of complicated financial arrangements. He never rushed to take on debt. As Don would get steamed up on a new idea, John would often pull back the reins.

— Now hold on a minute, John Tyson would say. Let's be realistic here . . .

John Tyson had his own esoteric set of rules of thumb for the company's finances. Tyson Feed and Hatchery could take on long-term debt only if the interest payments amounted to half the amount the company could deduct from its taxes each year for depreciation of its equipment. If the company could deduct $1 million for depreciation, for example, it could only take on debt with interest payments worth $500,000 or less.

This rule seemed arcane, but it was part of a philosophy that John Tyson drove home to his managers. Everybody could take on debt during good times. The banks practically threw money at you if they thought you would take it. But the real survivors thought about their debt in terms of the bad times that would inevitably come. Forty years later, when Don Tyson was running a company worth several billion dollars in annual sales, he would stick tightly to his father's rule of thumb about debt payments and depreciation.

As the meeting wrapped up, each man at the table had a fresh list of responsibilities for the week ahead. Don and John Tyson never looked over their managers' shoulders, and they never tried to do their work for them. But all the men knew they would be back in the smoky meeting room in one short week, and they'd be called upon to answer for everything they'd done.

The managers kept in mind the words on a plaque that hung in Don's office: "If there's any question about responsibility . . ."

They all knew how the statement was supposed to end.

Don was quick to tell them:

— The responsibility lies with you.

Just a year after he joined the company, Haskell Jackson began to see clearly that it was headed toward ruin.

By the summer of 1961, Jackson had gotten Tyson's books into relatively good order. And the financial picture that started to emerge was bleak. While Tyson had grown enormously since 1930, the underlying nature of the chicken business had not changed from the earliest days of tarpaper houses. It was still like a casino.

Starting in the spring, chicken prices began dropping sharply. Too many companies had seen the good profits to be made in the business, and they were flooding the market with too much product. Big meatpackers like Armour, Swift, and Wilson built poultry plants in the South, and they were joined by a crop of smaller upstarts like Tyson, Garrett Poultry, and Simmons. New farms were being built, slaughterhouses were being run at full capacity, and supply started to outstrip demand. Tyson was like a machine built to pump out huge volumes of meat, and it couldn't be ratcheted back easily. The company was shipping truckloads of ice-packed chickens, whether grocery stores wanted them or not, and its competitors were doing the same thing. Tyson salesmen haggled with grocers and restaurant owners to pay for loads of iced meat that nobody wanted, but their bargaining power was almost nil. Everyone knew that Tyson's truckloads of chicken would start spoiling in a matter of days. The salesmen dumped product at whatever price they could get.

At the beginning of 1961, chicken was selling for 25 cents to 30 cents a pound. By that summer, Tyson Feed and Hatchery was lucky to get 10 cents a pound. Some shipments were dumped on the market for

5 cents a pound. The slow bleed was undeniable as Jackson tallied it all up. For more than thirty weeks, the market price for chicken fell below the cost of production. Tyson was paying for factories, workers, and trucks that only dug it deeper into a loss with each shipment of chicken it produced. For all its intricate coordination of farms, feed mills, and hatchery, Tyson was being undone by the marketplace, the one sector of the business that remained entirely outside its control.

The mood at the Monday morning management meetings began to change. For Jackson and Buddy Wray, it was increasingly apparent they'd made a mistake in joining the company. Wray had walked away from the chance to get a master's degree from the University of Arkansas. Jackson had left a good job at an oil company. Both of them were regretting the gamble they made on entering the chicken business. On Monday mornings, the men filed into the meeting room as usual. They lit cigarettes and passed around their meeting memos for the morning. Jackson dutifully recorded the conversation. But in their hearts, Jackson and Wray thought this was the company's final act.

One person in the room never seemed to consider the possibility that the company would go under. Don Tyson went around the room and made each of his lieutenants report his week's performance and plan for the week to come. Don wasn't in denial. He made them recount the losses each unit had suffered, and he asked them for an unvarnished prediction of how bad things might be in the future. But against all available evidence, he was making plans for the future and laying out the company's strategy for a market recovery that he was convinced would eventually come.

— We will weather this storm, Don said.

He stood there and talked to them as if it was the high point of the market. He wanted their ideas, and he brainstormed along with them.

Don's confidence somehow fooled the men around him into being confident too. They began to buy into his idea that there might be a tomorrow for which to plan. The company began slowing its factory lines. It placed fewer birds in its network of farms. It tried to deliver just enough meat to stay in the good graces of its customers and keep a spot on their shelves without selling too much product at a loss. Don lined up a loan of $500,000 from Mercantile Bank in St. Louis to keep operations afloat.

What unfolded that summer was the first cycle in a long pattern that would define business for Tyson Foods. Don Tyson saw that the chicken business would never change. It clung stubbornly to cycles of growth and collapse. Good times induced more production, and then suddenly demand couldn't soak up all the meat on the market, and prices would plummet.

Don Tyson learned a critical lesson: The company's survival depended on how it weathered the downturns. The downturns became a death match between chicken producers. When the tide of profitability fell, it slowly exposed the weaknesses of each company. Week after week they lost money. Then the inefficient began to fall. In 1961 the poultry companies that hadn't followed Tyson's model of integration fell first. They had to buy feed and eggs on the open market, then sell birds for a loss. They didn't have Tyson's advantage of producing feed for itself. The smaller operators went under rather quickly. But the big meatpackers and the integrated producers remained.

Don Tyson talked with Haskell constantly. While Tyson couldn't control the market price for chicken, he became more obsessed than ever with the company's costs. The reason was simple: The cheaper he could produce a pound of meat, the lower Tyson's loss on each pound compared with its competitors. Companies that spent 10 cents to raise a pound of chicken went out of business before a company that spent 7 cents. The company that spent 5 cents would be standing after the other two were long gone. Don Tyson was resolved to be the 5-cent producer.

Jackson watched as Tyson Feed and Hatchery scaled back production and cut the number of new chicks it placed on farms. But Jackson noticed something strange. Don Tyson refused to trim his flocks of egg-laying hens. Those birds laid the eggs that filled Tyson's hatcheries and were later shipped to farms to be raised. But those farms were sitting empty. Still, Don Tyson insisted on paying to maintain the flocks of hens. Rather than place the eggs in the hatchery, Tyson sold them at a loss to a local factory that crushed them for food products. The hen operations lost money every week. But Don insisted on keeping them. Jackson wasn't about to challenge him.

Tyson's contract farmers were largely shielded from the downturn in 1961. But after the crash, companies like Tyson, Garrett Poultry, and Ralston Purina became miserly in what they would pay, citing the market crash that had almost put them out of business. What really worried farmers was the declining number of companies with which they could do business. The smaller firms had gone under, and others, like Garrett Poultry, were bought by competitors. It left farmers with little room to negotiate.

A group of farmers thought they would be better off if they banded together, so they formed the Northwest Poultry Growers Association. They figured it would be easier to bargain as a group for higher prices with the chicken companies that were becoming fewer and larger.

For many of the new members of the poultry organization, joining the group would be the worst business decision they ever made as chicken farmers.

As Don Tyson had predicted, the poultry business began to slowly pull out of its abysmal crisis of low prices after 1961. The market corrected itself, and it did so in a Darwinian way that came to define life in the chicken business. Everyone who couldn't hang on started to die. And when companies went out of business, the supply of chicken started to gradually decline. Soon the grocery stores and restaurants had a harder time finding the poultry they needed, and prices started to climb again.

When that happened, Don Tyson was ready. While other companies focused on cutting costs just to stay afloat, Tyson laid a plan in anticipation of good times returning. His plan relied on the chicken houses full of egg-laying hens, which Tyson quietly hung on to during the downturn, selling their eggs at a loss. As soon as he saw prices start to recover, Don Tyson diverted the supply of eggs into the company's hatcheries, which were running with just a skeleton crew. The hatcheries filled up quickly, and Tyson signed a fresh round of contracts with farmers, sending them new chicks the moment they were available.

As other chicken companies faltered and failed, Tyson ramped up production. The company's salesmen assured their customers that Tyson's production would be bountiful, predictable, and cheap. The company hardly seemed to be affected by a crisis that had plowed under its competitors. Where there was an opening, Tyson jumped in and filled it.

Jackson watched in amazement as the financial numbers rolled in. The column of losses from the egg-laying farms quickly transformed into profits. Sales started to climb. Profit margins returned.

But the crisis had left its wounds. The company had burned through all its operating capital just to stay in business, and it had taken on new debt. The company's balance sheet was getting dangerously close to looking like those for the farms that John had watched go upside down with debt in the 1930s.

Don had a solution: He wanted to take the company public. Tyson had proved to investors that it could survive bad times and turn a profit when times were good. It had a steady stable of customers and a team of salesmen winning more business every day. There would never be a better time to sell off an ownership stake to shareholders through a public offering. The bankers with whom Don met were eager to help him do it. Eventually, John agreed to go along with it. They called the new, publicly traded company Tyson's Foods, Inc.*

A photograph from 1963 shows a young Don Tyson standing in a banker's office in New York City. He is wearing an uncharacteristically dapper suit, with a dark jacket and skinny dark tie. With his broad forehead and thick, horn-rimmed glasses, he looks like a bookish accountant or civil engineer, rather than the newly minted owner of a publicly traded company. Standing around him is a group of investment bankers, big-city guys with well-coiffed hair and perfectly tailored suits. One of them is holding a series of cashier's checks, arrayed

---

* The company would later simplify its name to its current form, Tyson Foods, Inc.

in a fan. It was the kind of occasion for a young entrepreneur to exult for a while. But Don Tyson looks eager to get back home. He had just raised $1 million by selling 100,000 shares in the firm. And Don had already figured out how to spend the money.

Different people in the poultry business took different lessons from the crisis of 1961. For Charles Garrett, the lesson was clear: It was time to get the hell out of the chicken business.

Garrett owned Garrett Poultry in Rogers, Arkansas, near Tyson's headquarters in Springdale. He had survived the storm of 1961 in large part because he had imitated Tyson's model. Garrett Poultry was a wholly integrated company, with a slaughterhouse, feed mill, and hatchery bundled into the business. But Garrett didn't share Don Tyson's stomach for risk. The poultry crisis showed that for all the money Garrett invested in his infrastructure and equipment, his livelihood was as risky as a stock market speculator's. He wanted to sell his assets, take the cash, and use the money for something more stable.

It wasn't obvious to Tyson's managers why the company should buy Garrett in the wake of 1961's financial catastrophe. Having survived near bankruptcy, it made sense to save the cash from Tyson's public offering and build up a capital reserve for the inevitable bad times to come.

Don Tyson patiently explained his strategy. Getting bigger would help Tyson survive. The bigger a company was, the more it could drive down its costs. It gained efficiency through its size, using fewer managers to operate bigger slaughterhouses, for example, or buying feed in bulk. It was easier to be more efficient than the next guy if you were bigger than they were. That meant you could outlast them when the poultry business inevitably went underwater.

Tyson couldn't get bigger just by adding more farms or slaughterhouses. If the company expanded its own operations, it would put more chickens on the market, inevitably leading to oversupply. But buying a competitor neatly solved two problems with one move. Tyson could expand, and it could expand without boosting the overall supply of chicken. Tyson simply bought out its competitor's market share, without adding one bird to the market.

It was part of Don Tyson's new strategy, called "Expand or Expire."

Tyson's little-noticed purchase of Garrett Poultry Co. didn't make much of a ripple in the chicken business. But across the country, the fate of several dozen companies had just been sealed. Don Tyson had made his first acquisition. And he liked the feeling.

Nobody in the courtroom ever expected mercy from Jim Blair, which was good, because no one ever received it. A tall and athletic man, with a baritone voice and thick eyebrows that he let flare up in a violent arch above his blue eyes like prickly horns, Blair had intelligence that wasn't just impressive; it was weaponlike. It hurt people.

In northwestern Arkansas, a kind of awestruck lore had sprung up around Blair from his earliest days as a law student. He was rumored to have started reading books at the age of three. He graduated from college before his peers graduated from high school, and he finished his law degree before the age of twenty-one. He was known to be a brilliant investor who could make millions off the stock market with a shrug. He could have easily been a wealthy attorney in New York but decided to stay in Arkansas to be near the grandmother who had raised him in nearby Fayetteville. Circumspect about his childhood, Blair only acknowledges that it was harsh, his parents weren't around, and he was never handed anything in life.

Blair failed when he tried to start his own law firm in Fayetteville, running out of cash just a few months after he hung his shingle. He joined the law firm of Crouch and Jones, which counted John Tyson among its small roster of clients. From the late 1950s on, Blair handled more and more of the work for the Tysons and their burgeoning company. This provided him a deeper education in the chicken business than he ever dreamed of receiving. Don Tyson didn't think much of Blair at first, considering him a young pup of a lawyer, still wet behind the ears. But over time, Don began to respect the young attorney's intellect and aggressiveness. Decades later, Blair would tell a young lawyer his secret for success. When a client asks if they can legally do something, Blair didn't tell them: "No." He said: "Yes, and here is how we do it." The law wasn't a black-and-white series of prohibitions to Blair. It was more like a choppy sea that could be navigated by only the most accomplished mariners. And Blair was determined to help his clients chart new waters.

During the 1960s, many of the legal issues Tyson wrangled with revolved around labor disputes. Employees inside the company's hatchery, for example, demanded minimum wage, claiming they were entitled to it because they were basically factory workers. Tyson disagreed. The company considered itself a farm, so it was exempt from paying minimum wage or recognizing other workers' rights. When the U.S. secretary of labor sued Tyson over the dispute, Blair's boss and mentor Courtney Crouch fought the U.S. government and won.

Inside Tyson, there was a growing effort to make sure that unions didn't infiltrate the company's slaughterhouses, hatcheries, and feed mills. The company enlisted attorneys from Chicago and Little Rock to keep unions out, a practice that was common in Arkansas. But Tyson realized it faced another threat with which companies like Wal-Mart didn't have to contend. Tyson also risked organization among its chicken farmers. Although the farmers were heavily indebted, relatively uneducated, and dependent on Tyson for their livelihood, they had tremendous power over the company. If farmers organized, they could decide simply to shut down their farms and go on strike. If that happened, it would derail Tyson's entire business, possibly putting it into bankruptcy court within months. Tyson would have nowhere to place the tens of thousands of chicks coming out of its hatcheries. It would almost instantly lose its supply of chickens for its slaughterhouses, idling the plants and cutting millions of dollars in production overnight. Perhaps most significant, Tyson would have to tell its customers it couldn't deliver. That would leave the stores and restaurants empty-handed, giving them no choice but to switch to one of Tyson's competitors for supply. It was clear to Tyson and its lawyers that even though production was shifted to the farmers, Tyson needed to maintain complete control over them. If it didn't, the company would operate under the perpetual threat of a shutdown by unhappy contract growers every time they felt slighted or failed to make a profit.

New members of the Northwest Poultry Growers Association noticed a clear pattern. As soon as they joined the group, chicken companies like Tyson found a reason to cut off their supply of chickens. It seemed obvious the poultry companies were trying to put out of business any farmers who tried to challenge their authority. Farmers who were cut off discovered they couldn't even get a contract from the poultry companies that supposedly competed with Tyson. They felt blacklisted by the few remaining poultry firms, which seemed to be talking to each other, picking out which farmers were deemed troublemakers.

In 1965 the U.S. Department of Agriculture intervened on the farmers' behalf, filing a complaint against Tyson and two other poultry producers, Ralston Purina and Arkansas Valley Industries. The agency claimed the companies violated a 1921 law called the Packers and Stockyards Act. The law was passed to challenge the power of the infamous "meat trust" companies like Swift and Armour, and it prohibited a long list of behaviors those companies used to wring low prices out of ranchers and control the market for cattle and swine. The law was written vaguely enough to give farmers strong protections, penalizing companies for practices that could be deemed simply "deceptive" or "unjustly discriminatory." The practice of cutting off poultry contractors for joining an industry association seemed to be clearly illegal.

Jim Blair helped Tyson fight the complaint. And he learned from the experience. Tyson fought the USDA in a fashion that would come to define much of its legal strategy in coming decades. The company was aggressive, admitted no guilt, and was legally creative enough to look like it knew federal law better than the regulators.

Tyson responded to the USDA complaint by suing the agency in federal court. Rather than fight the charges head-on, the company made a novel argument, claiming that strong penalties under the Packers and Stockyards Act didn't apply to Tyson because it wasn't technically a meatpacker. It was a poultry company. When the law was passed, the biggest meat companies raised cattle and pigs, and John Tyson had yet to sign his first contract with a farmer. Poultry dealers, as they were called, weren't considered significant enough to earn a specific mention in the law's passages, which referred repeatedly to meat companies simply as "packers." The law was revised in 1935, just as John Tyson was getting his company started, and the amendments made mention of poultry companies in certain parts of the law. But as Tyson's lawyers pointed out in federal appeals court, when Congress updated the law in 1935, it hadn't gone through the law and inserted the words "poultry dealers" at every juncture where it mentioned "packers." Most important, the term "poultry dealers" was not inserted into a section authorizing severe penalties under the Packers and Stockyards Act. That meant the USDA could find Tyson guilty of violating parts of the law, but it could not impose penalties like the cease-and-desist orders it slapped on meatpackers. It seemed clear, according to Tyson, that Congress didn't intend to regulate poultry companies in the same way as beef and pork processors.

The federal appeals court agreed in a 1969 ruling. Tyson was something new under the sun, and the old laws didn't apply to it. The appeals judges in St. Louis threw out the USDA's complaint and ruled that the agency had no authority to regulate Tyson's relationship with its contract farmers.

Not surprisingly, the Northwest Poultry Growers Association faded into history. Its members knew they didn't have federal regulators to back them if Tyson decided to cut them off. The federal courts set clear law: The farmers would be on their own to negotiate with the company. And they would have to depend on Tyson to set rules that were fair.

By 1966, Don Tyson was eyeing his company's next acquisition. This deal wasn't just aimed at letting Tyson get bigger. It was aimed at changing the economics of chicken production.

Don had become interested in an East Coast chicken producer with the odd-sounding name of Washington Creamery. Don wasn't just interested in buying out the company's market share. He wanted to buy a new market altogether. Washington Creamery wasn't just selling ice-packed chicken; it specialized in selling "game hens," which were small birds sold in shrink-wrapped plastic. What caught Don's imagination about game hens was their price: 50 cents. Every bird carried that same price tag, 50 cents, regardless of what the underlying price of chicken was. Don saw this as a kind of Holy Grail: a chicken product that could hold its value even when the markets gyrated. There was something even better: Game hens were sold frozen. So if supply outstripped demand, Tyson could store its birds and wait until the market recovered before selling them again.

Selling frozen birds had yet another benefit, one that was clearly understood by Buddy Wray. After purchasing Garrett Poultry, Don Tyson needed a sales manager for the new poultry plant. He named Buddy Wray to the post after Wray had shown so much talent for signing up new farmers.

As a sales manager, Wray found his life had been ruled by a simple credo: Sell 'em or smell 'em. It was the law of selling ice-packed chicken that spoiled quickly. If companies produced too much chicken and couldn't find a buyer, the meat could go bad on the loading dock. It put salesmen like Wray at a perpetual disadvantage when they tried to bargain for a good price. The buyers knew that ice-packed chicken had to be sold quickly, and a poultry company would take a low price to get rid of it. Selling frozen chicken would erase that disadvantage for Buddy Wray.

Soon after Tyson bought Washington Creamery in 1966, the company began catering to the perception that game hens were some kind of luxury item, calling them "Cornish game hens." There was an exotic appeal to the product, the air of nobility to it, as if it were the kind of dish that was served by butlers after a fox hunt. Haskell Jackson marveled at the gimmickry of it. All of Tyson's chickens were Cornish birds, as Jackson and others in the industry knew. The Cornish breed had been selected as the industry standard because it grew fast. The only difference between a Cornish game hen and an ice-packed chicken was that you killed the game hen when it was younger. It was just a smaller chicken, wrapped in plastic and frozen, given a better name and sold at a fixed price. But the strategy worked. Cornish game hen sales expanded steadily, and, most important, the business provided a predictable cash flow. Tyson could always predict what the sales price would be. Soon Tyson was dedicating slaughterhouses in Arkansas to nothing but game hen production. The birds were frozen and shipped to markets as far away as New York.

Business was booming, and salesmen like Buddy Wray had finally been liberated from the law of sell 'em or smell 'em.

Haskell Jackson noticed that as the company grew, the roles of its founders were diverging. Don and John Tyson remained close, still meeting for lunch at Neal's and engaging in the usual back-and-forth during Monday morning meetings. But in important ways, the men were segregating their attention to different parts of the company.

Don embraced the intangible aspects of the business. He recruited new talent and trained a crop of young lieutenants. He was constantly reading and studying theories of business management. He absorbed the teachings of other great CEOs, and he sat around the office Saturday mornings to debate why one company failed as another thrived in the very same market. Don was fascinated with the methods that managers used to maintain control over a company's operations as firms grew bigger. He quizzed Haskell about the "span of control" a CEO could have over a big company. How big could an organization get before managers could no longer steer it? When did a corporation get so big that it lost its original culture?

John Tyson, by contrast, focused on the material side of the business. He haunted the slaughterhouses and made sure the equipment was clean and the slaughter lines were up to standard for federal inspectors. He looked over the steel conveyor belts and the suspended rows of hooks that carried plucked chickens. He imposed his standards of order and tidiness on the workers, creating a cleanliness regime that permeated Tyson's operations for decades. John milled around the hatchery and spent afternoons inspecting the company's trucks as they sat in the parking lot. John, the former fruit shipper, seemed most proud of the fleet of well-maintained refrigerated semitrucks. He quizzed the mechanics, looked over the vehicles, and made sure they all lived up to his expectations.

John Tyson grounded himself in what he knew best. And he was smart enough to let his son lead them into the unknown.

In 1967, John Tyson and his wife, Helen, were out on a Sunday drive, heading to a new cabin the couple had built on nearby Beaver Lake. They planned to watch the first Super Bowl on their new color television set there. The country roads around Springdale were overlaid by a web of railroad tracks that often weren't marked. Country drivers knew to stop and look both ways if they approached the tracks, wary of the steady traffic of boxcars carrying grain, coal, or feed to the local farms and factories. For some reason on that Sunday, John Tyson didn't spot an oncoming train. He and Helen were hit and killed on the tracks.

Don Tyson got a call at his house from his father's personal doctor, who told Don he needed to get to the hospital. His father and stepmother were dead, and Don needed to identify their bodies. Don went to his father's house and picked up his fourteen-year-old half-brother, Randall, whom Don took into his home. Don went to the hospital and identified his parents.

Later that day, Don took a call from a local trucking magnate named Harvey Jones, who had been a friend and business partner of John Tyson's going back years. Jones had some simple advice:

— Have your funeral quick, and go back to work, Jones told him.

Don complied. There didn't seem to be any sense in prolonging the most painful experience of his life. John and Helen were buried the next day after a ceremony at the Methodist church in Springdale. The pews were packed as the city laid to rest one of its most successful citizens, a man who arrived broke and desperate nearly forty years prior.

By Tuesday, Don was back in his office. Haskell Jackson, Buddy Wray, and others saw a hollowed-out look in his eyes, a dazed quality about him. Don went into his father's office and looked at the desk, the items that had been laid casually there on his father's last day at the company. Don saved the effects, and decades later they would be displayed on John Tyson's desk at the company's headquarters, arranged exactly as Don had found them.

At the Monday morning managers' meeting Don took the floor for the first time without his father at his side. He told his lieutenants they had work to do. There was still a business to run, still employees depending on them.

If Don Tyson was ever tentative about running the company without his father, he didn't show it. The restraining voice of caution and the Depression's hard lessons were gone. Don was free to push the company forward as aggressively as he wished.

If his father's death affected Don emotionally, he was loathe to show it to many people.

"If you're a farmer, see, you look at things a little different," he recalled later in an interview. "Things are born. Things die. People are no different."

CHAPTER 4

The Industrial Animal

(1970–1995)

DON TYSON became a billionaire in part because he never ate like one. Even after he got rich, Don Tyson preferred to dine at Neal's Café, the Springdale greasy spoon where he used to have lunch with his father. Don would show up at the airport for a business trip with his breakfast in a paper bag from McDonald's. He joined the growing herd of Americans who grabbed their lunch from a drive-through window. And Don took note of what he saw there. He noticed how restaurant patrons were in a hurry. When they bought lunch, they wanted something they could eat in a car, something they could get fast, and something they could get cheap. American eating was migrating away from the dining room and into the passenger seat. Don went to fast-food restaurants like Wendy's, Burger King, and McDonald's and watched the patrons who stared up at the backlit menu boards to order their dinner, and he saw the future.

The future had just one problem, in Don's estimation: Chicken wasn't on the menu. The fast-food industry was built squarely on the hamburger, and for good reason. Hamburger was a malleable meat, easy to shape into patties of various sizes, and to ship and speed-cook in cramped kitchens. Chicken, on the other hand, was still sold by the drumstick and the breast. Tyson had broken new ground by selling boneless breasts, which were easier to cook, but the product was still mostly served in homes or upscale restaurants. Don Tyson, before anyone else, saw that America's menu needed to change. Chicken was simply too cheap, and too plentiful, to be ignored any longer. Between 1970 and 1978 alone, the retail price of fresh chicken had fallen 11 percent. And it was less than a third the price of beef and less than half the price of pork. In the 1930s chicken had been a luxury dish: When Herbert Hoover talked about putting a chicken in every pot, he meant that every American family would achieve a certain measure of affluence. But Don Tyson had seen firsthand how the new model of chicken farming had changed that. The big chicken houses, the mechanized slaughterhouses, the advanced breeding, had all come together to make chicken the cheapest meat available. McDonald's, Wendy's, and Burger King couldn't afford to keep it out of their product lines. Don Tyson would make sure of it.

By the early 1970s, Tyson's Foods had moved out of its offices on the rundown side of Emma Street in downtown Springdale and into a new office building on a secluded hilltop west of town. The senior executives still held their Monday meetings, but, in a nod to the more civilized schedule of corporate America, Don Tyson moved the meeting from six o'clock to noon.

Haskell Jackson sat at the table as he always had, listening intently and taking notes. Buddy Wray joined him, having moved into marketing and sales full time. Joe Fred Starr was often there, as was Leland Tollett, the man who had recruited Wray into the company and now oversaw much of Tyson's operations. Since going public, the company had simplified its name to Tyson's Foods, from Tyson's Feed and Hatchery. The name change reflected a deeper change at Tyson, which now had the streamlined feel of a real corporation. This wasn't John Tyson's scrappy upstart anymore. It wasn't a hatchery, it didn't sell feed, and it was on its way to becoming one of America's biggest companies.

Usually, Don Tyson's managers went around the table and briefed the group on the latest events in their division. That kept everyone abreast of what was going on across the entire company. One afternoon, Don Tyson took the floor himself and said he had something important to announce.

— Somebody seated at this table is going to take over daily operations for me, he told his lieutenants.

Jackson was puzzled by the statement. Don wasn't resigning, but he was clearly laying out the proposition that he would be stepping aside at some point.

— The job is just getting too big for one man to do. So somebody sitting here is going to have to do it instead of me.

There was a kind of awkwardness in the room as everyone absorbed what he said. Each one of them had apparently just been given the chance to run the company. Don didn't indicate whom he preferred to take his spot. What was left unsaid was that each of them would have to prove they were up to the task, or were at least more prepared than their peers. The full meaning of what just happened sunk in slowly, but the resulting dynamic was clear to everyone. The top executives were competing every day, against each other, to prove which one would take the throne when Don stepped aside. Jackson noticed an almost immediate change in his coworkers. The men once operated like a well-trained football team. No one thought about gaining an advantage over someone else. But almost immediately after that meeting, a kind of quiet striving sunk into daily life at Tyson's Foods. Managers were quick to take credit for their work, and they often kept their best ideas to themselves. The race was on among the chiefs at Tyson. Little did they know the competition would last for more than twenty years.

The relentless competition within Don Tyson's leadership team helped drive the company into an unprecedented era of growth. A string of mergers brought dozens of large, independent chicken companies under the control of Tyson Foods. At the same time, Tyson refined its internal operations and created a well-oiled system of interconnected farms and slaughterhouses that could easily supply the nation's biggest food retailers. The system would help Don Tyson execute his vision of a new kind of poultry company, and it would ultimately reshape the industry.

Don Tyson's obsession with fast food made him a difficult man to locate. He often couldn't be found at his desk, or anywhere at company headquarters. He disappeared for days on end, taking his private airplane to destinations he kept to himself. Only Tyson's inner circle of advisors, men like Joe Fred Starr and Jim Blair, knew he was spending an inordinate amount of time in Illinois, where McDonald's was based. Don Tyson had an obsession with McDonald's that seemed entirely outside of rational proportion. He had made a personal fortune by specializing in chicken production and nothing else, and yet he spent several years of his life hounding a hamburger company that had never sold so much as a drumstick. Don Tyson called on McDonald's with all the grace and restraint of a magazine salesman going door to door in the rain. He set up meetings with buyers and executives, telling them they were missing the boat on chicken. Chicken could be served just like hamburger—and at half the price, he said. Chicken could be put into sandwiches, or served in boneless patties. When the McDonald's executives and buyers politely thanked him for his time and sent him home, he called back to set up another meeting. He took his jet to trade shows and industry meetings. He became an evangelist for chicken and its potential as a cornerstone of the fast-food menu.

He also made it clear that Tyson, and only Tyson, could deliver millions of pounds of meat to a national food chain with an around-the-clock distribution system. His pitch was simple:

— Look, we'll dedicate a whole plant to your production. We'll cost it out, where you give us a reasonable margin. And we'll just run your product. We can do this cheaper for you. And because it's a dedicated plant, you can look over our shoulder on quality control all the time.

Back in Springdale, Don Tyson focused almost exclusively on the McDonald's account for long stretches of time. As he explained it to Jim Blair and Joe Fred Starr, Don planned to piggyback on McDonald's franchise system to bring processed chicken to every street corner. In his estimation, McDonald's had the best distribution system of any fast-food franchise in the country, and that's what drew him to the company. Rather than deliver Tyson's product to several depots of refrigerated warehouses, Tyson could deliver to just one location: the McDonald's distribution center. Then the restaurant chain would use its own trucks to ship the product out to its network of stores.

It only took fourteen years for McDonald's to come around. But eventually, the company called Tyson and said it had a product deal in which he might be interested. McDonald's had developed a chicken product that would fit in with its menu of sandwiches and French fries that were easy to eat on the run. It wasn't just a chicken burger but a whole new kind of product. McDonald's food scientists had figured out how to mince chicken breast meat, mix it with stabilizers and other ingredients, then partially fry it in a special breading that enveloped the meat. Customers could hold a piece in their hand and eat it out of a box. It was dubbed the "McNugget."

As Don Tyson promised, his company retrofitted a plant in Nashville, Arkansas, to make nothing but the McNugget. By 1983 Tyson was supplying the McNugget to McDonald's stores around the country. Don Tyson had finally found a chicken product whose price didn't fluctuate with the wholesale market for fresh chicken. It freed Tyson, at least in part, from the vicious commodity price cycle that tortured the industry.

As Don Tyson had envisioned, chicken products slowly began to creep onto menus across the country. Eventually, chicken would overtake beef and pork as the most-consumed meat in America.

Although he didn't know it, Haskell Jackson hired his replacement when he brought on board a bright young accountant named Gerald Johnston. Johnston came to Tyson with one mission: to drill down into Tyson's business operations and get a clearer picture of the company's costs. To do that, he invented a new accounting system that went beyond anything Jackson had thought up. It wasn't enough to know how much Tyson spent to grow and process each chicken. Johnston figured out how much it cost to produce each *piece* of chicken Tyson sold. He broke down the bird into its component limbs—the thigh, the wing, the breast, and the waste products—and developed a way to track the cost of each piece of meat. The cost of producing the thighs and wings was just a subsidy of sorts to get the money-rich breast meat to market.

Don Tyson was impressed with Johnston's new cost models. He began inviting Johnston to the Monday afternoon meetings, even though Johnston was technically far too low on the totem pole to warrant it. Don often quizzed him about the company's costs during the sessions, and he asked him to explain his cost models to the other executives. With his square jaw and easygoing demeanor, Johnston had a sociable air about him that Jackson lacked. Jackson was pleased his new hire was working out so well.

The competition among the executives under Don Tyson had grown fiercer with each passing month.

Don asked Buddy Wray and Leland Tollett each to look over an impending acquisition and tell him their thoughts on it. It was clear he was judging their reasoning ability, as much as he was looking for advice. Don had asked Jackson to hire an architect to design Tyson's new headquarters building, and Jackson had gotten a great design that had every specification Don had asked for. Don seemed pleased with it. Then Don selected Joe Fred Starr as the general contractor for the project, which came as a surprise to Jackson. Starr gutted the design Jackson had submitted, cutting the project's costs and saving thousands by using cheaper building materials and lighting. Don went with Starr's plan, paying him a bonus for saving money on the project. When the building was almost completed, Don took a tour and exploded at Jackson, who had come up with the idea to put nameplates on each office door.

— Why are there nameplates on the doors? I told you we don't have goddamn nameplates on the doors here!

Jackson took the nameplates down. He didn't ask why, but he figured they carried an air of formality or presumption that Tyson objected to.

Soon Jackson discovered his responsibilities were being shifted to others. He was being sent on the road most of the time, visiting new poultry complexes as Tyson bought up its competitors. Jackson helped get the accounting in order at each complex, making it conform with Tyson's system. He spent weeks on the road, away from his wife and kids. He knew the work he was doing was important to the company, but he also suspected he was put on the assignment in an effort to drive him into the ground, or least keep him out of the office. On both counts, it was working.

Haskell Jackson liked to play basketball with Gerald Johnston and other Tyson managers at a court in downtown Springdale.

One evening, Jackson grabbed a pass from Johnston and began sprinting down the court, when he felt a sharp pain, as if a knife had been thrust into his stomach. Jackson went sprawling onto the floor, and he lay their doubled up in pain. He thought he might be having a heart attack, but at the hospital he was relieved to find out it was only an ulcer. When the doctor asked Jackson if there were any particular stressors in his life, Jackson might have laughed if the pain wasn't so bad. Jackson's whole life was a stressor. He spent days on end driving from plant to plant, putting in untold hours of overtime for Tyson, just to feel like he was still falling behind. At that moment, in the hospital, Jackson came to the conclusion that he would most certainly die if he kept working for Don Tyson.

Not long after that, Jackson noticed a job opening for a senior accountant at George's Poultry, one of Tyson's smaller competitors in Springdale. He jumped at the job. In his last days at Tyson's Foods, he wondered if he should say something to Don. They had spent eighteen years together, building this company from a tiny operation on the wrong side of downtown Springdale. Jackson decided against saying anything, figuring Don would approach him before he left. But on his last day at the company, in 1978, Jackson left without so much as saying goodbye to Don Tyson. And he never spoke to him again.

After Haskell Jackson's departure Gerald Johnston rose through the ranks and eventually became chief financial officer. With his new title, Johnston's role at the company changed. In essence, he went from controlling costs to raising cash for Tyson's expansion. This wasn't a matter of simply attending road shows and attracting money from investors on Wall Street, although he did that too. To function day-to-day, Tyson needed bank loans and revolving lines of credit, but most institutions were still wary about lending to chicken companies. Put simply, Tyson Foods was a strange hybrid, part factory, part farm, and bankers didn't know what to make of it. What little track record the industry had showed it was still wildly volatile. When Johnston took over as CFO, he was shocked to discover that Don Tyson personally covered millions of dollars of the company's debt just to make banks willing to loan to the company.

That changed during the 1980s, in part thanks to Tyson's neighbor to the north, the retailer Wal-Mart in Bentonville. Sam Walton's rural discount chain was growing at a remarkable pace, opening new stores across small-town America, and his business drew a steady stream of New York and Chicago bankers who were hungry to loan Wal-Mart money. Johnston made sure to catch these bankers while they passed through town. He set up meetings and explained to them why Tyson was a safe bet for their money. The company wasn't a farming operation anymore but was more like an appendage of big retailers like Wal-Mart and restaurant chains like Wendy's and McDonald's. As long as those companies sold food, Tyson would be in business. The company worked backward from the deals it forged with these national suppliers, giving Tyson's farms and slaughterhouses a predictable cash flow.

Johnston became more proficient at his sales pitch, and he helped raise millions to fund Tyson's expansion. With each new loan he got, more banks became interested in the business, and soon he had loan officers competing against one another to lend Tyson money at the cheapest rate.

Don Tyson was happy with the performance. He already had big plans for the money.

Jim Blair didn't want to raise unnecessary attention. The Fayetteville attorney made a few discreet phone calls, worked some personal connections, and quietly arranged to buy a $10 million bond note that was owned by the investment firm Stephens Inc., in Little Rock.

A bond note is a form of corporate debt, and in this case the $10 million in debt had been borrowed by Clift Lane, a poultry magnate from central Arkansas. In all likelihood, Stephens was more than happy to unload the debt at that point, in the early 1980s. Lane was looking like a shakier borrower by the day as his company foundered, due to weak sales and high interest payments. Lane almost certainly had no idea that Blair was buying up his debt, but he would find out soon enough. Blair handed over the note to his biggest client, and Lane's most hated rival, Don Tyson.

Tyson had cajoled Blair into becoming general counsel for Tyson's Foods, a high-pressure job Blair was hesitant to take. He didn't need the money, having become independently wealthy by 1980 from a series of shrewd stock investments. In spite of his personal wealth, he found himself working far more than he wanted to on the Tyson account. Blair had a job that was never done, and to call him Tyson's general counsel was to miss his larger role at the company. He didn't just handle lawsuits or regulatory matters. He was more like a well-trained attack dog, with a deep and creative understanding of U.S. law. Don Tyson kept him on a short leash.

In a typical exchange, Don once complained to Blair that a small supplier was giving the company trouble. Jim was quick to give his advice.

— I'll put him out of business for you, Don. Just give me ninety days.

Don declined. He considered the supplier a personal friend. So Blair took the easier path and simply wound down Tyson's business with the supplier rather than push the man into bankruptcy.

During the 1970s and 1980s, Tyson kept Blair at his side for a series of hostile acquisitions. It took more than a lawyer to get these things done. It took a fighter who was equally conversant in securities law, bankruptcy law, contract negotiation, and antitrust regulations. Jim Blair was the rare man who fit the job.

Tyson's model to "expand or expire" became an intrinsic part of the company's operations. The poultry business was still defined by cyclical market swings when prices would rise, production would increase, and then prices would inevitably crash. When the business went into a slump, people like Don Tyson and Clift Lane went on buying sprees, snapping up smaller and weaker competitors. Then the survivors reaped even larger profits during the next upswing and were ready to acquire more companies during the next crash. All the while, the overall size of the industry kept expanding, dominated by larger and larger companies at the top.

Don Tyson explained it to Jim Blair.

— Companies come and go, but you'll notice that the chicken plants never actually close. They just paint over the name on the front of the building, and business keeps going under new ownership.

So it was that in the early 1980s, Don Tyson employed Jim Blair to go after Clift Lane's crown jewel, a high-tech chicken-processing company called Valmac Poultry. Valmac processed about 153 million birds a year, just slightly less than Tyson's Foods. Valmac was among the best companies in the industry, but Lane had made a serious miscalculation when he borrowed millions to expand. The poultry down cycle lasted longer than he thought, and Lane was having a hard time paying off the debt. Don Tyson, having followed his father's strict rules for limiting debt during the upswing, was ready to buy Lane out.

The fight to take over Valmac wasn't a business dispute; it was a duel of vanities between Tyson and Lane. Both men had built multimillion-dollar empires. Both got cocky about their ability to survive the downswings of a tough business. Both had built brand-new office buildings in their small hometowns, Lane in the central Arkansas town of Grannis, and Tyson in Springdale. Lane wasn't about to see his prized possession get painted over with Tyson's name. Years later, Clift Lane said in a separate lawsuit that he would have rather seen his company go out of business than go to Don Tyson.

When Lane refused to sell to Don Tyson in 1982, Blair got creative. He bought the $10 million bond note, which was backed by Valmac's stock. Clift Lane quickly discovered that not only did he owe an unholy amount of money, but he now owed it to Don Tyson. And Don Tyson was about as gracious about the debt as Lane expected: He immediately tried to foreclose on him. By calling in the loan, Don Tyson would win ownership of the stock that backed it, giving him de facto ownership of the company.

Lane fought the foreclosure in court, then stealthily flew to North Carolina and declared bankruptcy, defaulting on the $10 million bond. Blair argued in court that Tyson should still have rights to Valmac, but Lane managed to sell the company out from under them to a Texas investment firm called Bass Brothers Enterprises in 1983.

Don Tyson and Jim Blair had lost the battle for Valmac. It was a defeat that lasted all of thirty days. Don scrutinized the Bass brothers' investments and then called Jim. He thought the Basses would sell Valmac for the right price.

— You know, the Bass brothers are doing a deal with Disney, and they need money. They don't know what they've got here. We better buy that before they know what they've got.

Blair was stunned when Tyson told him the offer price: $30 per share. It was more than a third higher than what the Bass brothers had paid, and nearly double the price Tyson had originally offered.

Blair thought the price was far too high, and it would mire Tyson in a money-losing venture.

— Trust me. I know it's worth more than that, Don Tyson told him.

Not surprisingly, Bass Brothers Enterprises was willing to let Valmac go at the seemingly exorbitant price. Don Tyson and Jim Blair flew to Fort Worth to sign the papers, closing the deal in September 1984. Don excused himself from the meeting early, leaving Blair behind to iron out the details, and took his private plane for a flying tour so he could look down on the new Valmac plants he had just acquired.

Shortly after the Valmac deal closed, chicken prices surged. The Valmac purchase paid for itself in six months. Tyson doubled its annual production and picked up a slew of new clients. (Valmac had specialized in selling chicken products that were partially cooked, which were ideal for fast-food restaurants.)

Clift Lane eventually declared personal bankruptcy. Tyson bought the remainder of his poultry holdings. The former headquarters for

Lane Poultry in Grannis sat empty. Tyson had no use for the building. Blair tried to donate it to the U.S. Forest Service, but the deal fell through. It wasn't much of a concern, though, because Tyson's Foods had what it needed: a brand-new network of poultry complexes.

Among Gerald Johnston's more unpleasant tasks was firing other CFOs. As Tyson bought one company after another, it had no choice but to cut the senior management, an unenviable task that often fell to Johnston. He met with the CFOs, good guys, almost all of them, and knew he could have easily been in their shoes. He tried to let them down easy. And then, when they were gone, Johnston got to work.

Johnston saw the same pattern in virtually all the companies Tyson acquired. On the upswing in the chicken price cycle, the companies got fat. They added staff; they bought coffee machines for the break room and upgraded equipment. Then, when the crash came—and it *always* came—they were caught flat-footed and had to shed jobs and cut expenses.

Johnston helped usher in a new way at these companies: the Tyson way. Rather than get fat on the upswing, Tyson looked to strip out costs. The company minted millions of dollars in profit every year, but it was obsessed with cutting expenses whenever possible. Goodbye, coffee machine. Goodbye, extra travel expenses. Goodbye, extra secretary. It was the only way to survive.

As Tyson expanded, acquisition by acquisition, this culture spread and soon came to dominate the growing chicken business.

One of the slaughterhouses that Tyson bought during its acquisition spree was Valmac's poultry plant in Waldron, Arkansas. After the deal was closed, employees at the plant began learning firsthand how Tyson did business. It was a hard lesson for people like Jerry Skeen.

Jerry Skeen had loved his job back in 1983, when Tyson bought the Waldron plant. A field veterinarian, Skeen was good at what he did, and he enjoyed it. He was the only field technician on staff who specialized in laying hens: the birds that laid eggs for the hatchery. Most other field men at the plant, like field veterinarian Tommy Brown, visited farms that grew so-called "broiler" chickens, bound for the slaughterhouse.

Skeen was jovial, a tall and gangly man with an easy way about him. He has a tattoo on his right arm that looks like a woman wrapped around a beer bottle, a leftover from his wild, younger days. Skeen had since settled down, and his wife is a devout Christian who liked the quiet life in Waldron. Skeen got along well with the farmers he visited. He got along with everyone. It was his nature. Only in retrospect was it clear that this joviality, this bond Skeen had with farmers, would end his career.

There was a change in tone that was unmistakable when Tyson's Foods took over the Waldron plant. Tommy Brown noticed it right away. According to Brown, when Tyson's manager over the field technicians arrived, he gave them one explicit instruction:

— Go out there and piss the farmer off! the manager bellowed at his field techs.

The bravado seemed bizarre to Brown, but the manager's point was clear: Tyson's field technicians needed to show quickly, and firmly, exactly who was in control. Tyson called the shots, not the farmers. If the company started to lose its grip, it might never be able to keep hundreds of farmers in line.

Skeen noticed the change play out in more subtle ways. The field technicians were asked to leave written tickets on the farms they visited. The idea was to outline all the things that needed improving. The tickets did more than simply replace the friendly advice that Skeen used to pass on to farmers in person. The tickets made a paper trail, a way for Tyson to prove farmers were doing things wrong if the company ever needed to cut them off.

Both Brown and Skeen noticed the overarching change that Tyson brought to their work. If anything went wrong, they were told to blame the farmer for it. It was inevitable that bad chicks would come out of the hatchery every now and then, inevitable that one batch of feed would be mixed improperly. Skeen used to acknowledge the slipups openly to his farmers. But under Tyson's management, it was clear the mistakes could never be admitted. The story was told through the tickets the field men left behind, and the tickets blamed the farmer.

After a while, Skeen simply quit leaving the tickets. To hell with the company, he thought. I know how to do my job.

But ignoring Tyson's direction wasn't easy. Tension grew between Skeen and his managers until he became sure that he was close to being fired. He hated going into work every day. He found himself brooding and tense on Friday nights, already angry because he knew he had to go back to work Monday morning.

Still, Skeen refused to use the company's playbook, blaming farmers for mistakes they hadn't made and for bad results that were beyond their control. Skeen tried several times to get jobs outside of Waldron, but somehow they always fell through. He was supporting his family, and there was only one viable employer in Waldron. He was stuck, and the anger, the powerlessness, started to twist his insides. His wife worried he might have a stroke.

Then one day, the new manager at the complex, a young man named Gary Roper, called Skeen into his office. Roper informed Skeen he had two weeks left as a field technician. Skeen left the meeting assuming he'd been fired, but another manager told Skeen he could take a different job at the plant if he wished. Skeen ended up driving a forklift in the warehouse, for half the pay he made before.

For nearly a decade, Skeen ran the forklift and moved pallets of chicken products. He grew to enjoy the job over time. Skeen never had any hard feelings against Gary Roper for firing him, even many years later. Like a lot of people in Waldron, Skeen respected Roper as a hardworking family man. Skeen always felt like Roper was just doing his job. It wasn't Roper's decision alone to demote Skeen—it was just the way Tyson's Foods operated. Besides, Skeen's new job wasn't so bad. At least he didn't hate himself every morning as he headed into work.

When Tyson bought Valmac, it also bought the services of that company's young head of operations, David Purtle. He was a man who spent his career in the poultry business, and he had almost a gut instinct about the way it worked. Within two years, Tyson promoted him to head of operations for the entire company.

Purtle's job was to make sure all of Tyson's complexes ran as efficiently as possible. If one complex spent more money to raise chickens than another, he had to know why, and how to fix it. But one thing made this hard to do. Even into the 1990s, each Tyson complex operated with a certain level of autonomy. Through its chain of acquisitions, Tyson Foods had stitched together a constellation of poultry plants with different management teams, making different products and raising different sizes of birds. It was nearly impossible to measure their efficiency because each complex had the freedom to choose what formula of feed it gave its farmers. Complex managers had their own special recipes, winning formulas they were convinced put the most meat on a bird's bones. That made it hard for Purtle to figure out which managers were running a more efficient ship. Whenever he tried to judge their operations, they always blamed the feed mixes for the results.

Purtle put an end to it. He standardized the feed formulas that all of Tyson's plants used. With all of them forced to use the same recipe, Purtle removed the most critical variable for their differing results. Now, Purtle made it clear to the complex managers, their management decisions alone accounted for how efficiently they ran. It was like putting each Tyson complex under a powerful X-ray, with Purtle able to see which ones could produce the most pounds of meat with the resources they were given. Slowly, a competition began between each complex. Managers were called to account for their shortcomings against complexes several states away.

This turned the managers' focus outward, toward the networks of contract farms that provided the plants with chickens. Purtle thought the contract farms were the critical link in Tyson's production chain that could keep the company efficient. And, dangerously, that was the one link in the chain where Tyson did not have direct control. Purtle wanted his complex managers pushing farmers to run as lean as possible.

The tournament system of Tyson's chicken contracts was critical to this process. It eliminated the bad farmers and the older housing stock that wasted Tyson's money as it fed millions of birds at each complex. During the 1990s, Purtle ensured that complex managers focused on running the tournaments among farmers, pushing the farms to upgrade equipment rather than toying with their feed formulas. And the results were clear. The company improved its efficiency across its complexes. The bad managers, and the bad farmers, were quickly rooted out.

By 1995, Purtle was executive vice president over all of Tyson's operations, and he oversaw its network of poultry complexes and farms. He had no illusions about where this put him in the pecking order among Tyson's executives. The marketing team ruled the roost at Tyson, because they generated all the company's profits. Men like Buddy Wray and Don Tyson dreamed up the new products, the nuggets and tenders and boneless patties, and they signed the contracts to sell them. Then the work was turned over to Purtle, whose job was to execute on the marketing team's vision. He turned around and reverse-engineered Tyson's farms and slaughterhouses to make the products.

Purtle saw firsthand how Tyson's business model could remake small towns like Green Forest, Arkansas. Green Forest was an isolated hamlet in the Arkansas Ozarks in the mid-1990s, nobody's destination for a daytrip. The decayed stone buildings along the north end of Main Street were cheerless and worn by the elements. There were a couple of antique shops, a bank and gas station, and a few remaining stores that catered to an economy built on the chicken business, like Country Rooster Antiques and Reliable Poultry Supply.

At Purtle's direction, construction crews arrived in Green Forest from throughout the rural counties around town, hauling heavy equipment, machinery, and cement mixers. The crews worked seven days a week, and Purtle kept up avidly with their progress. He knew it was a priority for Don Tyson, and he didn't want to disappoint.

The Green Forest plant was being transformed to make a product that would have been all but unrecognizable to consumers just fifteen years earlier. It was producing chicken-based products, not chickens. Purtle oversaw the installation of machinery worth millions of dollars that would mince, press, and reconfigure chicken meat, which was then breaded and partially cooked to form a handheld product called a "tender." In a sign of the times, the product was to be sold exclusively to the hamburger chain Burger King.

Jealous of McDonald's runaway success with the McNugget, Burger King felt that it needed a product to compete. Even though the business was built on charbroiled burgers, Burger King wanted diversity on its menu to draw customers through the door. Tyson landed the contract to make the tender, supplying both McDonald's and Burger King as they battled for customers. Chicken was pushing its way onto more fast-food menus, even at chains that had resisted it for years.

Crews worked urgently to retrofit the Green Forest plant in time to meet Tyson's delivery contract with Burger King. Construction crews tore out the old machinery and added new factory space in the slaughterhouse. They installed several new assembly lines, with conveyor belts and ovens and steel slides built into them, running up to three hundred feet long. The plant began operating full time, cranking out truckloads of chicken tenders shipped to Burger King restaurants nationwide. Consumers around the country began eating millions of chicken tenders without the foggiest idea that they were made in Green Forest. Although the businesses along Main Street in Green Forest didn't do much better than before, the city became a remarkably profitable center for chicken production.

The Green Forest plant became the face of the modern poultry industry, and the foundation of a new American diet, where drivethrough windows had replaced the dining-room table and chicken had become the cornerstone of fast-food menus. The plant reflected the poultry industry even in how it was built: from the marketing idea outward. It started with the contract to sell chicken tenders, and it reorganized production in small-town America to supply the new product on an industrial scale. In 1969 the average American ate about 39 pounds of chicken each year. By 1995 he ate an average 70 pounds of chicken a year, a transformation made possible, in part, by the efficiency and scale of Tyson's factories.*

---

* By 2013 the average had risen to 81 pounds of chicken a year.

Projects like the plant in Green Forest generated millions in new revenue for Tyson, but they also served another purpose. The expensive complexes became the first line of defense against real competition, an increasingly high barrier to entry into the business of chicken production. Tyson was able to lock up the market through its very bigness, being one of the only companies that could viably deliver tens of millions of pounds of chicken a week to customers like Wal-Mart or Burger King. To compete with Tyson, an upstart would have to be willing to spend tens of millions of dollars or more to build plants like the one in Green Forest. With each new deal it signed, and each new plant it built, Tyson made that prospect increasingly unlikely.

In 1994 Tyson Foods made an acquisition that helped the company cement its place at the top of the chicken industry. It bought a relatively obscure company called Cobb-Vantress. Tyson didn't win any additional market share through the deal, but that wasn't the point. Buying Cobb-Vantress let Tyson absorb the very core of the chicken industry's profits.

Cobb-Vantress was the premier poultry breeding company. It owned a flock of genetically elite birds that spawned the vast industrial flocks raised on farms around the country. Companies like Tyson bought hens from Cobb-Vantress to use as a kind of seed stock to supply their hatcheries. The exact genetic traits of elite birds were a closely guarded secret, and these were largely responsible for the historic drop in chicken prices of the last fifty years.

Cobb-Vantress and a handful of other companies used advanced breeding techniques to select birds that grew twice as fast as their ancestors, putting more meat on their bones for every pound of food they ate. The company created a breed of chicken that could be slaughtered at a far younger age, compressing the amount of time needed to raise it on the farm. In 1925, it took fifteen weeks to raise a chicken that weighed 2.2 pounds. By 1990, it took only about four weeks. Just as important, Cobb-Vantress developed a bird with a bigger breast, the ideal vehicle to make the highest-value meat.

These advances were the foundation of Tyson's profits. Cobb-Vantress helped create the ideal industrial animal. The birds could grow comfortably in confinement, and their physiology could be changed in just a few short generations to meet the whims of the marketplace. If the chicken weren't a willing biological partner, Tyson wouldn't have been able to build a factory food system around it. But there were some problems as Cobb-Vantress developed a modern flock that met Tyson's needs and supplied McDonald's and Wal-Mart with meat. The demands of the marketplace eventually outstripped the chicken's physical capacity to support them. The bird's breasts became too big for its legs and skeleton to support. The animals grew so fast they couldn't supply oxygen to all their tissue and muscle, causing fluid to build up in their body cavity. The chicken's immune system suffered, and some birds simply keeled over after a few weeks. Many of these problems didn't manifest themselves until the flocks of birds were on the farm and being raised in large numbers, puzzling farmers who were using the same techniques they always had, only to discover their birds were sick or dying off.

Over time, the genetic manipulation changed chicken meat itself. As the birds grew faster, their meat became more pale and soft, a problem that geneticists struggled for years to overcome. Ultimately, the softer, paler meat didn't hurt the industry. Above all, the market demanded meat that was produced cheaply, at high volume, and on schedule. The taste of the meat was often covered over by breading, frying, and flavor additives.

With the purchase of Cobb-Vantress, Tyson Foods brought under its control the final component of chicken production: the animal's very DNA. It owned the most coveted flocks of breeding birds, and it had now integrated the final chain of the marketplace. Now it controlled production from the genetics to the final shipment of breaded, partially fried McNuggets.

Tyson's wave of acquisitions wasn't easy on Jim Blair. He spent his time traveling to courtrooms from Delaware to North Carolina, arguing on

Tyson's behalf, fighting at every hearing to give the company an edge over competing bidders or owners who were reluctant to sell. Don Tyson was relentless in his search for new companies. It wasn't just to win more market share. If a company looked like it might be vulnerable to takeover, Tyson felt obligated to buy it just to deny a competitor a chance to do so and get bigger at Tyson's expense.

Between 1962 and 1997, Tyson Foods bought at least thirty-three companies. Some were relatively small, like Garrett Poultry; but deals like the Valmac purchase doubled Tyson's size and made it the biggest chicken company in the United States by the mid-1980s.

In 1979 Tyson's annual sales were $382.2 million. One short decade later the company had grown almost sevenfold and was pulling in $2.5 billion a year.

As Tyson went on its buying spree, the company shaped the modern chicken industry into what it is today: a highly concentrated business controlled by four companies. By the mid-1990s, Tyson controlled about 25 percent of the U.S. chicken market and competed against just a handful of giant companies that controlled the rest. The top four chicken producers controlled over half the U.S. poultry business, supplying massive volumes of meat to the biggest national grocery chains and restaurants, like Wal-Mart and McDonald's. The remainder of the market was controlled by smaller versions of Tyson, vertically integrated companies that were still enormous by historical standards. By 1992, 88 percent of all chicken in the United States was produced in the kind of large, heavily mechanized slaughterhouse that Don Tyson built in Springdale. In 1967, by contrast, just 29 percent of chickens came from big processing plants.

Jim Blair didn't have much time to think about the way Tyson's acquisitions were affecting the meat industry. He was working up to one hundred hours some weeks for Tyson, living in hotel rooms and spending his days arguing before judges. At one point years earlier, during the long buying spree, Blair had been all but exhausted, and as he and Don talked over their strategy, Blair looked up and asked a simple question.

— Don, what are we trying to do here?

Don looked at him, and he replied as if the answer were all but obvious.

— I want to be worth fifty million dollars by the time I'm fifty years old, he said.

Tyson's father, John, always made sure he owned the newest Chevrolet in Springdale. Don, a child of poverty, seemed driven by the same calculus, just on a bigger scale. He aimed to acquire a great fortune, no matter the means.

Fifty million dollars would ultimately be a rounding error in Tyson's personal worth. Over the next decade, Tyson Foods would grow by a factor of ten. This growth had an impact far beyond the fortunes of one corporation. As Tyson Foods bought competitors and solidified its grip over the nation's poultry industry, it began to change rural America. The culture of one company became the defining culture of towns that Tyson Foods dominated. Tyson's law became the law of the land in places like Waldron, Arkansas, where generation after generation would try to make a living in the system Tyson had created.

CHAPTER 5

Cage Match

(2004–2012)

DURING 2004, it was common to see groups of Laotian immigrants touring the ruined farms around Waldron. When someone like Jerry Yandell or his neighbor Edwin went bankrupt or decided to sell his place, he could count on the arrival of big white rental vans full of visitors. Groups of Laotians would step out of the van and walk the grassy lots around Waldron, touring big empty chicken houses and speaking among themselves in their native tongue. The local farmers had only the vaguest ideas of where these groups came from, but it didn't matter. It was clear they were willing to borrow hundreds of thousands of dollars to buy farms that locals were desperate to unload.

And so it happened that in 2004, a short Laotian man named Boonau Phouthavong* walked the length of a chicken house just outside Waldron in 2004, scanning the building for signs that it could turn him a profit. The houses he looked over belonged to a local farmer named Edwin, who had grown to despise and even fear the old buildings, which Edwin considered to be Ground Zero in a long chain of events that ruined his life. Edwin had given over years of his life to working on the barns, only to end up on the edge of bankruptcy. They were a lodestone around his neck, a sinkhole of debt he longed to escape, and a shabby-looking monument to the misfortune that Edwin believed had swamped his life.

But Boonau looked over the buildings with different eyes. He saw promise, and he saw a future. He eyeballed the houses, measuring their

---

* Pronounced *Boo-now Poot-uh-voong.*

square footage and the size of the flocks they would hold against the loan payments he would take on to buy the place. The math seemed promising to him. Boonau knew he'd have to borrow at least several thousand dollars to update the chicken houses, but he thought he could make it work.

Boonau might have been looking to buy a ruined business venture in Edwin's farm, but he was nobody's fool. As he looked over Edwin's buildings, he had good reason to believe he could make some money off the place. Boonau was already operating five chicken houses, three of them on a farm west of Waldron and another pair near his own modest farmhouse south of town. He had moved to Waldron four years earlier.

Immigrants like Boonau brought with them to Arkansas a sense of visceral optimism that was often missing in longtime residents around Waldron. The Laotians believed in hard work, believed in farming, and believed that Tyson could provide them a path to the American Dream. Boonau and his wife approached the chicken business in much that same way Jerry and Kanita Yandell did in the 1970s. The Laotians thought that hard work would pay off and that the seven-day work-weeks would eventually make them independent farmers, free of debt.

Laotian immigrants seemed like the one group that could make a go of it as Tyson chicken farmers. They were frugal to the extreme, willing to live in conditions many local farmers considered impoverished. The Laotians helped each other do farm work to keep down labor costs, and they seemed to have no complaints about working the long hours. But in the end, even they found it difficult to keep their farms out of bankruptcy.

This is because the immigrants were just pieces in Tyson's ongoing game, players in a grinding tournament that the company orchestrated to pit one neighbor against the other. Tyson Foods dominated the poultry industry so thoroughly by the time Boonau bought his farm that the company could easily manipulate the price it paid farmers for their work. Tyson exercises this power in a way that systematically depresses the prices it pays to many farmers, creating a new breed of high-tech sharecroppers who live on the ragged edge of bankruptcy. The Laotians unwittingly joined this tournament and helped drive local farmers, and then one another, out of business. The rules of this tournament illustrate the logical conclusion of vertical integration, and what it means for farmers and rural communities when one company gains control over the levers of meat production. And at the heart of this tournament is Tyson's secretive system for paying farmers.

At the end of any given week, a series of letters is mailed out from the Tyson complex in downtown Waldron. The thick envelopes carry a crisp, bright red TYSON logo as the return address, and each bears the name of a company farmer behind a clear, plastic screen. These letters carry an economic verdict that is meted out to each farmer, determining who will survive and who will be driven out of business.

The letters are several pages long and packed with complicated financial figures. The farmers call them settlement sheets. The one critical piece of information the settlement sheets contain is the going price of chicken, or, more accurately, the price that Tyson deems appropriate to pay.

Each farmer receives their own price, determined by the tournament system that ranks each farmer against his neighbor. At the end of each week, Tyson makes a competitive pool out of all the farms that have delivered chickens to the plant. Tyson managers in the complex run a series of calculations that compare the efficiency of each farm against the others in the pool. The company has far more data about the farms than their owners; the company can compare how much feed each farm consumed compared to its neighbors, how many birds died and how much weight they gained overall. The company can measure a farm's performance down to the number of calories the birds consumed, a figure that is helpfully included in the letter.

All of this information is fed into an equation that spits out a simple ranking: the most efficient farms on top, the least efficient at the bottom. The key metric that Tyson uses to pick winners and losers is how much feed it takes a farmer for his chickens to gain one pound of meat, a neat little number the company calls its "feed conversion."

As each farmer opens the envelope, he or she sees a cover page with a ranking of every farm that delivered birds the previous week. There are twelve neat rows of figures just to the right of the rankings, showing how many birds were placed at each farm, how many pounds each farm delivered, and what the feed conversion ratio was at each operation.

But there are critical pieces of information that Tyson keeps secret. The company doesn't tell the farmer whom he competed against in a given tournament. On the far left side of the settlement sheet, where the names of the farmers should be listed next to each farm's results, there is just a large void of white space. When someone like Jerry Yandell, Doug Elmore, or Boonau Phouthavong reads over his settlement sheet, he sees only his own name, sitting there alone in the field of white, placed wherever he landed in the ranking. Sometimes near the top, sometimes at the bottom.

If a farmer ranks near the top, he might earn 5 cents a pound for his labor. If he ranks in the middle, he would get paid 4.5 cents. Close to the bottom, he would make 4.1 cents. Cattlemen, corn farmers, and hog producers nervously watch the futures markets to see the price change for their goods. A swing from 5 cents a pound to 4 cents a pound is terribly significant. But rather than look at the futures exchanges, a modern chicken farmer nervously reads over his settlement sheet, seeing where his name ranks against a phalanx of his anonymous neighbors.

The differences in pay are severe. One farmer who lived just outside of Waldron watched helplessly during the winter of 2008 as he fell lower in the tournament, his ranking and his pay driven downward with every settlement sheet he received.*

A survey of the farmer's settlement sheets in 2009 shows just how severe the results of the tournament could be. When this farmer ranked 6th out of 14 farms, he was paid 5 cents a pound. He later fell to the rank of 16th out of 20, and he was paid only 4.5 cents a pound. That meant he took a pay cut of $846, making his total payment $7,618.

---

* This farmer chose to remain anonymous because even discussing his ranking in the tournament, let alone sharing his ranking information as he did, could get him sued into bankruptcy by Tyson.

Later in the year, this farmer did even worse, ranking 12th out of 14 farmers. For that flock of birds his pay was docked $1,428, leaving him just $6,596. He took an 18 percent pay cut because of where he ranked in the tournament.

With gas and electrical bills to pay, a pay cut of $1,428 could make the enire flock of birds a loss. The farmer, in other words, often worked for free, seven days a week for six weeks, to deliver as much as 161,000 pounds of meat to Tyson.

When a farmer gets hammered in the tournament, it might seem prudent for him to approach his neighbors and ask what they were doing differently. This is tough to do, and not just because the names on the tournament ranking are left blank. Each page is clearly marked with the warning: "Confidential and Proprietary Information of Tyson Foods, Inc." If farmers were to meet and compare their settlement sheets, or show them to a journalist or lawyer, Tyson can sue them for leaking confidential information. To put it lightly, this has chilled the flow of information about the tournament among farms.

Only Tyson has access to the centralized pool of information that it uses to rank each farmer, giving it immense power over how the tournament is played. Tyson determines which chickens will be sent where, and when they will be picked up for slaughter. That means it chooses which farms compete against one another in any given tournament. If the company wants to leave a farm out of a given tournament, it simply delays picking up the chickens at that farm by a couple of days. Conversely, it can throw a farm into competition against others of Tyson's choosing by picking up birds there a few days early.

Only Tyson can see clearly how the game is played, watching the tournament through its centralized databases that tally the results. For the farmers, the tournament unfolds almost like a game of chance when they open their settlement sheets and get the latest rankings.

Around 2008, longtime farmers who raised chickens for Tyson Foods in Waldron noticed a change in their paychecks. It happened slowly, but it was unmistakable. It was as if some kind of bad weather system had come rolling in over the mountains, plunging the barometric pressure. An invisible force hung over their farms, steadily driving down their paycheck each month.

The change was a prime topic of conversation at Scott County Tractor, a repair shop that passes for a social hub on rural Highway 80, about a dozen miles east of Waldron. The tractor shop is really just a glorified shack with a tin roof, located just across a broad gravel driveway from the small house of its owner, Coy Butler.

On a typical morning in the fall of 2008, Butler sat at his desk just inside the shop's front door, next to crowded shelves of spare auto parts and piles of paper. Men come and go from the shop all morning long, chicken farmers most of them, dropping off broken mowers or tractors or looking for replacement parts.

Richard Moore is a frequent customer, although more often than not he stops by simply to catch up on local gossip or bring fresh vegetables from his garden. Moore is a tall and rangy man in his sixties, with a sharp face and white hair. Both he and Coy Butler have grown chickens for Tyson Foods since the 1980s. The men sit around the shop and talk business, trading stories and news about Tyson and their farms.

Having been in the business for decades, Butler and Moore have the air of men who have seen it all. They survived the still mysterious plague of 2004, when flocks of sick birds were delivered to farms around Waldron and drove many of their neighbors out of business. They know which farmers are doing well and which are on the edge of bankruptcy. They are survivors, old-timers who seem to have figured out how to make it work in a difficult business.

Moore in particular seemed to have an inside line when it comes to Tyson, having been a manager at the slaughterhouse downtown for more than twenty years. He had known many of the Tyson managers since they first arrived in town, and he seemed to know all the Tyson field technicians by their first name.

But for all its familiarity, the countryside around Moore was changing. The most noticeable transformation was the death of farms that were owned by his longtime neighbors and the arrival of immigrants who had taken their place. Increasingly, the motorists whom Moore passed on the highway as he drove to town were Laotian. They nodded and waved, but they didn't speak the language. He didn't know their families, and they didn't know his. Moore drove past the same hills and leaning wooden barns he had always known, but the men who tinkered on machines there and worked on the farms looked as if they inhabited a different nation altogether. It was as if Moore had been transplanted to the rolling hills of some Asian country that only closely resembled his own.

At the age of sixty-eight, Moore has known a life of stability. He and his wife, Joyce, live in a big white house with a porch and painted columns on Highway 248, east of town. He and Joyce thought they were on an easy path toward a quiet retirement, a peaceful life of long afternoons on the porch with the occasional noisy visit from the grandchildren. They own four long chicken houses, a sizable farm that yielded steady pay over the years. After twenty years in the business, Moore knew what he was doing. He knew how to ride out the bad times and stay afloat.

But now the farming business was like riding a Brahmin bull. From one month to another, Moore was never sure what he would be paid for his work. He worked his hardest, put in seven days a week, and delivered a flock of chickens to Tyson that he considered among his best, only to find that the price they fetched wouldn't cover the cost of raising them. While there were wild ups and downs, Moore noticed that overall his pay was steadily declining. Some grinding, quiet force was pushing down the price he was paid for his birds.

Moore and Butler had their suspicions as to what was behind the economic changes they faced. It had something to do with the Laotians who were moving to town and their willingness to take on huge loans to retrofit the old farms they bought.

"We're competing against them—it's hard to beat them," Moore complained. "They're at the top of the list!"

There wasn't much overt racism against the newest farmers in Arkansas, but nor was there real closeness. The social pattern followed closely what happened a decade before in Tyson's slaughterhouses, when immigrants from Latin America and Mexico filled jobs that locals found too low-paying and dangerous. Hispanic immigration reshaped backwater towns like Green Forest and Berryville, Arkansas, which suddenly boasted their own strip malls of bodegas and clothing stores with signs written only in Spanish. The immigrant community lived side by side with Arkansas natives but never truly integrated. The Hispanics and Laotians spoke little if any English, and the Arkansans didn't bother to learn a second language.

In the absence of real communication, each group invented stereotypes about the other. Laotian farmers in Waldron were convinced their white neighbors got special breaks from Tyson and favoritism from the field technicians. There were rumors that the white farmers always carried guns, so Tyson's men were scared to ever criticize them.

The local farmers, by contrast, spun wild theories about the shady forms of financing the Laotians must be using to build their farms. The most common assumption was that the Laotians had access to some sort of cheap government loans because they were minorities.

"I don't know how their money works," Moore complained. "They get it cheaper than we do."

Of course, the ethnic differences between each group were ultimately meaningless when it came to determining their success or failure as chicken farmers. That was determined by Tyson Foods. And it hinged on mathematical equations and the rules that Tyson set for its tournament.

Tyson and its defenders say the tournament price incentivizes farmers to work hard, and it rewards the good farmers over the bad. That might make sense if farmers had any control over their operations, but they don't. Anyone with any experience growing chickens cannot argue one basic point: The success of any given flock of chickens rests primarily on the quality of the feed birds eat and the healthiness of baby chicks when they are delivered. A farmer can be a genius and can put in ten-hour days, seven days a week, but he will not raise a good batch of chickens if his feed is bad or he gets sickly chicks. The farmer can have an impact on the margins: If he completely neglects his birds, they won't gain as much weight. If he is in the chicken houses constantly, they will gain a little more.

Very few people understand this better than C. Robert Taylor, a professor of agricultural economics at Auburn University. Pretty much any farmer who has sued a chicken company over the last thirty years has hired Taylor to help him. He has made a small cottage industry out of being an expert witness for big lawsuits. This role has given him a unique perspective on the tournament system. He has reviewed massive databases of confidential information from the poultry companies themselves, including Tyson, showing exactly how much they pay farmers through the tournament and how the system really works. Taylor has looked over the tournament for tens of thousands of flocks of chickens at different poultry complexes, but confidentiality agreements bar him from releasing the data he has seen. But Taylor dryly notes that the confidentiality agreements don't bar him from sharing what the data has taught him.

To understand what the tournament truly incentivizes, Taylor looked over farmer settlement sheets, including one from Waldron, and used the data in them to reverse-engineer the secret equation that Tyson uses to rank and pay its farmers:

$$Pay_i = [AFC - c_i + .05] \cdot q_i$$

This formula is exactly as arcane and difficult to understand as it looks, which in Taylor's view is the primary reason Tyson is able to get away with using it.[*] This way, farmers have a tough time truly comprehending the mathematic realities of the payment scheme. Chief among these hard mathematical truths is the fact that the tournament is a zero-sum game.

The figure "AFC" represents the weighted-average cost of all the flocks in the tournament, and that's the benchmark used for the ranking. Farm-

---

[*] For those who can understand this kind of thing, Taylor describes the equation this way: "AFC" is the weighted average flock cost, "ci" is flock cost for the "ith" flock (flocks 1-20), "qi" is the net pounds sold for the "ith" flock.

ers aren't ranked against some sort of industry average cost, or even the average cost of growing chickens in their area. They are ranked against each other. That means that no matter how well they do, about half the farmers will end up taking money from the other half. Even if a group of farmers does extremely well during a given week—if they all happen to raise chickens at a remarkably efficient rate and use way less food to grow a bird than the typical farmer—they won't all get a big bonus payment for their work. Under Tyson's system, half of them still end up losers. The average cost of production for that remarkable week of growing becomes the benchmark against which the farmers are ranked. The top performers, even if the margin is slim, take payment from the bottom.

This incentivizes farmers to fight one another economically, rather than focus strictly on good performance. Each farmer knows his survival is dependent on his neighbor's loss. And his neighbor's gain comes at his expense. This leaves the farmer desperately seeking to get any edge he can to push his neighbor into bankruptcy.

The equation also spells out a critical function of the tournament. It helps push the financial risks of farming from Tyson to its farmers. The tournament allows Tyson to set a base price, letting it predict how much it will pay for chickens, even as pay fluctuates for the farmer. That's because Tyson shifts the base pay around for its farmers, but only by shifting pay from one to another. A simple breakdown shows how this works. The best farmer makes six cents a pound, but he takes that money from the bottom farmer, who makes four cents a pound.

FARMER	RANKING	BASE PAY	TYSON'S AVERAGE COST
Farmer #1	1	6 cents	5 cents
Farmer #2	2	5 cents	5 cents
Farmer #3	3	4 cents	5 cents

The tournament, then, lets Tyson predict exactly what it will pay for chickens while making the farmer's income wildly volatile. Who wins and who loses doesn't change anything for Tyson Foods. The farmers are left to fight that out on their own and determine who gets to stay in business.

Boonau Phouthavong's background made him an ideal chicken farmer. He knew how to endure, and he knew how to sacrifice. His personal definition of hardship entailed sleeping in the jungle, scrounging for food, and being hunted like an animal by government soldiers. Chicken farming wasn't so bad by comparison.

After buying Edwin's chicken houses, Boonau enjoyed his most profitable run of years as a chicken farmer. He invested roughly $60,000 into the houses, adding computer systems that automatically controlled the climate and new fans that cooled the birds in a wind tunnel. He and his wife, Pat, lived in a mobile home nearby three of their chicken houses, sharing the small quarters with their two children.

Boonau took to chicken farming with relish, donning his white facemask and entering the cavernous industrial barns to work every morning with the happy resolve of a man who had finally found his good station in life. Pat had to work at the Tyson plant in town to make ends meet, but the sacrifices the couple had to make seemed tiny compared to those in their past.

When he was sixteen, Boonau was drafted into the army, during a time when the United States dropped more bombs on Laos than it deployed during the entirety of World War II. But even Boonau's time in the army was easier than what came afterward, when his country fell to a Communist regime in 1975. Boonau hated the new centralized government and the fact that his family no longer owned their land, or even their harvest of rice. Communist bosses decided how much money Boonau's family could keep from their labor, and their decisions seemed arbitrary and corrupt. When he was in his early twenties, Boonau fled to the jungle and joined a ragtag band of resistance fighters. He split his time between the jungle and a refugee camp in Thailand.

Boonau eventually emigrated to the United States, pressured by his parents, who didn't want to see him killed in combat. He arrived in the Midwest with nothing and got a factory job in Chicago.

By the mid-1980s, Boonau was working as a factory machinist and living in a small apartment. He had a few weeks of job training and spoke enough broken English to get him through a trip to the grocery store or a restaurant. Even then, Boonau dreamed of owning his own land and a house and setting money aside for retirement. He wanted the kind of economic independence his parents and grandparents enjoyed as property owners in Laos.

A relative told him about the business of contract chicken farming. It was hard, smelly work, but there was stability to it, a steady paycheck. There was good money in it, Boonau heard. And independence. This job, above all the others, captured his imagination. He would live in the green countryside, on land he owned. There was no job more self-sufficient than being an American farmer.

Starting in 1985, Boonau worked in the factory every day and dreamed of the farm he would own, the house where he would live on some wooded hillside somewhere. He married a fellow Laotian refugee named Pat, and they had two children.

Boonau and Pat Phouthavong saved everything they could, which turned out to be quite a lot. If there is ever an Olympic event in saving cash from a meager paycheck, there is no question Laotians would dominate the sport. Members of the Laotian diaspora opened McDonald's franchises, hardware stores, and restaurants in the decades after they arrived in the United States, all with money they somehow saved away while living near the edge of poverty. The Phouthavongs were no different. They lived with the kind of frugality only practiced by people whose early life was steeped in deprivation.

Fifteen years later they had amassed roughly $70,000 between them, and they owned a house worth near $80,000. In 1999 they used their life savings as a down payment on a better life, buying their first farm outside Waldron and signing their first contract with Tyson Foods.

Local farmers were quietly puzzled as to why someone like Boonau would sink their fortunes into chicken farms that barely turned a profit. But he himself felt comfortable with the investment. Tyson was good to him. The company paid Boonau a Christmas bonus, and it was quick to answer his calls when he needed help. Boonau ranked well in the tournament system and was turning a steady profit off each of his houses. Like Jerry Yandell in the late 1990s, Boonau was a man who did well by the chicken business.

But because of the way the tournament system was structured, his success came at his neighbors' expense.

Greg and Donna Owens had done well in Tyson's tournament system for nearly a decade, placing at the top sometimes, or more commonly toward the middle. Then some invisible hand seemed to grab hold of their operation, dragging them lower in the competition. They started placing last and couldn't seem to break the average mark. And for the life of her, Donna couldn't figure out why.

It didn't seem to be a problem with the farm. The Owenses ran a small place, two chicken houses off a winding gravel lane called Lick Skillet Road. They bought the place in 1998 from Jerry Yandell, who was Donna Owens's distant in-law. Yandell was looking to unload some of his property to scale back. The Lick Skillet farm was a profitable one, he assured them.

The Owenses couldn't really afford the place, but Donna's parents agreed to cosign a loan with them for $114,000 to finance the purchase, putting up their own 120-acre farm as collateral. For Donna Owens, it was the down payment on a dream life. She had worked at the Tyson plant since high school, and by the late 1990s she was having back trouble from standing all day on the concrete floor of the slaughterhouse. The couple's new farm was a fresh start, a dignified way to make a living and a chance for the Owenses to set their own schedule.

For years, the farm paid off well. The Owenses afforded a modest life, with occasional meals out in Waldron and new clothes for their son and daughter. Donna's husband, Greg, was no stranger to hard work. Looking like a figure who stepped right out of a Civil War photo, he didn't bother to shower or shave when entering the modern world. He's as tall as a bear, and he has a thick matted beard. Greg wears grimy denim overalls around the farm, and he has a habit of notching his thumbs into the overall straps and pushing outward when he speaks, puffing out his chest. Greg's hands hang like big stones at the ends of his arms, and it would seem unwise to provoke him into swinging them.

For all of his size and apparent strength, Greg would wince and slouch his shoulders like a schoolboy at the mention of Gary Roper's name. Roper, the manager at Tyson's complex who oversaw the Owenses' farm, was in increasing contact with the couple throughout the winter of 2007 and spring of 2008. Donna was calling him and pestering her field man, trying to figure out why the couple couldn't place better in the rankings. The Owenses' field man simply criticized everything they did in response. After a decade in the business, it seemed as if they had forgotten the rudimentary elements of raising chickens. They were told to run the fans longer, work on their water lines, make more passes through the house to collect dead birds. None of it helped. They sank lower in the rankings, their paychecks shrank, and eventually Tyson sent them a letter saying they'd been placed under Intensified Management Status. Under this program, farmers get three final chances, three flocks with which they must beat average cost to get released from the program and keep their farm. If two out of three consecutive flocks are below the average, and a certain measurement of their birds' weight is in the bottom 10 percent for farmers in their network, Tyson can cancel their contract.

The Owenses didn't make it. Greg Owens drove to the complex to meet with Gary Roper and ask him how Tyson could cancel their contract after so many years in the business. In response, Roper used a dog-racing metaphor he apparently thought Owens could easily understand.

— If you were running a dog race, and you were getting outrun all the time, then there wouldn't be much use in you being in it, Roper told him.*

Owens understood he was the dog who wasn't winning the race, the dog that wasn't making Tyson enough money.

---

* The account of this meeting is based on Greg Owens's recollection of it. The general tenor and substance of the meeting conforms with the accounts of other chicken farmers in Waldron who found themselves unable to meet the demands of Tyson Foods. Tyson Foods refused to make Gary Roper available for interviews.

Roper offered Owens a way out. Owens could take out a loan for hundreds of thousands of dollars and update his chicken houses, adding new fans and walls and insulation to make them more efficient. It would indebt the Owens family for years, another decade at least, at a time when their current mortgage was already eating most of their paycheck from Tyson.

— I can't do it, Greg said. So you're just going to cut me off? Just cancel my contract?

A letter from Tyson made it official. Their contract was canceled. The farm on Lick Skillet road was out of business. Months later, Donna Owens was still trying to figure out what had happened and puzzle out what had driven them down in the rankings so quickly.

The tournament system isn't built to produce enduring winners. This fact became evident to Boonau Phouthavong around 2008. By that time Boonau should have been at the pinnacle of his career as a chicken farmer. He was nearly a decade into the business and had plenty of experience that taught him the tricks and techniques of industrial animal production. He was a veteran, and he'd spent years paying down the loans on his chicken houses, giving him the first glimpse of the profits that come from operating a chicken farm that was free and clear of debt. He had sold the two chicken houses he bought off Edwin at a tidy profit and was able to plow the money back into the other five houses he operated.

But in spite of all he had going for him, Boonau noticed that his paychecks were steadily declining. He seemed to be ranking lower and lower in the tournament system and couldn't seem to pull above average no matter what he tried. His houses might be considered slightly out of date, at least compared to the brand-new operations being built around him, but they were hardly obsolete. They weren't even halfway through the thirty-year lifespan of loan taken out to build them. On paper, the farms Boonau operated should have had decades left of good production.

To understand why he was losing money, Boonau only needed to take a short drive down the country roads east of Waldron. There he would have seen the reason for his troubles. There was a freshly cut gravel driveway leading off the side of the road, and next to that a metallic sign advertising one of Tyson Foods' newest farms. The sign simply said: N&N Farm.

The chicken houses on N&N Farm command the high ground and are lined up in a neat row like the barracks of an occupying empire. The houses have locked steel doors and no windows. At each end of the houses are two wide-mouthed fans as big around as swimming pools, thrumming and sucking air inside to make a wind tunnel that cools the flocks.

There is a small green farmhouse at the bottom of the hill, and very early one October morning the glass door on its back porch slid open and out stepped Nue Yang. Nue is a slight woman, and she stepped gingerly past a pile of shoes her kids left by the door in the Laotian tradition. She walked down the sidewalk and toward the yard, where her husband, Nouk, was already outside, wiping dew off the windshield of an all-terrain vehicle. Nouk was working quietly, wearing a kelly-green hat emblazoned with the yellow script: "Nothing Works like a Deere."

Nouk and Nue (hence the name N&N farm) were new to Waldron. Their farm was only a few months old, and the gravel drive leading up to the houses was newly cut into the ground. Nue got into the ATV Nouk was cleaning and started driving up the hill, toward the chicken houses. There was a white bucket in the seat behind her that she used to collect dead chickens as part of her morning routine.

Jerry Yandell wouldn't recognize the farm Nouk and Nue operate. The couple had borrowed nearly two million dollars to build the complex. Each chicken house has a small control room with a computer inside that controls a system of thermometers, feed-bin monitors, and water-level gauges, constantly monitoring the environment inside, where more than twenty-five thousand birds eat and grow. Because the houses are so big, with so many animals crammed inside, the birds can start dying within fifteen minutes if anything goes wrong. So the computers in each house are wired to a pair of cell phones Nouk and Nue carry at all times. If a water line clogs or a fan quits running, even for a short time, the computers call Nouk and Nue. Some nights, the cell phones are like fussy infants, squalling every forty minutes, reporting everything from tiny glitches in the fan system to water pipe failures that require an immediate trip up the hill.

The Yangs' most recent batch of nineteen-day-old chickens had been relatively easy. Nue stopped the ATV outside and grabbed the white bucket before walking into a small plywood shack adjoining the first chicken house. Inside, she looked at the white computer monitor on the wall and entered a pass code. Several screens popped to life with digital readouts. The temperature was 78.5 degrees, while the thermostat was set at 76.6 degrees. Not a worrisome spread. The fans were temporarily off, and the feed lines were steadily piping food to a network of trays inside the house.

Nue opened a small door, slid a white facemask over her mouth, and walked inside the barn. A clucking echoed up from the sea of birds as she walked through the flock. She passed slowly down the length of the barn, past round heating globes that hung at regular intervals from the ceiling. Nue looked down as she walked, scanning from left to right. She spotted dead birds, half buried in the litter, and bobbed down quickly to grab them, throwing them into the bucket in her hand.

Plunk, plunk, plunk, she threw them in the bucket. She walked the length of a Wal-Mart parking lot to the end of the barn, then turned around to come back along the opposite wall, collecting dead birds along the way.

Back outside, Nue opened a plastic freezer and dumped the dead birds inside. The chicken houses behind her looked imposing, the exhaust fans protruding from them impossibly huge. A farmer with older chicken houses could look upon the buildings and know they were outgunned. The automatic ventilation, the airtight insulation, and the computer-controlled feeding systems shaved precious pennies off the cost of raising each chicken. And because of the way the tournament system was structured, those pennies would be taken away from any farmer unlucky enough to be pitted against N&N Farm.

In 2009 Boonau Phouthavong discovered he was a failure as a chicken farmer. Tyson laid out the extent and scope of his shortcomings in a series of detailed letters the company sent Boonau throughout 2009. At first, his failings had been made clear by his low rankings in Tyson's tournament, which never seemed to improve. Because he ranked below the average for three flocks in a row, Boonau had been put on Intensified Management Status, and given a Performance Improvement Program. He was told that if he did worse than the average on any two out of three consecutive flocks, and if a six-flock average of his birds' weight was in the bottom 10 percent for farmers at the Waldron complex, Tyson could cut off his contract.

On May 19 Tyson sent Boonau a letter outlining the nature of his improvement program. The message was brief:

> "Basic management practices are an important part of getting good performance out of the birds. Areas that need to be carefully controlled are: Consistent brooding, correct water and feed line height, temperature control, house ventilation, and feed management, such as keeping the lines at the proper height and depth so the birds do not waste feed. You must constantly strive to manage the birds and equipment on a daily basis to get maximum performance and be competitive."

In essence, the letter only said: "Be a good farmer. Work hard." There weren't recommendations for new equipment he could buy to upgrade his houses, or substantial changes he could make to improve. Tyson's letter made clear the company could put him out of business if he didn't improve his performance, but Boonau couldn't figure out what to do differently. He tended the birds daily and made sure the water and feed lines were clear. But still, he kept sinking lower in the tournament rankings.

Then, on December 14, Tyson sent Boonau another terse letter. He hadn't met the company's criteria for getting off the management program. He was also provided a series of documents that portrayed the economic performance of his farm with a level of breathtaking detail that Boonau, the farm's owner, would never have been able to ascertain on his own.

There were graphs that charted the growth rate of chickens on his farm going back to 2006, comparing it to the average rate for farmers in the Waldron complex. The spiky line of Boonau's growth rate fluctuated wildly from flock to flock but always seemed to come in below the average. Another bar graph showed his farm's average cost to produce a pound of meat, compared to the average around Waldron, going back to 2006. Boonau did better than the average on only five out of twenty-one flocks.

Boonau read over these documents as he sat in the kitchen of his small farmhouse south of Waldron, wearing a green baseball cap and rubber boots. His English was proficient, but he still had a hard time truly comprehending what the letters told him. Tyson seemed to have measured every ounce of feed and every chicken that had passed through his operation and had deemed his farm wasn't worth their time or money.

But Boonau shouldn't have taken it personally. His failure exemplified one of the most important elements of Tyson's tournament. The system does more than simply push risk onto the farmer. It also allows Tyson to control the one element of meat production that is owned by the farmer: the physical infrastructure of the farm. With each flock being a risky, life-or-death competition against neighbors, farmers turn to the one thing they can do to boost their efficiency. They spend more on equipment, hoping it will boost their efficiency just a little, whether it's profitable in the long run or not.

It's true that a farmer's ranking can be almost random within a tournament, given that he has no control over his birds or feed. But there is one clear trend within the competition. The bigger, newer houses tend to rank above the smaller, older houses when they compete against one another. The correlation isn't perfect, but, overall, farmers with newer houses do better than the farmers with older houses.*

C. Robert Taylor, the Auburn economist, has seen the trend clearly in the data he reviewed. What this means, over time, is that the tournament acts like a kind of anti-Robin Hood, taking money from farmers with older houses and using it to subsidize construction of newer houses that compete against them. Big, wind-tunnel houses like those at N&N Farm steadily take pay from the older houses like Richard Moore's. So the farmers who have been with Tyson the longest end up paying for newer farmers to borrow more money and build new houses. The deductions come out of their paycheck, thanks to the tournament, and the money flows to the newer housing. The competition isn't just between immigrant farmers and local farmers. It is between older farms and newer farms, and whoever happens to occupy them.

On Valentine's Day, 2010, only the children were home at N&N Farm. It was a Sunday, and none of the kids knew where their parents, Nouk and Nue, had gotten off to. The Yangs' twenty-one-year-old son, Tua, was watching the house, home for a weekend visit from college in nearby Fort Smith. That morning he babysat his twelve-year-old brother and ten-year-old sister.

The kids were excited. There was a Valentine's party planned that day at the Laotian church downtown, and the next day was President's Day, so they had the Monday off from school. But Tua dutifully reminded his siblings there were chores to be done before they could head to the party.

---

* Tyson Foods acknowledges pitting newer houses against older houses, but says the arrangement is necessary to reward farmers who spend money to upgrade their facilities. The company pointed out that it also reinvests in its slaughterhouses and other facilities.

Tua's ten-year-old sister donned a puffy purple coat and pulled big rubber boots over her pajama pants emblazoned with white clouds and yellow stars.* Tua put on a hooded sweatshirt while his twelve-year-old brother grabbed a windbreaker and his favorite baseball hat with a Baltimore Ravens logo on the front. They went outside, where gray clouds had rolled in over the mountains and brought with them a biting, cold wind. Tua and his siblings each grabbed a white plastic bucket, then headed up the gravel road toward the chicken houses.

Tua opened the door of the first house and they all went inside. It was dim and warm, an enormous cavern where the air was hazy with ammonia that burned the throat. Chickens clucked and warbled, and the two young kids walked away from Tua and down toward the end of the houses. Their path was lit by big heating lamps that hung at regular intervals from the ceiling, clicking on automatically with a hiss and exuding orange flames.

The kids collected dead birds. As they walked through the flock, the birds dispersed in a broad arc, revealing little pale carcasses stuck in the chicken litter. The kids picked them up and tossed them in the bucket.

Only Tua was old enough to be worried about how many dead birds they found that morning. His parents had told him there was something terribly wrong with this flock, though they didn't know what. Ever since the Tyson trucks delivered the birds in January, the animals had been dying in waves. The Tyson trucks had delivered 39,000 chickens to each of the Yangs' seven houses. In the first week on the farm, it would have been normal for about 390 birds to die in each house. Instead, Nouk and Nue hauled out more than 2,000 birds from each building. By the end of the second week, they had taken between 2,000 and 5,000 dead birds from each house.

After working for a while, Tua's sister set down her bucket, which was overfilled with dead birds and too heavy for her to carry. Tua walked over and helped her lug it out of the house.

"Man, so many," Tua muttered. He flipped the bucket upside down

---

* The Yang children will remain anonymous because they are minors.

and dumped its contents into a beige plastic freezer. Although Tua didn't know Jerry Yandell, he was discovering that the fundamental rules of chicken farming hadn't changed that much since Yandell's day. In spite of all the high-tech equipment at N&N Farm, the Yangs were still vulnerable to the same factors that drove the Yandells out of business. The Yangs never owned the birds they raised and couldn't control the quality of the feed Tyson delivered.

Tua stood outside and tallied the dead as the kids left each house. He is a slight man, wearing oval-shaped eyeglasses that would easily let him pass for a teenager. But his face bore the wrinkles of a very worried grown-up that morning as he squinted at the worksheet and counted the dead birds from the flock.

Tua knew what the mortality rate meant for the farm and his parents' future. By the end of two weeks they had lost about 27,000 birds, or 10 percent of the flock. That took about $15,000 out of their paycheck, while the mortgage payment stayed the same and the heating bill climbed because of the propane they pumped into the houses.

The Yangs had no idea what kind of disease was burning through the birds. Nouk called the family's Tyson field technician and told her what was happening. She visited the farm while he was not there and left a note. The field technician speculated that the birds might have some sort of respiratory problem, something that could have originated in the hatchery.

Nouk tried to keep the birds alive, but there were only so many levers he could pull to alter the environment inside the chicken houses. He ran the fans faster, then slowed them down. He pumped up the heat, then cooled it off. But the birds kept dying, hundreds a day.

Tua and his siblings went through the houses, came out, and dumped the carcasses into plastic freezers that were brimmed full with dead birds. At one point when they came out of a house, they saw it had started snowing, with thick white flakes swirling down from the clouds, sticking on the tops of the aluminum feed bins and melting on the wet orange clay ground between the houses.

The kids tilted their heads back and caught snowflakes on their tongues.

"Hey!" Tua's little brother said, smiling. "It's snowing! I told you I could see the future!"

By the time N&N Farm got up and running, Jerry and Kanita Yandell were well ensconced in their new life. The couple lived in a small trailer off Highway 80, not far from their old place. Jerry worked on the county road crew, Kanita worked at a nursing home. Both earned low wages and couldn't afford to buy a home, but Jerry considered it a step up from the chicken business.

After a long day of hot work along the asphalt highways, Jerry stood on the couple's small wooden porch, where morning glory vines crawled over a rickety wooden trellis and provided him shade. He didn't like to think about Tyson or farming much at all now that he had moved on. But he couldn't help but be curious about the new tide of Laotian farmers moving into the area. When he heard that Nouk and Nue Yang had borrowed $2 million to build the complex of seven houses nearby, Yandell took a long, contemplative drag from his cigarette.

"They're doomed," he said.

Nouk Yang spent his long weekend days alone on N&N farm. One Saturday in February, his wife, Nue, left town to go to a church event in Oklahoma with the kids. But with the birds still dying off at a rapid pace from some unknown disease, someone had to stay behind to monitor the flock. So Nouk stayed home. But beyond checking on the birds, there was little he could do to stave off their sickness. With nothing but time on his hands, Nouk took a BB gun and walked over a hill to a small lake on his land, where he shot glass bottles placed on fence posts. Nouk had one attribute that made him a particularly gifted chicken farmer: He knew how to wait. He had spent much of his youth in refugee camps in Thailand, waiting for each meal, waiting to find out when he would get a ticket to the United States.

Waldron was Nouk's better life. And he was able to embrace it because of a second quality that made him a great chicken farmer:

his deep sense of fatalism. Nouk believed destiny smiled on some and scorned others. It wasn't up to people to decide their fate. He, for example, wondered how anyone was able to get a job that entailed sitting in an office all day, enjoying air-conditioning and wearing nice clothing. Work for him entailed wearing a facemask, breathing rank ammonia, lifting white buckets full of dead chickens. He worked a seven-day-a-week schedule. The air of the chicken houses infected his clothes. He knew it must be unhealthy to breathe it, and for his children to breathe it. But what was he to do?

Nouk sat on a concrete slab next to one of his big chicken houses that sunny Saturday afternoon in February, while the birds died inside, and pondered things. On paper, he was a rich farmer. He owned property worth nearly $2 million, with seven massive chicken houses and a white propane silo installed next to them. More than $300,000 in cash passed through his hands every year. But for all that money, Nouk couldn't afford to repair the long gravel driveway that ran from the road up to his chicken houses, which was getting rutted by Tyson's trucks. He had less than $10,000 in the bank account, a fraction of what he would need to cover his bills if he lost money on this flock. He and Nue avoided doctors because they could not afford health insurance.

Nouk seemed resigned to this. Almost comfortable with it.

"When I lived in Laos, I never had health insurance. You know, if you're going to die, you're going to die," he mused.

His destiny was out of his hands. He was stuck between Tyson, which gave him his income, and the banks, which demanded his mortgage payments. He had learned from other Laotians that the banks wouldn't blink before foreclosing on him if he didn't make his payments.

In the end, Nouk and Nue Yang were lucky. Because their farm was virtually brand new, they were able to drop their contract with Tyson Foods and get picked up by its competitor, OK Foods out of Fort Smith, Arkansas. Most farmers don't have this choice. Chicken companies usually demand massive new investments in a farmer's chicken houses if the farmer wants to switch companies. For people like Doug Elmore or Jerry Yandell, the extra cost is prohibitive. Switching is made more difficult by the paucity of choices—many farmers live close enough to only one chicken company with which they can do business. After the Valentine's Day weekend when Tyson's birds died off in huge numbers, Nouk and Nue were ready to make a change, and OK Foods accepted their bid.

Nouk Yang discovered that the chicken business was almost unchanged under OK Foods. He was still paid through a tournament system, and he still had no control over the health of his birds or the quality of his feed. His financial picture didn't change at all after making the switch. Plenty of money still flowed through the farm, but the Yangs kept very little of it.

On a hilltop south of Waldron, an old farmhouse has been painted in wild tropical colors, with burgundy walls and a vivid tableau above the front door showing Buddha, meditating serenely with a mountain range behind him, surrounded by loyal supplicants. A hand-painted sign nearby identifies the building as "Wat Lao Sirithummo of Waldron," the Buddhist temple where local Laotians gather to pray.

Inside, Laotian chicken farmers gathered around a broad table one Saturday night for a community meeting. A Buddhist monk sat at the head of the table, dressed in a bright orange robe. Boonau Phouthavong was next to him, sitting upright with the quiet dignity of a village elder. As one of the earliest Laotian settlers in Arkansas, Boonau was considered a dignitary of sorts, having helped many of his fellow immigrants get acclimated to the area when they first arrived. He didn't speak often during meetings, but when he did his words carried weight.

In the winter of 2010, the Laotian community was beset by bankruptcy and farm failures. People were coming to Boonau for help and advice. Many farms had gone under within just one or two years of being bought. The Laotians were amazed at the economics of chicken farming, once they finalized their loans and started accepting chickens from Tyson or OK Foods. Their checks barely covered the cost of propane and electricity needed to raise a flock of birds. When they ranked poorly in the tournament, they actually lost money for their labor. Tyson's field technicians seemed unable or unwilling to help them. One after another, farmers in Arkansas, Oklahoma, Missouri, and elsewhere simply gave up. In some cases they walked off the farm, leaving behind their life savings.

With his own farm on the edge of failure, Boonau was at a loss to help. After sending him the letter on December 14, Tyson refused to deliver any more birds to his chicken houses. He had just signed a contract with the company on October 26, 2009, that was supposed to supply him birds through October 2012. But it didn't seem to matter. All five of his chicken houses sat empty. One of the houses had collapsed because of an ice storm, and he didn't have the money to repair it. Boonau sold off cattle he grazed near his chicken houses to keep up with the electricity and other utility bills.

After a long Saturday morning of work in 2011, Boonau Phouthavong sat on the front porch of his small trailer home, overlooking a rolling green meadow and the hulking, silver-roofed chicken houses in a neat row. Out beyond the chicken houses, the tree-covered mountains made a jagged wall. The air was clean, and a cool breeze blew through the valley. In this quiet moment, with the stillness and greenery all around him, Boonau seemed to be living the life of a real farmer. He looked content.

Tyson had withheld delivery of its birds for about a year. Boonau begged and cajoled, but it made no difference. The bank agreed to delay part of his loan payments, so he didn't have to declare bankruptcy. Then in the spring of 2011, Tyson called out of the blue and asked him if he'd be willing to accept a load of chickens. He said he would. The company only agreed to deliver birds to his farm west of town, where he sat on his porch. The other farm sat empty, but he still paid the mortgage on it. In spite of that, he was able to keep afloat as long as Tyson delivered birds, so he accepted the work.

Tyson seemed to have found the ideal farmer in Boonau Phouthavong. The company held complete power over his destiny, and Boonau had come to peace with that fact. It was not as bad as the Communists. Not as bad as Laos.

Boonau didn't question whether Tyson was a good or bad business partner. Good and bad weren't his concern. What was important to him was that Boonau understood Tyson. He knew how to work with it. In Boonau's eyes, Tyson's business was not unlike a feudal monarchy. Its employees had the arbitrary power of medieval lords, a power they so willingly displayed when they shut him down for nearly a year. And these new-age barons were all part of a closed society, in Boonau's estimation. Tyson hired its own managers and gave them control of the farms regardless of what any outsiders thought. Skill and knowledge had nothing to do with their power. Often these men didn't seem to have the foggiest idea how to run Boonau's farm, but still they told him what to do. And, being a quick student, Boonau had learned how to cope with this. He simply stayed quiet. He didn't talk back. He didn't ask questions. He didn't threaten to sue when the company said it would shut him down. He accommodated Tyson, and he survived.

It might seem curious that a bank would be willing to lend $2 million to a couple like the Yangs, or hundreds of thousands of dollars to a farmer like Boonau. The Laotian immigrants are living on the ragged edge of bankruptcy even though some operate monstrous, state-of-the-art farm complexes. The high failure rate among farmers is well known. But the banks keep lending easy money for farms, so new operations can replace old ones when Tyson's tournament drives farmers out of business. The reason for this is simple: The banks have a very powerful patron to bail them out if the farm loans go bad: the U.S. taxpayer.

The tournament system is kept afloat by an obscure federal organization called the Farm Service Agency. The FSA spends hundreds of millions of dollars in taxpayer money to make sure that there will always be cheap loans for a new chicken farm when an older one is put out of business.

Ron Burnett is a loan officer in Arkansas who has seen how the farm loan program works firsthand and how it has changed over the last few decades. In 1983 Burnett became a loan officer for a small division of the U.S. Department of Agriculture called the Farmers Home Administration. Few people ever heard of the agency, whose nominal goal was to ensure that struggling farmers had access to credit. But from his vantage point in the Arkansas branch of the agency, Burnett watched as it grew and ultimately made taxpayers responsible for billions of dollars in loans for industrial chicken farms.

The Farmers Home Administration (FMHA) was created in the 1940s because private banks had backed out of the business of extending farm loans, fearing that the business was too risky. The FMHA's job was to loan money directly to farmers. It also had a side business of guaranteeing farm loans made by private banks, promising, in essence, to bail out the bank and pay it the value of the loan if the farmer defaulted. Burnett's FMHA office in Arkansas was a relatively sleepy little operation when he joined back in the 1980s. It extended loans to cattle ranchers so they could buy livestock, and it loaned money to row-crop farmers so they could buy or repair equipment. The FMHA extended some loans to chicken farmers, but that was a small part of the agency's business because it wasn't allowed to lend out more than $300,000 at time, which was hardly enough money to build a big chicken farm.

Burnett and other loan officers noticed a change in the mid-1990s, when the FMHA got wrapped into a large agency called the Farm Service Agency. At that time, private banks started getting edgy about loaning money to poultry farms. The business was getting riskier, even as it was expanding and companies like Tyson were reaping record profits each year. In spite of the growth, more farmers were going under and selling their operations at a loss to get out of the business. It seemed increasingly routine for Tyson to cancel a farmer's contract if he didn't meet the company's expectations.

But the rate of chicken house construction didn't slow, because bankers figured out a new way to keep money flowing to Tyson's network of contract farms. They turned to the Farm Service Agency. While the agency was limited in how much money it could loan directly to farmers, it had far more leeway in the size of the loan it could guarantee. Under the guaranteed loan program, the FSA would pay back the bank more than 90 percent of the loan value if a farmer defaulted. The bank also got to keep any down payment the farmer made, plus any fees, interest payments, and other money it collected from the farmer before he went bankrupt. This meant the bank had nothing to lose if it could land an FSA guarantee for a poultry farm. One bank after another discovered this lucrative pool of taxpayer-backed loans, first regional banks in towns like Danville and Fort Smith, Arkansas, then national operations like U.S. Bank.

The FSA became a pipeline of credit for chicken farms by the time Boonau Phouthavanong, Nouk Yang, and other Laotian farmers were ready to enter the business. In 1999 the Arkansas FSA guaranteed $49.9 million in new farm loans, with well over 90 percent of the loans going to chicken farmers, according to Burnett and other loan officers. By 2001, when Boonau was settling into Waldron, the FSA guaranteed $68.4 million in loans.

As more Laotians moved south to buy up poultry farms, the value of loan guarantees exploded. The Arkansas FSA in Arkansas guaranteed $101.9 million in 2002 and $103.4 million in 2003. Banks were rushing to get in on the deal making. Backing the risky loans for poultry farms wasn't a problem for the USDA. At the FSA, the biggest concern seemed to be that loan officers would get in trouble if they shut out aspiring farmers by failing to guarantee the loans. The USDA was confronting a dark legacy of discrimination against black farmers and other minorities, and it was eager to show it treated all new farmers the same.

Between 1999 and 2009, the Arkansas FSA office alone guaranteed more than $797 million in new loans, leaving taxpayers on the hook if the farms failed.

"We don't discriminate against nobody," Burnett said. "If it'll cash flow in any way possible, we'll make the loan."

The loans for new farms around Waldron were parceled out by small banks with local branches, like Chambers Bank of Danville, Arkansas, or Regions Bank in Alabama. These banks became a loan mill, churning out hundreds of loans to Laotian immigrants so they could overhaul existing farms or build new ones.

The paperwork for these loans reflected the same sort of hazy math and willful blindness that characterized the wave of subprime mortgages being extended from Las Vegas to Florida. To get a loan from Chambers or Regions Bank, farmers had to submit a Farm and Home Plan that justified the amount of money they would borrow. The plan was meant to show how much money the farmers could reasonably expect to earn from their operation, balanced against the amount of income they would need to keep the farm running and support their family. If earnings from the farm were enough to support the family and cover expenses, then the loan could be approved.

A review of the Farm and Home Plans submitted by a single loan officer in Arkansas named Larry Skeets reveals the sort of rigor that went into the process.*

The paperwork for Tria and Mai Xiong, for example, shows that the couple and their son planned to spend about $20,000 a year for their living expenses. That budget made their loan application look pretty feasible, leaving the family a total annual income of about $61,000 a year after expenses.

Curiously, it appears that farmers Lue Her and Mai Yang also budgeted $20,000 a year in living expenses, according to loan documents, even though it was just the two of them, with no children. Strikingly, a farmer named Tou Lee also budgeted $20,000 a year in living expenses. So did Lao.

All these families decided to budget their living expenses at $20,000, which was luckily just the right amount to make their farms appear profitable on paper.

Maybe a banker reviewing Skeets's loan documents would think the $20,000 was some traditional Laotian family budget, a number they all used in the same way they decorated houses with identical plastic flowering vines. But the numbers start to look really strange in the case of Pa Chay Xiong, who also, not surprisingly, budgeted living expenses of $20,000 on the loan application for a farm. The thing about Pa Chay

---

* The loan documents described here were uncovered by Fayetteville attorney Mark Henry.

was that he had seven kids. That means he budgeted $6.11 per day to feed each person in his family, or $42.74 a week. Xiong's neighbor Don Lee seemed to make an identical calculation, budgeting $20,000 to feed his family of nine.

These rubber-stamp numbers did not seem to raise serious objections for senior loan officers. All of the loans went through. Throughout Arkansas, Oklahoma, and Texas, similar loans were being approved. Laotians had no trouble borrowing $500,000 or $2 million at a time for their operations, even as local farmers declared bankruptcy, had their contracts canceled by Tyson, or simply put their farms up for sale because they couldn't pay their bills.

It's difficult to determine how much money taxpayers spend every year to support Tyson's system of contract farms. Clearly, billions of dollars underpin the construction of new chicken farms in the United States. This steady flow of easy credit allows Tyson and its competitors to cast off farmers without worrying that banks will hesitate to lend money to the next chicken grower in line.

One reason it's difficult to put an exact dollar amount on this subsidy is that the government itself does not know. The FSA knows the total value of loans it guarantees every year and the total value of bad loans that it has bailed out. But it doesn't track its loans by industry, meaning the agency doesn't know how many loans each year go to buy new tractors and how many go to build new chicken houses.

Jim Radintz, who was an officer in the FSA's farm loan division in Washington from 1989 until late 2010, said the agency isn't required to track which type of agriculture consumes most of the agency's money. The FSA was created to support all farms equally, so it doesn't need to track how much money is used to bail out poultry farms versus, say, catfish hatcheries. Congress didn't set up the FSA as a profit-making enterprise, Radintz said, so it ultimately doesn't matter if one kind of agriculture is a bigger drain on taxpayer money than another.

According to one internal FSA audit, the agency guaranteed more than $568.9 million in new loans for poultry farms in just 2008 and 2009 alone, the only two years for which it tracked the number. The internal audit didn't track the value of losses paid out for bad poultry farm loans. The FSA paid a total of $468 million to bail out bad farm loans between 1999 and 2008, but what proportion went to poultry farms is unknown.

While the FSA office in Washington doesn't track the value of loans to poultry farmers, its local offices do. Each loan file says what kind of business the money was used for. But a series of open records requests sent to the nation's biggest poultry-producing states met with mixed results. Some states, like Mississippi and Alabama, quickly responded with precise figures showing the value of loans they guaranteed for new poultry farms. (Alabama said it guaranteed $287 million in loans for chicken houses over the last decade, while Mississippi said it guaranteed $150 million.) Other states, like Arkansas, provided less detailed records that showed only the total value of all the loans they guaranteed (loan officers in Arkansas said well over 90 percent of all the loans were for chicken farms).

Several of the biggest chicken-producing states, including Oklahoma, Texas, Tennessee, and Georgia, refused to provide records for their guaranteed poultry loan programs. The loan files were indisputably public information. But FSA officers in these states said they were not obligated under the law to dig through their files and compile information about poultry loans that were extended in different counties, as several other states had done.

If the FSA is hesitant to disclose its figures, it is easy to understand why after looking at the figures from Arkansas. Even as the state was guaranteeing more loans each year over the last decade, it was simultaneously paying out ever-larger sums to cover losses. The state paid just $125,237 to bail out failed farms in 1999. By the middle of the decade it was paying at least $2 million a year, and by 2009 it paid out $4 million. Over ten years Arkansas spent $20.6 million to cover loan losses.

One thing the loan program has going in its favor is that most chicken house loans aren't a complete loss when farmers default. In the vast majority of cases, a bank is able to sell off a farm and recoup at least some of the loan value, sparing taxpayers the burden of paying off the entire debt.

But farmers don't get any of that money. A system that was once designed as a safety net for struggling farmers now serves the opposite purpose. The FSA is a safety net for Tyson, the banks, and the tournament system.

The farmers are left to fend for themselves.

Rural Americans have a word for what has happened to the economy of towns like Waldron and what has happened to the livelihoods of people like Boonau, the Yangs, and Jerry Yandell. They have been *chickenized*.

It's a silly sounding word to outsiders, *chickenized*, but farmers and ranchers spit it out with all the vitriol of a racial epithet. The word describes a miserable state of existence, a powerlessness that Boonau and others have come to accept as the inevitable state of the American rural economy. Chickenized. It describes what happens to farmers like Boonau who struggle to eke out a living in Tyson's shadow. It describes a system where massive federal subsidies help keep a company like Tyson afloat at the expense of working families.

As Tyson Foods expanded during the 1980s and 1990s, so too did the reach of chickenization.

Tyson's domination of the chicken industry became so complete by the late 1990s that the company could take it no further. Jim Blair, Don Tyson's top attorney, repeatedly reminded his boss that U.S. antitrust laws prohibited Tyson Foods from taking over the entire market. There were limits to how big Tyson could get, no matter how much cash the company had on hand to buy competitors or build new plants.

But that didn't mean Don Tyson was content to stop growing. There were other horizons the company could conquer, other businesses in which the company could compete.

There were billions of dollars in profit being made each year in the livestock industry, for example, a fact that did not escape Don Tyson's attention. Even by the 1990s, rural America was still home to a patchwork of independent cattle ranches, feedlots, and hog farms, whose owners still operated the kind of midsize operations idealized by Thomas Jefferson two hundred years ago. They lived on their farms, owned their animals, and sold their herds on open, competitive cash markets. Cattle ranchers and hog farmers still made a good living, and the towns where they lived prospered much more than Waldron did.

Perhaps it was inevitable that Don Tyson and his lieutenants would eventually set their sights on the lucrative business of raising cattle and hogs. The company had to look outward, beyond the poultry sector, in their search for more profit.

The livestock industry was one of the economic pillars of small-town America. And it was ripe for the taking.

PART 2

THE GREAT CHICKENIZATION

CHAPTER 6

Pig Cities

(1973–1994)

I N THE early days, Don Tyson's hog farms were only a sideshow compared to the company's chicken business. The company funded a few scattered hog barns primarily as a way to discard used chicken feed, letting hogs eat it rather than throwing it away.

But over time, Don Tyson saw something special as he looked over the balance sheets of his small network of experimental hog farms. He saw a possible new future for his company, one that made it less vulnerable to the brutal swings of the poultry market. Tyson Foods could raise pigs without spending too much money, and it made a decent profit when it sold them to meatpackers like Armour. Tyson realized that pork prices rose and fell on a completely different cycle than chicken prices. If Tyson kept growing hogs, it might buffer the company from chicken's permanent boom and bust pricing cycles. The hog barns could be an insurance policy of sorts, a hedge against the volatility that drove modern chicken companies out of business. While Tyson's competitors were focused on chasing the next order for drumsticks, Don Tyson quietly funded his small cluster of hog houses.

Tyson's strategy was based on short-term profits. But it launched a sweeping change that would overtake traditional ranching and hog farming, transforming them into the industrial meat system that exists today. Farming as it had been practiced for centuries would be replaced in a matter of decades by a centralized, tightly controlled system modeled on the poultry business.

The takeover started in 1973, on a nondescript farm in northwestern Arkansas. A young man named Bill Moeller lived on the property, and he woke up early every day to start his farm work. Moeller was a full-time employee of Tyson's Foods. His job wasn't simply to raise meat or even necessarily to make money. Moeller's job was to learn. The farm he ran was a hidden experiment, an investment that would ultimately yield Tyson billions in profit.

In the predawn hours, Moeller donned rubber boots and work clothes and walked from his small house out to a group of low-slung sheds that sat secluded on a stretch of green pasture. When Moeller opened a shed door and went inside, he was greeted by the acrid smell of feces. There was a rustling and grunting sound, the clattering of hooves as a pink mass of bodies shied away from Moeller and bumped into one another, the startled whining of pigs crammed into a small space. The barn was a novel invention, a hybrid between a pigsty and a chicken house. It was a gamble on Tyson's behalf, a learning center where the company tested the theory that pigs could be raised under the same industrial model as chickens.

There was ample reason to doubt the gamble would work. Chickens and pigs were leagues apart biologically. Chickens were simple creatures, docile birds that could be packed next to one another for the six short weeks they were scheduled to be alive. Pigs, on the other hand, were not only bigger than most people, but they were far more biologically similar to humans than to birds. The internal organs of swine are so close to a human's that the animal became a favorite for medical dissections and tests of the digestive tract, stomach, and heart.

For over ten thousand years, pigs had been raised mostly outside, like cattle or horses. They wallowed in mud, they furrowed for food. The females suckled their young and cared for them with all the attentiveness of a mother cow or dog. It seemed unlikely the animals would be able to adapt to the production model of a chicken house, crammed into a barn, shoulder to shoulder, all four hundred pounds of a boar pressed up against all four hundred pounds of his neighbor. In many ways, it was the biological equivalent of putting hundreds of large people in a barn with no toilets or running water, and very little heating or cooling.

Moeller, however, was game to try. He was a cattleman by heart, raised about fifty miles east of Springdale in the town of Berryville,

Arkansas. He graduated from the University of Arkansas and planned to get into the ranching business. But his wife wanted to live near home, in northwestern Arkansas, which meant Tyson's Foods was his best bet for a job. He applied, willing to take what the company offered, and was a little taken aback when one of the nation's biggest chicken companies told Moeller they wanted him to work with hogs.

In the beginning, Tyson raised hogs only to get rid of its excess chicken feed. Before it had hog barns, Tyson used to cart unused chicken feed from one chicken farm to another. But Tyson's veterinarians were worried that the feed might be carrying diseases along with it as it got shipped to other farms. The company came up with a novel solution: It decided to feed those leftover chicken rations to hogs. That way it would get the grain off chicken farms but still put it to good use.

Moeller was hired to work on Tyson's flagship hog farm. It consisted of a few large sheds that could each hold five hundred pigs. Each day, Moeller fed the animals leftover chicken food, gave them water, and kept the barns clean. And he observed the animals. He learned about them. It quickly became clear that disease was the biggest hurdle to raising hundreds of hogs in confinement. When one pig got sick, the others caught it quickly. They didn't have space to roam, and they weren't moving around outside where they could build up natural immunities. The barns were a hothouse for disease. Moeller had an orderly mind and meticulous work habits, attributes he assigned to his German ancestry, so he quickly adopted rigorous hygiene protocols for the farm. Workers scrubbed themselves thoroughly, and the company used different sets of equipment for different barns, even using separate trucking fleets to transport different batches of hogs. Pig waste was another problem. Weighing hundreds of pounds, each animal produced a tremendous amount of feces and urine. On a typical hog farm, this waste was an asset. Farmers spread it on their crop fields and it enriched the soil. But big hog barns had just the most primitive form of sewage systems: open lagoons and pits where the waste built up quickly. At such highly concentrated levels, hog manure became toxic waste. If it leeched into local streams, it could kill fish and other aquatic life. The stench was bad enough to make people want to leave their homes nearby.

Over the years Moeller and a handful of other workers improvised a new set of rules for raising pigs in a factory environment. They were highly effective at their job, and the hog farms turned a profit. Don Tyson saw the opportunity to expand into hog farming, even though chicken production was his company's foundation.

The incentive for doing this was clear for Tyson's Foods. There were billions of dollars of profit at stake if the company could figure out how to raise pigs in the same way it raised chickens. In 1973 there were about 736,000 hog farms in the United States, which collectively made about $7.7 billion a year. It was a business still characterized by mom-and-pop producers scattered across theAmerican countryside. If Tyson could beat them at their own game by raising pigs more cheaply and voluminously, the company could steal the lucrative market for itself. If Tyson could dominate hog production, it could take on the cattle business after that.

The task was daunting, and it amounted to nothing less than the fundamental redrawing of the livestock economy. Tyson had created an industrialized chicken business out of whole cloth, but the hog and cattle businesses were different. They were already entrenched, already profitable, and populated by millions of owners and workers who weren't about to give away their businesses easily.

Luckily for Tyson's Foods, the livestock industry was becoming more vulnerable to a takeover in the 1970s and 1980s. This vulnerability was a direct result of Tyson's growing chicken business. The rise of modern poultry consumption came at the direct expense of the beef and pork industries. When consumers started eating more chicken, they didn't increase their overall meat consumption. So chicken pushed beef and pork off the dinner plate and the fast-food menu. That meant that cattle and hog producers were watching their markets shrink during the 1980s and 1990s, as their customers were stolen away by cheap chicken.

To compete with the chicken industry, hog and cattle producers could follow the model that Moeller was slowly building for pig farms. They could chickenize. Tyson's chicken contracts could come to dominate hog production. Cattle producers could also fall in line, with ranches and feedlots organizing themselves around the principles of coordinated supplies and contracts inspired by chicken farms. The meat from cattle and hogs would become more uniform and cheaper, all the better to compete with chicken. Pork lobbyists would even spend millions trying to convince consumers that pork basically *was* chicken, or the "other white meat," as they called it. The sirloin steak and pork loin of years past would be replaced by factory meat, delivered reliably on schedule and with qualities that were the same from restaurant to restaurant, and Wal-Mart to Wal-Mart.

To make this happen, the livestock industries would have to resemble the chicken business in another, critical way. They would be dominated by a handful of giant corporations that could finance, coordinate, and control complex industrial farms. Shifting power into the hands of a few corporations wouldn't be an easy task. Regulators were taking notice of the power grab, from farm state attorneys general to USDA antitrust officials in Washington. Federal efforts to curb the power of meat corporations were halting during the 1980s. But a handful of regulators took notice of the big meat companies. The degree to which these regulators fought back would determine who won and lost in the new agricultural order.

But before Tyson could get to any of that, the company had to overcome one hurdle: the biology of the pig.

Moeller's business plan was almost thwarted by piglets.

Chickens procreate through the wonderfully factory-friendly industrial unit of the egg. Eggs can be lined up in crates and stacked in neat rows and heated in hatcheries. When chicks pop out, they're ready to ship to a waiting farm. Pigs, on the other hand, are born in broods. The babies need to suckle at their mother's teats. It takes weeks for a wobbly piglet to be strong enough to be shipped anywhere. And like other mammals, pigs evolved over the eons to protect their young. The animals have strong, innately bred social instincts that made it all but impossible to raise them in close quarters. Packing hundreds of female sows into a barn means some of them are going to kill the others. Jealous mothers fiercely protect their young. The male boars fight off competitors and kill the runty weak among them. In short, unattended hog barns easily turn into a big, messy carnival of violence. And that's not good for business. Stressed-out animals don't yield good meat.

Then there was the waste to deal with. Chicken litter can smell horrible, and it gets noxious when it builds up inside a big barn. But hog manure makes chicken litter smell sweet by comparison. As Moeller worked the barns each day, the smell of pig waste seeped into the very fibers of his clothing and the follicles of his hair. No amount of soapy washing and scrubbing could easily remove the stench. Pig waste is more similar to the excrement of a 350-pound human than it is to chicken litter. It piles up quickly inside hog barns.

Over the years, Moeller and his team of coworkers solved each of these problems, inventing their own solutions and borrowing others developed by outside companies, farmers, and universities. To house the animals, Tyson stuck with the basic blueprint of a chicken house. But the company subdivided the floor of the houses into smaller pens, keeping the animals segregated so they wouldn't kill each other. They built a gangway that ran down the center of the barn so workers could walk between the long rows of pens. When it came time to load the pigs onto a truck, the pens were opened up and the pigs were herded into the central gangway and then out the front door.

To handle the waste, Tyson designed deep pits beneath the hog houses. The floor of the pens was replaced with slats, which let the waste fall through into the pits below. The manure and urine was pumped outside the hog house into a pit resembling a primitive lagoon.

Perhaps the most important innovation dealt with the suckling pigs. Moeller and his fellow researchers broke hog production into two, distinct stages. In stage one, female pigs give birth to piglets in special barns. In stage two, those piglets are fattened to slaughter weight.

During stage one, pregnant sows are confined in special pens, called "farrowing crates."* These crates are narrow metal cages, no wider than the sow's body, which keep the mother pig immobilized, unable to turn

---

* "Farrowing" is the term for giving birth to piglets, and the big sow houses soon became known as "farrowing barns."

right or left. On each side of the sow, there are smaller cages where the piglets reside and where they can suckle from their mother through metal slats. By keeping the mother pigs penned, there is no chance that the piglets might be crushed in the melee of a crowded barn. Workers walk up and down the gangway between rows of crated sows and easily pluck squealing piglets from their pens when they are old enough to be shipped away.

At this point, the piglets enter phase two of the new hog industry. They are shipped to the "feeder farms," where their life consists of nothing but eating and getting fat.

The feeder barns were also modeled on chicken houses, with slatted floors and subdivided pens. They were equipped with big feed bins, automatic water lines, and fan systems to keep the animals cool.

By the late 1980s, Tyson had built a small network of hog farms based on Moeller's system. Don Tyson was pleased with the results. He was focused almost entirely on the chicken business at that point, but he couldn't deny there was money to be made in hogs. Moeller proved it. Moeller attended Tyson's Monday meetings at headquarters and reported impressive profits from the swine division.

Don Tyson gave Moeller his marching orders: It was time to grow. Tyson would build a network of hog farms from scratch, expanding Moeller's operation to an unprecedented size.

Moeller had the money, the model, the technology, and the workforce he needed to expand. But he needed to find just the right place to do it. Arkansas seemed like an obvious choice. But after some searching, Moeller and his team settled on a remote location in the neighboring state of Oklahoma. It was a trek to get there from Springdale, but the place had everything to offer someone who wanted to launch an industrialized hog industry.

Downtown Holdenville, Oklahoma, is like a ragged grid of inner-city ghetto, inexplicably dropped down into the middle of desolate prairie.

There is nothing around Holdenville but green hills covered in scrub grasses that stretch out to a lonely horizon. The town is stranded, but it was prosperous once. The brick buildings along Main Street speak to the grandeur of Holdenville's past, with ornate stonework and cornices adorning the skyline through the middle of town. But the elements have been hard on the buildings, and the economy unable to preserve them. Windows are boarded up, bricks are crumbling, and paint peels off the walls.

Businesses downtown reflect an economy that long ago quit growing and now exists by cannibalizing itself. An inordinate number of pawn shops dot the strip downtown, while several check-cashing and payday loan shops advertise the opportunity to borrow money against the meager paychecks most residents earn. The unemployment rate is among the highest in Oklahoma, and those citizens lucky enough to have a job earn just a fraction of the average pay of their relatives who left for big-city jobs.

When Bill Moeller saw Holdenville, he knew it was perfect. The city had a population that was hungry for work and would welcome a new company in town. Perhaps more important, the soil surrounding Holdenville was well suited for hog farming. The contract farmers would need somewhere to spread the waste from the farms when lagoons filled up, and the pastureland of Oklahoma was ideal.

Bill Moeller drew up plans to make Holdenville the beachhead for Tyson's expansion into the hog industry. The company recruited local farmers to become contract hog producers. Local banks eagerly jumped into the business, offering loans of hundreds of thousands of dollars to finance new hog buildings. Tyson's Foods invested millions to build a vertically integrated hog complex outside Holdenville, complete with a feed mill, trucking line, and veterinary services. Perhaps the most important part of the complex was a small building that Moeller affectionately called "the nursery." Moeller knew that the nursery would be the linchpin of Tyson's success as it competed for more control of the hog business.

The nursery was basically a large holding pen for piglets, which were brought to the building from farms all around Holdenville. The building let Tyson control which pigs were delivered to which contract farms, and on what schedule. Tyson's trucks visited special sow farms where piglets were born, gathering up the young animals and bringing them to the nursery, where they were mingled with piglets from other farms. It was critical to do this in a sterile, controlled environment to ensure that disease didn't break out when the piglets were most vulnerable. While the company depended on outside farmers to raise its animals, the nursery kept Tyson squarely in the center of the production chain. Being in the center meant that Tyson was in charge.

Tyson hired some of the best geneticists in the field to breed its pigs. The company was pushing ahead of the industry, breeding pigs that were far leaner than their ancestors, with thicker legs that could support their fast-growing haunches. The animal's skeleton was bred to be a sturdy meat rack, ideal for an animal meant to grow as large as possible while never leaving a pen more than a few square feet wide. The sows were engineered to be superior breeding machines, big, fat mother pigs that could give birth to, and suckle, huge litters.

Moeller read the pork industry trade magazines, and he laughed. They contained stories about world-record-holding boars that had the leanest meat and the widest body. Moeller knew that Tyson was beating those records, secretly, inside the company's swine nursery. Tyson chose to keep its records and its breeding secrets to itself. As more farms were put into production, Moeller and his team grew even more adept at breeding and raising the animals, building a herd that was superior to any family farmer's.

In 1992 Don Tyson called Bill Moeller. Tyson had orders for him. He wanted Moeller to buy one of the nation's biggest hog slaughterhouses, which was located in Marshall, Missouri. Moeller helped push the deal through, and with it he closed the final link in Tyson's production chain. The company now controlled its hog business just as tightly as its chicken farms, from the genes of the pigs to the farms where they were raised and the factory where they were slaughtered and butchered for sale. And just like in the chicken industry, Tyson collected a profit at each link in the chain, money that it would pour into expansion.

Throughout the 1990s, industrial hog farms began sprouting up across rural America. More farmers signed contracts to grow for Tyson Foods, outside the company's complex in Holdenville and even farther away in states like Arkansas and Missouri. The meat produced on these farms began taking up more shelf space in grocery stores around the country, squeezing out pricier pork produced by independent farmers and expensive beef raised by ranchers. The tide of chickenization was well under way. And it was about to accelerate.

CHAPTER 7

The Next Generation

(1995–2006)

THERE WAS a sense of grandeur, by the mid-1990s, at the Tyson Foods complex in Springdale. New office buildings had been erected of black steel and glass. The buildings housed several floors of workers, who labored in cubicles and helped direct the new age of centrally controlled agriculture. From these offices, it was determined how many chickens would be raised in a network of farms that stretched from Missouri to Georgia. It was determined what breed of chicken would be raised to provide Americans their poultry. Workers directed a growing number of hog farmers where pigs were raised under contract, controlling the size of the herds with a few strokes on their computer keyboards.

If there was anything close to a broad vision that drove Tyson during the 1990s, it was the belief that Tyson could control anything it wanted and crush any competitor. The company dominated the chicken market and supplied all the major food companies, from McDonald's to the corner grocery store. It was one of the largest hog producers in the United States and was toying with the idea of cattle production. Tyson Foods even made a $243 million bet that it could control the seafood industry with its purchase of Arctic Alaska Fisheries. There was no corner of the meat industry that Tyson was not set to conquer.

The 1990s was the age of dominance for corporate agribusiness. Tyson Foods alone earned $86.9 million in profits in 1996 and $219.2 million the year before. The company's assets were worth about $4.5 billion, and sales were growing 17 percent a year.

Having built this empire, Don Tyson finally decided it was time to step aside in 1991. He spent more and more time on his personal yacht, having developed an affinity for fishing the deep seas or Caribbean waters. It was time to let someone else deal with the day-to-day headaches of running his company.

Don Tyson's lieutenants had vied for decades to take his spot at the top of the company. Many of them seemed to have already earned the right to take it. Men like Buddy Wray and Leland Tollett had decades of experience, and they had helped make Tyson a multibillion-dollar corporation. But ultimately, none of these men would be the leader who ushered Tyson Foods to its ultimate destination as the undisputed king of U.S. meat production. That task would fall on the shoulders of a younger man, whose last name happened to be on the marquee sign outside company headquarters.

He was always "Johnny." Even when he took over the corporate suite, the oval office with the brass eggs for door handles and the big desk where he called all the shots, even then, he was still "Johnny." He was "Johnny" to his dad, and" Johnny" to the cadre of old men who surrounded his dad. He was even "Johnny" to the secretaries and farmers and lowly office workers who would never possess a fraction of his fortune.

The name was his childhood name, and it stuck, seeming to imply that he would always be Johnny Tyson, Don's son. This was curious in a way, because Johnny Tyson was clearly his own man. He was better-looking than his father. He was not so short, and his face was not so round as a bulldog's. Johnny inherited the square jawline of his grandfather, whom Johnny knew only when he was a child.

But the good looks never really translated for Johnny. The good looks only went so deep, and beneath them there wasn't the magnetic charisma that defined Don Tyson. When Don Tyson met a person, that person wanted to be near Don Tyson and wanted to impress Don Tyson. Don often visited the slaughterhouses he owned, and he walked down the long line of workers in their white hairnets as they cut apart chicken carcasses on a conveyor belt. And when the workers turned and saw him, he put out his hand and said: I'm Don. And those workers lit up. They shined. They smiled and shook his hand and told the story later.

People didn't light up when they met Johnny. Johnny seemed to inherit the brittle, explosive temper of his grandfather without inheriting the warm attraction of his father.

This wasn't helped by the fact that some of the men around Don Tyson never respected Johnny, even decades later, when they had left the company and retired. While Don Tyson fostered competition among the executives who worked below him, he also forged strong personal bonds with them. When the former chief financial officer Gerald Johnston was still a young accountant at the company, he was asked to go along with Don Tyson and other executives on a trip to Chicago. The men arrived early at the airport and waited for their afternoon flight in a lounge. The executives all ordered drinks, but Johnston said he didn't want anything. He didn't drink alcohol, and he felt awkward about ordering a soda. As the men drank and talked business, Don Tyson noticed that his young new hire wasn't drinking. Don got up, went to the bar, and ordered a Coke, bringing it back to the table and setting it in front of Johnston. Johnston never forgot that moment, even years after he became Tyson's chief financial officer. It was the kind of small thing Don Tyson did that cemented an unbreakable loyalty in the men below him.

Some of the old-guard executives didn't think Johnny held a candle to his father when it came to thinking like a businessman or being a leader. They scoffed at the mention of Johnny's name and dismissed him with a wave of their hand and a half smile. Johnny was tolerated by the men around Don Tyson.

It was clear Johnny wanted to be part of the company, and Don tried to show him the ropes. As a boy, Don Tyson had shoveled feed in a warehouse and looked over the company's ledgers in the kitchen at night. Johnny came of age when Tyson Foods had its own corporate suites, private jets, and a constellation of multimillion-dollar poultry complexes that dominated towns like Waldron. Don tried to tutor his son in the basics. He sent Johnny to North Carolina, to take the helm of a series of contract hog operations Tyson bought there. In Springdale, whispers spread among the executives that Johnny had abandoned his post in North Carolina. His underlings were doing the work for him. This didn't seem to surprise anyone, nor annoy them. Johnny was Don's problem.

Johnny Tyson later admitted to heavy drug and alcohol abuse as a young man. At work, he bounced from job to job. But even when he was in North Carolina, about a thousand miles away from Springdale, no one in the executive suite had any illusions that Johnny was going to stay gone for too long. They all knew he would be back.

By 1991, Johnny Tyson wasn't ready for the top job at Tyson Foods. Don Tyson decided that the first CEO to succeed him would be Leland Tollett, the University of Arkansas graduate who joined the company in 1959. But Tollett's tenure would be relatively brief, and it would set the stage for Johnny's ascendance.

Even when Don gave Leland the title of CEO in 1991, Don didn't surrender his control over the company. Don stayed on as chairman of Tyson Foods, and he used a special legal maneuver to ensure his power over the company could never be diluted. Don created his own special class of stock, called "Class B" shares. Each share of Class B stock gave Don ten votes on any shareholder resolution. When taken together, his special class of stock would give him roughly 80 percent of all the votes available to Tyson's shareholders. The voting power gave him extraordinary control over a corporation that was publicly traded, and at least in theory owned and controlled by its outside shareholders. Don's special stock ownership gave him veto power over any decisions at Tyson Foods, an arrangement he never relinquished. Don Tyson could fire the entire board of directors and the CEO if he felt like it. Any and all shareholder proposals had to pass muster with one person, and one person only.

Under these circumstances, Leland Tollett exercised what authority he could. Tollett was meticulous, and he executed his business plans with attention to the finest details. Tollett made the galaxy of moving parts mesh smoothly at Tyson, but he was never a visionary. There was no new chicken McNugget. Don Tyson had driven the company from a regional firm to one of the world's biggest corporations by seeing things that other people couldn't see. He exploited new opportunities that had not existed before. Tollett was brilliant at keeping Don's creation moving, and even growing, but Tyson Foods never reinvented itself as it did during the 1970s and 1980s.

Investors weren't impressed. The market measured Leland Tollett's tenure as a kind of stewardship, a safekeeping of everything that Don Tyson had built. Tyson's stock price plateaued during the 1990s, ending a steep climb in value that had continued almost uninterrupted for decades. While Tollett tinkered with the company and tried expanding into different kinds of meat production, Tyson's stock wiggled back and forth in a narrow band. The shares were worth about $14 in 1991, when Tollett was named CEO. They hovered around $15 a share until 1995, when Don Tyson finally let go of his role as chairman and gave Tollett full control of the company. By the middle of 1996, the stock was worth about $14.

Leland Tollett quit in 1998. In the public announcement of his departure, he blamed his poor eyesight, claiming that a chronic ocular disease made his job harder to do every year. Tyson needed someone who could see into the future. The company needed its next visionary.

In September 1998, Tyson's senior managers were called to the company's auditorium on the Springdale campus. This was just before Leland Tollett announced his resignation, and the managers didn't know what to expect when they filed in and took their seats.

Then Johnny got up onstage. He had an announcement. Johnny was to become the chairman of the company, the role his father had filled when Tollett became CEO in 1991. In one swift move, Johnny had swooped past the CEO's office. The managers learned that Leland Tollett was leaving, and the CEO's job would be filled by Wayne Britt, the company's chief financial officer. It wasn't clear to anyone how Johnny Tyson and Wayne Britt would divvy up their authority.

"It's hard to run a football team when you have two quarterbacks," one board member said.

Many people questioned what qualified John Tyson for his new job, other than his last name. But Johnny Tyson had made at least one change since his early days in the company: He had gotten sober. He quit drinking in 1990, and his free time seemed to be largely occupied by church services.

Just as Johnny took the helm, however, the mid-1990s executive culture of arrogance began to exact its costs. In its effort to take over the world of meat production, Tyson had overreached. The company's Seafood Group showed nothing but losses, quarter after quarter. Tyson Foods eventually dumped the division at a $20 million loss. The hog business, which John Tyson had overseen directly, also began to languish. Tyson was being quickly outpaced by its competitor Smithfield Foods, which snapped up smaller companies and crowded Tyson out of the marketplace.

Tyson's stock price sank steeply after John Tyson and Wayne Britt took the helm. The shares were worth $19.15 when John Tyson became chairman. A year later they were worth $15.41. A year after that they were worth $9.44.

Wayne Britt left the company in April 2000, leaving Johnny alone at the top. Johnny set to work restructuring the company and replacing top executives. The company was his to run now, and he wasn't going to be shy. While none of these efforts did a thing to lift the stock price, Johnny Tyson had one thing going for him. The U.S. taxpayer was about to give Tyson a gift worth billions of dollars. It was a one-time bonus from Washington, D.C., that would underpin the profits of every major corporate meat producer for more than a decade.

The farm subsidy programs of 1938 had transformed over decades, growing from a series of emergency bailout programs into a permanent agricultural bureaucracy.

The original laws were amended and re-amended by a revolving door of Democratic and Republican administrations, each of which added new layers of provisions, forging ever-deeper links between government bureaucracy and the food business. By 1994, taxpayers were spending $7.9 billion every year in direct payments to farmers. The money kept the price of food low and helped big farms prosper regardless of market prices for their crops.

The free market had very little to do with the U.S. food market anymore. The USDA, for example, centrally controlled how many acres of corn were planted each year. This wasn't as completely Soviet-esque as it sounds: The production controls weren't mandatory. Farmers could plant as many acres of corn or wheat as they wanted. But if they didn't comply with the USDA's state production levels, the farmers got cut out of government subsidies. In essence, the USDA bribed farmers to go along with its central planning regime. And it worked remarkably well.

But there was always something about the farm programs that didn't sit right with Americans. Central controls and subsidies didn't seem to fit with the ideal of the American farmer as a small-business owner and anchor of the rural economy. When Republicans took over Congress in 1994, farm subsidies were on their list of government programs to scale back or end.

In 1996, Congress ended the farm subsidy program with a new farm bill called the Freedom to Farm Act. Strangely enough, Freedom to Farm only enlarged the farm subsidy program and made it much more expensive. Farmers had their direct subsidies cut, but the government wasn't willing to throw them to the wolves of a free market when times got tough. So the normal subsidies were replaced with "disaster" payments. The food business is always in a state of disaster in one way or another—if it rains it's too wet, if it doesn't rain it's a drought—so the disaster payments became another semipermanent cost to taxpayers. In 1998 taxpayers handed over $12.4 billion to farmers, and in 1999 they paid $21.5 billion, nearly triple what they paid before Freedom to Farm was passed.

While it didn't end subsidies, Freedom to Farm made one critical change that benefitted Tyson Foods. The law disbanded production controls. Farmers got their government checks, and they could grow whatever they wanted. When the production controls went away, farmers did what they do best: They massively overproduced. The world was glutted with corn, wheat, and soybeans. Prices plummeted, farmers bemoaned the low prices, and taxpayer subsidies grew rapidly to cover farmers' losses.

This cycle led to a remarkable gift for meat producers. Feed grains were the biggest cost that Tyson Foods had to pay to raise animals. If feed grains got too expensive, the company's profits could quickly vanish. Freedom to Farm didn't just make grains cheaper for Tyson. The federal program went so far as to produce an upside-down food economy, where corn was actually cheaper to buy than it was to grow.

This inverted market had a strange effect. It made it economically irrational to be a diversified farm, the once-traditional kind of operation where farmers raised hogs, cattle, soybeans, and corn. A farmer lost money if he or she grew corn and fed it to animals that he or she owned under Freedom to Farm.

This was financial jet fuel for the new breed of industrial meat producers. The companies weren't diversified farms, after all. They bought corn; they didn't grow it. For industrial hog producers alone, Freedom to Farm delivered about $947 million a year in savings, according to one study.

Freedom to Farm let corporate meat producers reap huge profits just by virtue of their business model. A company like Tyson made millions of dollars in profit every year even if its business strategy was marred by errors, bad investments, and questionable leadership.

As Don Tyson pulled away from daily operations at Tyson Foods, so too did his friend and lawyer Jim Blair. But the two often spent time together, and Jim Blair helped Don Tyson with a number of legal jobs, such as doing his estate planning. For Don Tyson, estate planning involved a lot more than simply figuring out to whom he was going to leave his money. It involved the sticky questions of how Don Tyson would bequeath his company stock, and therefore his power, to certain heirs and not to others. Along with his son, Johnny, Don had three daughters. And his sister-in-law, Barbara, had a major stake in the firm.

As they talked over the estate, Don suddenly mused out loud to Blair:

— You know, you're not very kin to your grandchildren.

Blair didn't understand.

— You forget. I used to be the company geneticist, Don explained.

As head of Tyson's breeding program, Don had selected the "grandparent" line of breeder hens. Those grandparents were the best-of-the-best breed. But the next generation carried only about half their parents' genes. And the generation after that only carried a quarter. By the time the great-grandchildren rolled around, their genetics were just an eighth of their grandparents'.

The rolling wheel of genetic change slowly diluted the character of a family. It was inevitable.

Jim Blair took the point.

Johnny's early tenure as CEO was rocky. Media accounts of his rise to the top almost inevitably began with the fact that he was once addicted to cocaine and alcohol. He got divorced and had to juggle single fatherhood with work. He presided over a company in turmoil as Tyson Foods began to unravel the big bets it had made to expand beyond the chicken business.

The loss Tyson Foods suffered by unloading its Seafood Group was bad enough. But more worrisome for Johnny Tyson was the struggling swine division, which he had overseen.

By entering the pork business, Tyson's success had started to create its own problems. And the biggest of those problems was Smithfield Foods. The birth of the factory hog farm sent a clear message to the industry: Adopt Tyson's model or go out of business. Smithfield had chosen the former option and spent millions pursuing it.

It became clear that Tyson was losing at its own game. Smithfield Foods had copied Tyson's playbook, almost to the letter, and had now taken the dominant position in the hog business. After building its own network of tightly controlled farms based on Tyson's chicken-farming model, Smithfield had gone on a buying spree just as Don Tyson had, snapping up smaller competitors until the company controlled a majority of the market.

When Smithfield's growth left Tyson behind, it put the company exactly where Don Tyson never wanted to be: following the leader.

None of this seemed to deter Bill Moeller, who had built Tyson's swine division from scratch. Moeller was impressive during the senior leadership meeting at Tyson Foods headquarters in Springdale. Those around him could count on Moeller to boast about the swine division's profits and growth prospects. There were plans to expand with new hog farms in states like South Dakota. Every month seemed to deliver better profits from hogs.

But Jim Blair was unimpressed. Moeller seemed a little too eager to make his unit look good at the meetings, Blair thought. The facts on the ground seemed to say otherwise.

Blair got the impression that Tyson's swine division was juicing its profit figures in part by taking money out of the pockets of the hog farmers. The hog contracts had a number of provisions that docked farmers' pay and dinged them for any losses in production. Even Tyson's massive hog plant in Marshall, Missouri, didn't give the company the scale it needed to compete against Smithfield.

There was only one path to take: Tyson Foods was getting out of the hog business. The company sold its plant in Marshall and even tried to sell its farms in Holdenville to Smithfield Foods. The deal fell through because Smithfield liked to operate bigger hog barns than the ones Tyson had built. Tyson wanted to keep its hog barns small enough that a contract farmer could still feasibly borrow the money to build them. Smithfield, on the other hand, often owned its own barns and liked to make them much bigger.

Tyson kept its Holdenville complex, which continued pumping out hundreds of thousands of piglets to supply contract farms.

In 1999, Bill Moeller retired. The experiment he had begun was largely cast off by Tyson Foods. The one division Johnny Tyson had overseen had ended in failure.

Tyson's stock price continued to fall under Johnny Tyson's leadership, in spite of the company's dominance in the poultry industry. Investors didn't see a future of explosive growth now that Tyson had locked up its control of the fast-food market and big grocery chains.

And Tyson was getting overshadowed by other companies. Just as Tyson's hog farms helped create Smithfield Foods, the rise of factory chicken created a grinding pressure on the cattle industry. Beef was the most expensive meat, and the old-line meatpackers like Armour and Swift were desperate to find ways to compete with cheap chicken. This pressure helped create Tyson's twin in the beef industry, a corporate giant of unprecedented scale, called Iowa Beef Processors.

Just about everybody hated Iowa Beef Processors* from the first day the company opened its doors. The unionized slaughterhouse workers hated it. The grocery store butchers hated it. Ranchers came to hate it. Even the other big meatpackers hated it. The company's first thirty years were one long trail of antipathy as IBP fought these forces and overcame them, making billions of dollars in profit as it dominated the American beef business.

People hated IBP for the simple reason that it was upending the beef industry. The change IBP represented was evident in the very location of the company's first slaughterhouse, in Denison, Iowa. All the meatpackers built their big slaughterhouses in cities like Chicago, Detroit, and St. Louis. This is where the cattle stockyards and the labor force were based, so it only made sense that old-line beef packers like Swift and Armour would be rooted in urban areas.

But a guy named Andy Anderson decided to change that in 1960. Poultry companies like Tyson had built big slaughterhouses in the middle of nowhere, in tiny towns like Springdale, Arkansas, and they

---

* The company was initially called Iowa Beef Packers.

reaped massive profits from doing so. Anderson thought he could gain a clear advantage building a beef company that followed suit. Unions weren't as strong in small towns, so the labor force was cheaper. And remote places like Denison or Storm Lake, Iowa, didn't have as many big companies, so workers were happy to have jobs. The unions never forgave IBP for slipping out the back door and taking thousands of good-paying slaughterhouse jobs with it. Union strikes, sit-ins, and violent protests defined life at IBP plants in Iowa and Illinois as the company grew. Don Tyson had the luxury of building his workforce from scratch in nonunionized southern states, but IBP had to do the ugly work of making unionized slaughterhouse workers realize that the meat industry had changed. Northern beef packers would have to live on southern poultry plant wages.

There was another advantage to being located in rural areas that seems remarkably obvious in retrospect: All the cattle lived in the rural hinterlands. By building its plants right next to the ranches, IBP didn't have to pay as much to ship the cattle to its front door. IBP made the cowboy obsolete, since the cowboy was nothing but a commercial artifact of the old meatpacking industry. The cowboy's primary purpose was to herd cattle from distant pastures into the stockyards.

Andy Anderson was able to redraw the meatpacking business in part because he was new to the industry*. He was a city boy, whose first job in the meat business was in an urban butcher shop, not a slaughterhouse. This last part helps explain perhaps the most important innovation behind IBP, the one that made the grocery store butchers loathe the company.

Just like Tyson, IBP figured out that it could butcher meat more efficiently at its meat factories than butchers could do in their stores. IBP was the first company to popularize a product called "boxed beef." Rather than ship whole carcasses to retail locations, like the other meatpackers, IBP cut up the cattle along a factory line. It bagged the

---

* Anderson didn't launch IBP alone. He was helped by his partner, Currier Holman, according to the excellent history *The Legend of IBP*.

parts in airtight packages and shipped them in boxes in refrigerated trucks. Boxes, needless to say, could be stacked in a truck a lot more neatly than carcasses. IBP didn't ship the parts of a cow that butchers cut off and threw away. Boxed beef was the most efficient way to ship beef, and IBP had developed its own shipping network to do it, saving money every step of the way.

Boxed beef drove butchers out of business and caused many of them to launch boycotts against IBP. But the boycotts were pointless. The American appetite for convenience made boxed beef a fixture in all the big retail chains during the 1960s and 1970s. Beef finally started to catch up with chicken as something that could be plucked off the shelf and cooked in a hurry. By 1975, 60 percent of U.S. beef was boxed beef. IBP did the same thing in the pork market, buying up hog slaughterhouses and refurbishing them to make boxed pork products.

IBP became the chicken company of beef packers. And its primary reward for doing this was survival. From 1970 on, times were not good for the cattle business. American consumption of beef declined steadily. Beef was more expensive than chicken and people were avoiding red meat because they thought it was fattier and unhealthier. The total number of cattle raised in the United States declined and has fallen steadily ever since. Meatpackers went out of business, and the most inefficient went first.

But IBP grew even as the industry shrank. It took market share from everyone else. Like Tyson, IBP was expansionist from the moment it started, buying up competitors whenever it could. The company started in 1960 and opened one plant. It owned four plants by 1964. The growth never slowed. IBP snapped up dozens of companies through the decades.

But even by 1980, the beef industry was hardly chickenized. The four biggest companies controlled only about 25 percent of the total market. Those companies still competed aggressively against each other to deliver the best product at the lowest price. And there was still an open, competitive cash market where virtually all cattle were sold.

IBP would change all that in about fifteen years. And the revolution would start in a remote little place called Garden City, Kansas. Garden City would become home to IBP's experiment in building the next generation of cattle production, one that rested on contracts rather than markets.

There wasn't a slaughterhouse in existence like the one IBP built outside Garden City in the early 1980s. It was a beef factory that could kill over five thousand cows a day, one every eleven seconds or so over two eight-hour shifts. The plant produced millions of pounds of boxed beef that could be shipped to retailers and restaurants from Seattle to Florida. By making its slaughterhouse so big, IBP spent less to slaughter each cow compared with the existing meatpackers, giving the company a critical cost advantage.

But like Tyson before it, IBP realized that one of the biggest obstacles to running a meat factory was getting a dependable supply of animals. If fewer than five thousand cattle arrived every day at the plant, it meant downtime on the factory line that translated into wasted money and slimmer profit margins.

There had been scattered experiments around the country to vertically integrate cow production, just as Tyson had vertically integrated chicken and hog farming. But these efforts were all stopped short by two of the cow's internal organs: the rumen and the uterus.

The rumen is part of the cow's four-chambered stomach, and it allows the cow to do something most mammals can't: digest the cellulose in grass. Young calves live off a diet of grass and their mother's milk for a period of at least several months. Calves can't eat corn or other grains. The stubborn rumen ensures that cattle need acres of pasture on which to graze when they are young, requiring lots of land and lots of money.

The more daunting challenge is the uterus. Cows have only one baby at a time. They don't have litters of ten, like a pig, and they don't lay a battery of eggs like a chicken. The formula is depressing for a factory farm man: one cow, one calf. And it takes about one year for a cow to have each of those calves.

Taken together, these pieces of the cow's biology mean that a factory cow farm is a tremendous waste of money. It would require feeding a confined mother cow grass for a whole year, just to produce one calf, which would then also have to be confined for several months and fed grass and milk. And grass, unlike corn or soybeans, isn't subsidized.

Senior executives inside IBP realized that raising cattle was a waste of money. So at Garden City, IBP employed a new way to procure a steady stream of cows. It was called the "formula contract."

The formula contract created a way for IBP to lock in a steady supply of cattle without having to go out on the open market and haggle for them, as meatpackers always had. Instead, IBP signed contracts with a rancher or feedlot, agreeing to buy a set number of cattle at a set date.* The price for those cattle, when they were delivered, was based on a formula rather than a competitive bid.

IBP created a formula price that allowed the company to start controlling its cattle supply in a way that mimicked Tyson's methods for controlling its chicken supply. IBP couldn't simply dictate what kind of animals it slaughtered, the way Tyson did, but it could use contracts to exert influence over the ranches.

IBP's formula contained a series of discounts and premiums that rewarded some qualities in the cow while punishing others. These discounts were crude levels that IBP used to shape the kind of cattle ranchers raised. Early on, for example, IBP controlled the size of the cows ranchers delivered by discounting those that were too big and those that were too small. The formula acted as a market incentive all its own, slowly bending the characteristics of the cattle herd to IBP's specifications. It was still a long way from the exacting control Tyson had over its chicken flocks, but the formulas would evolve over the decades.

Once IBP secured its cattle supply, it began a chain of acquisitions that ended the highly competitive beef industry. IBP's big plants drove smaller producers out of business. The few surviving meatpackers, like

---

* Typically the contracts called for delivery within a certain date range, which could be as wide as a matter of weeks.

IBP, bought their competitors to survive. During the mid-1990s alone, IBP is estimated to have spent $1.5 billion buying other firms.

By 1995, IBP wasn't just Tyson's mirror image in the beef business. It was much bigger and more profitable than Tyson. IBP had large slaughterhouses scattered through the Great Plains and the Midwest, and it earned profits of $321 million in 1999, with total sales of $14.1 billion. Tyson, by contrast, earned profits of $230 million with total sales of $7.4 billion.

Still, IBP wasn't a direct threat to Tyson because the companies competed in different markets. IBP dominated beef and pork production, while Tyson controlled the chicken market. But all that would change.

In late 2000, a group of IBP managers decided they wanted to take the company private by buying it from its public shareholders. The managers put together a bid with a private investment company and presented it to IBP's board of directors.

Smithfield heard about the deal and decided to make a bid of its own. IBP had become the nation's second-biggest pork producer. If Smithfield bought IBP, it would be the indomitable leader of beef and pork production, boxing Tyson into the chicken business alone. It seemed inevitable that, one day, the company would buy Tyson as well. Only the biggest could survive.

Johnny decided he wasn't going to let that happen. Tyson Foods would buy IBP. The company would have to borrow billions to do it and it would need to pony up a huge portion of the company's stock. Johnny would be mortgaging everything his father and his grandfather had built. It was the riskiest acquisition the company had ever contemplated. Everyone around him realized that when Johnny looked at IBP, he finally had his vision.

Don Tyson thought the IBP acquisition was a bad idea. The company had been burned during the 1990s for straying outside the chicken industry and trying to buy its way into markets it couldn't control and that didn't fit with its primary strategy of vertical integration.

Buying IBP would overshadow the chicken operations of Tyson Foods and saddle the company with cattle and pork businesses that Tyson executives poorly understood.

The amount of debt Tyson took on to buy IBP would have repulsed Don Tyson's father. The deal required too much leverage, and it would leave Tyson Foods vulnerable to the inevitable industry downturns.

But Johnny Tyson pursued the deal regardless. History was within his grasp. He could be the CEO who oversaw his grandfather's company when it became the biggest meat producer the world had ever known. In December 2000, Tyson Foods submitted a bid to buy IBP for $4.2 billion, while agreeing to take on an additional $1.4 billion in IBP's debt.

Gary Combs, an Arkansas real estate developer who was married to Johnny's sister Carla, had never seen Don Tyson so angry with his son. Combs saw the anger boil over while he was in the lobby of a hospital where Carla was recovering from an illness. Don and Johnny both arrived to visit Carla Tyson, and when they met each other in the lobby Don exploded:

— You've ruined us! We'll lose the company over this. It's going to destroy the company!

But even Don Tyson's disapproval could not stop his son. There was too much at stake for Johnny Tyson to bend to his father's wishes.

If consummated, Tyson's merger with IBP would create an unprecedented level of concentrated power in the meat industry. One USDA estimate predicted that 5 percent of the average American's grocery bill would go to one company, the new Tyson Foods. The era of big was about to be replaced by the era of titanic.

Lawyers for Tyson Foods were working feverishly to draw up the necessary contracts and paperwork to close the company's acquisition of IBP. There wasn't going to be any stiff resistance from federal antitrust regulators. The Bush administration gave the proposed merger its consent, largely on the grounds that it wouldn't increase consolidation in any one meat segment. While Tyson was gaining unprecedented control over the production of U.S. beef, chicken, and pork, the company was not increasing the overall level of concentration within a specific industry. It appears there would have been more opposition if Tyson had purchased another regional chicken company, boosting its market share in poultry, rather than creating the world's biggest meat producer.

While federal regulators gave the deal their blessing, Don Tyson never did. He thought that Tyson Foods paid too high a price for IBP, and the returns would never justify the debt. After talking with his longtime attorney Jim Blair, Don Tyson pushed a plan to back out of the merger.

Tyson found an excuse to drop its multibillion-dollar buyout offer when IBP announced that one of its small divisions would restate some earnings figures to the Securities and Exchange Commission. The amount of money at stake was laughably small compared to IBP's total revenue, and it would hardly have made a dent in the company's overall results. But Tyson argued that the issue was serious enough to warrant scrapping the merger altogether. IBP sued Tyson, saying the company could not back out of its offer. A court in Delaware agreed, and the merger went through.

When the papers were finally signed, Johnny Tyson's legacy was sealed. He had made his mark, and he was head of the biggest meat company the world had ever known.

As he took on the role of CEO at Tyson Foods, Johnny Tyson seemed to be obsessed with one overriding goal: improving the company's image. He set about to redraw what people thought of the company and to burnish the Tyson name in the mind of every consumer. He wanted to transform the company from a commodity meat producer into a branded consumer company along the lines of Kraft Foods or Proctor and Gamble. Tyson was going to become a household name, and a fondly thought of brand.

Operationally, the company changed very little. The headquarters of IBP, based in South Dakota, remained open for business. Some key IBP executives moved to Springdale to be closer to the new company's headquarters, but they didn't alter much of the way IBP did business. At the same time, Tyson's poultry operations chugged ahead as they had before the merger was proposed. But things did change on the marketing end. Tyson was now able to offer big customers like Wal-Mart an unprecedented menu of products. One company could now offer all the beef, chicken, and pork products that a retailer would need.

As the new Tyson Foods hummed steadily along, John Tyson began to overhaul the corporate leadership. He held meeting after meeting, telling his subordinates how the new firm would be reshaped into a consumer-friendly corporation. A devout Christian, Tyson began a program to place clergy members in the company's slaughterhouses. The company hired marketing experts, formed a new strategy team and a human resources team. Johnny Tyson began to talk tirelessly about something he called "People Development," which seemed to amount to making every one of the company's 120,000 employees love the Tyson name and training a new generation of leaders.

Many of the executives under Johnny Tyson were no-nonsense meat industry guys. The strategy of People Development didn't resonate.

"It was as confusing as that term can be," a baffled executive said.

Johnny Tyson was undeterred. And if people questioned him, he had a track record of big profits that made his wisdom as CEO seem beyond question. The company's profits more than tripled between 2001 and 2004. As the profits grew, so did the corporate workforce. Tyson Foods ran out of space at its headquarters and began renting outside office space at several locations around Springdale.

The company hired a woman named Faith Popcorn to help make the Tyson name cozy. The marketing team hired outside consultants and performed in-depth testing on focus groups.

In the late summer of 2004, Johnny Tyson publicly unveiled the fruits of these efforts at an investors' conference in New York. The company was launching an unprecedented advertising campaign built around the slogan "Powered by Tyson." The company would run national television ads and sponsor gymnasts and NASCAR pit crews to promote the slogan. There was talk of hiring street performers in New York to "create buzz" about the brand and the new campaign. The Powered by Tyson campaign would cost more than $75 million in the first year alone.

Dissension started to spread among those who reported to Johnny Tyson. The company was becoming too top heavy, in their eyes. The thought that Tyson would become the next Kraft Foods seemed ridiculous. Tyson's meat was served anonymously in McNugget boxes, cafeterias, and butcher shops. Yet the company was about to spend hundreds of millions to bolster a brand name that would never be attached to those products.

But Johnny Tyson didn't listen. His path was clear. He had a reputation for dressing down colleagues who questioned him and exploding at those who made him angry.

So his lieutenants took matters into their own hands.

Don Tyson was in England when he got a phone call from his old friend, the former Tyson Foods CEO, Leland Tollett.

Tollett was the front man for an internal coup at Tyson Foods. A group of senior officials at the company had approached him and asked him to deliver a simple ultimatum to his old friend, Don. Tollett's message was simple. A group of the most senior leaders at Tyson Foods was prepared to walk off the job unless Johnny Tyson was fired. The executives would stay only if he was given some kind of honorary title but was stripped of any line authority over operations.

In a normal corporation, an ultimatum like this would likely have been taken to the company's board of directors. But at Tyson, it was taken directly to Don, through his old friend Leland. The board of directors had no real authority over operations. In many ways, the CEO was powerless as well. Don Tyson had authority to fire the entire board and any executive he chose. As long as Don owned the special class of stock that gave him 80 percent of the shareholder voting power, he was the ultimate authority over operations at the world's biggest meat company.

Don Tyson caught a flight home, and soon he was back at his small office at company headquarters. Johnny Tyson still resided in the CEO's oval office, just down the hallway from Don Tyson's more modest workspace. Don Tyson sent out word to more than twenty senior leaders of Tyson Foods. He wanted to meet with them in his office. He wanted to listen to them, hear them out on any problems they might have with where the company was headed. He wanted to talk to them about Johnny. The senior executives were free to air whatever grievances they had, and Don Tyson promised he wouldn't hold it against them.

For roughly three weeks, Don Tyson held court in his office, closing the door behind each executive as he came inside to talk. Just down the hall, Johnny Tyson continued to act as the company's CEO, fully aware of what his father was doing, and he wasn't good at hiding his feelings. The tension was thick inside the long corridor of executive suites.

Don Tyson could not have been happy with the stories he heard. Managers below Johnny Tyson felt that he was dead-set on turning the company into a big, branded enterprise, like Kraft Foods. Johnny Tyson wanted the brand to be a household name, respected and loved by consumers around the country. But his managers didn't think the company had the profit margins to support that vision. Tyson Foods was still a commodity company at heart. It was a business built around producing huge volumes of cheap, consistent meat, seven days a week, every week of the year. Tyson didn't sell the kind of higher-profit foods that Kraft Foods sold, like Philadelphia Cream Cheese, Oreos, and Ritz Crackers. Those were products that lived or died by their brand names. Most of Tyson's meat products didn't even carry a label.

It appeared as if Johnny Tyson had forgotten the fundamental lesson that was burned into Don Tyson's consciousness during the poultry crashes of the 1960s and 1970s. The company's core strategy was to make food more cheaply than the competitor. Adding in costs made a company vulnerable to the inevitable downturns. John Tyson was building a multilayered pantheon of costly initiatives on top of this business. The marketing costs, the advertising costs, and the personnel that were being added at headquarters were all making Tyson too top heavy. The company was vulnerable in a volatile meat industry with thin profits. This was what Johnny Tyson's lieutenants believed. But they couldn't get the CEO to listen to them. They felt like he was leading the company to inevitable ruin.

Don Tyson heard these executives out. And then he had to decide what to do about his son.

Tyson's board of directors gathered for their regular meeting in May 2006. They were told that Johnny Tyson had an announcement to make.

Johnny Tyson told the board he was stepping down. In public, the company portrayed the move as part of a long-planned succession plan to hand leadership off to Richard Bond, the company's chief operating officer and former president of IBP.

Tyson Foods quietly scrapped its Powered by Tyson campaign. The company focused less on People Development than it did on running its slaughterhouses at full speed. It was time to realign the company with its primary goal of pushing down costs and selling meat for the highest profit it could.

In a way, it didn't matter too much who was in the CEO's office by 2006. By that point, thanks in no small part to Johnny Tyson's ambition and leadership, the company had become a system far bigger than any one person could control. It was the biggest meat company in the world. No other firm could claim as much power over all three major meat industries: chicken, beef, and pork. But Tyson had done far more than just become the biggest player in the business. As it expanded, the company had redrawn the rules of meat production, reshaped the markets by which meat was sold, and changed the power structure of rural economies across America. To truly understand the nature of the changes Tyson wrought, it is helpful to look at the company from below. To see it from the perspective of hog farms and cattle ranches that were once independent but that now operate in Tyson's shadow.

CHAPTER 8

Squeal

(1996–2011)

IN 1996, an Iowa farmer named Chuck Wirtz walked along a piece of property his father had owned, a plot of land where Wirtz would build his future as an industrial hog farmer. Wirtz was inspecting a new pair of buildings unlike anything that had been built on his family's property. He had borrowed $300,000 to erect the twin buildings and invested hundreds of thousands of his own dollars as well. He was going all-in on the hog business.

Wirtz watched over the construction crews as they laid the concrete foundations and installed the heavy timber trusses of the new buildings' roofs. While the two long barns resembled chicken houses on the outside, they were far more fortified and technologically sophisticated on the inside. They had automatic fan systems that kicked on when the temperature rose, and a series of sprinklers that sprayed a fine mist if fans couldn't cool the air fast enough. The floors were slatted to allow manure to fall through, and a mazelike series of gates would keep the pigs inside separated into manageable groups. Each house would hold about two thousand pigs.

Just a decade earlier, Wirtz would have considered the idea of raising four thousand hogs preposterous. But by the time Wirtz built his first set of confinement feeding barns, it would have been economic suicide to raise a herd any smaller. The number of slaughterhouses in Iowa was decreasing, and those that were left were getting bigger. The companies wanted pigs by the semitruck load, and they didn't want to deal with farmers who sold their animals in small batches at roadside sales stations. Wirtz wasn't interested in committing economic

183

suicide. He was ready to embrace the future and learn how to raise hogs on an industrial scale. And he was ready to mortgage his farm to do it.

What Wirtz didn't know at the time was that his success or failure as a modern hog farmer would not be determined by the verdicts of free market or competitive enterprise. The old rules of farming no longer apply. What determines the fate of industrial hog farmers is the raw power of companies like Tyson Foods. Open markets have been replaced by contracts. Independence has been replaced by close relationships with transnational corporations. Wirtz's foray into the hog business would reveal just how much control Tyson exerts over the hog business and anyone who tries to make a living doing it.

Wirtz was raised on a farm in Iowa, near the town of Whittemore. Like its neighboring communities, Whittemore wasn't much more than a few streets laid out in a neat grid, with a feed store, restaurant, and post office, surrounded by an oceanic expanse of cropland. Kids in Whittemore, like Wirtz, knew a life of pigs, cows, and combines. Wirtz rode on the back of his father's tractor as it rolled over the emerald fields of baby corn. He felt the wind blow through his hair and saw nothing but blue sky and open land around him. Because of moments like that, Wirtz knew he would do nothing else with his life but farm.

Wirtz owned his first pig when he was seven years old, and he named it Pinky. He fed Pinky grass clippings and table scraps. He held the piglet in his lap, and he watched it flap its ears and scamper around the grassy yard.

One day, Wirtz's father told him it was time to take Pinky to market. The pig was fully grown, and it would be shipped to a nearby sale barn and then to slaughter. Wirtz cried when it was time to load Pinky onto the truck. He had spent years coddling and raising the pig, and he knew Pinky's quirks and character traits in the intimate way that city kids know their dog's. But his father explained that pigs were raised to be eaten, just the same as a stalk of corn or soybeans. So Wirtz helped load Pinky onto a truck and took him to a roadside barn where his father haggled with a man and settled on a price for Pinky's flesh, and he said goodbye to his pig.

Pinky was the last pig that Chuck Wirtz cried over. As he grew older, he showed a real talent for raising hogs, and he evolved toward his father's view of seeing the animals as a kind of crop. Wirtz and his siblings built a hog shed in the backyard: a squat, rectangular little building with a mud floor where the pigs gathered for shelter. There was a muddy pit and a feed bin in front of the little shed where the great fat pigs wallowed and grunted and ate grain as their floppy ears hung down over their eyes. Mother pigs are called sows, and Wirtz knew his sows by name. Each sow had her own little pen with a bed of straw where she gave birth to a brood of piglets. She would lie down in there and let the piglets suckle until Wirtz came and opened the pen's gate, letting the sow out to root through the mud and have her dinner. When the sow was finished, she would walk back to her pen and wait outside for Wirtz to notice her and come to open the gate and let her back with her piglets.

Over the years, Wirtz watched over countless generations of piglets, and he learned how to spot the sick and weak ones with a quick glance. In Iowa, pigs that grow the fastest are called the "best doers," and Wirtz was quick to spot good doers in a litter. There was real money to be made in this skill. Pigs were steady earning machines. The animals were known as "mortgage lifters" because farmers used them as a source of cash to pay down the debt they took on to operate the rest of their farms. It was hard to lose money raising pigs, and easy to turn a big profit. Pigs earned good money because the grain to feed them was cheap and the market for pork was still strong, yielding high prices for hogs. If the market price fell, farmers could simply cut back the size of their hog herd and wait for the price to rebound before adding more piglets to their farm. The profits of hog farming drove jealous competitions at the county fair, where local boys showed off their prize hogs and competed to raise the finest, most succulent pork chop.

Chuck Wirtz did well at hog farming. He added more sows to the shed behind his family's house and a number of "A-hut" buildings in the fields out beyond their yard—triangular little huts where the pigs lived in an open field of grain, more or less feeding themselves and raising their piglets with relatively little supervision.

Chuck Wirtz's hog herd became his family's mortgage lifter. It helped anchor his family to their land, as his brothers took on the job of tending their father's fields of corn and soybeans. In this way, the Wirtzes became a wealthy family, in the quiet way that Iowa families do. But it was hard to look at Wirtz and see a rich man. He often wore beat-up collared shirts and worn work pants with mud along their hems. Because of the way he made his living, Wirtz constantly exuded the slight whiff of hog manure. But together, he and his brothers built a family farm worth millions.

Such was the economy in Iowa during the 1960s and 1970s that hard work on a farm could still generate wealth for an extended family. The wealth supported an archipelago of clean, prosperous towns throughout the state, with busy town squares, bustling department stores, and a thriving middle class.

Indeed, it is helpful to think of Iowa not so much as a state but as one enormous farm. A visitor can travel day upon day over the two-lane highways of Iowa and pass nothing but cropland, a broad expanse of corn and soybeans, wide as the horizon, whipping by uninterrupted. Iowa is a flat table of black soil, some of the richest in the world, and towns like Whittemore were built on top of it with the single goal of raising as much food as possible from the fertile ground.

The most noticeable structures are the towering, concrete grain silos and the little clutches of houses built at their feet that make up Iowa's towns. The ground is crisscrossed with railway lines that carry corn and soybean loads from little towns to river ports where it is shipped to a global market. In towns like West Bend and Emmetsburg, there are lighted marquees that in other states would display the time and temperature but which in Iowa carry the most important metrics of life: the going price for a bushel of corn or soybeans.

Over several generations, families like the Wirtzes built Iowa into a food-producing machine that remains the envy of the world. It is more efficient to raise a hog on a plot of ground in Iowa than almost anywhere else on the planet, due in no small part to the abundance of cheap corn and soybeans. Feed rations are the most expensive part of raising livestock, and it is cheaper to buy corn in towns like Whittemore, West Bend, and Emmetsburg than almost anywhere else. Iowa hog farmers have a critical cost advantage over farmers around the globe. Just saving a few pennies on each bushel of feed can mean millions of dollars in profits for a major pork producer. That's why Iowa has historically been the epicenter of pork production in the United States, and will likely always be. In 2011 there were more pigs in Iowa than there were humans in Manhattan. It is estimated that at any given time, 10 percent of these 19 million pigs are on the highway, meaning 1.9 million swine are rolling across the state's blacktop on their way to a slaughterhouse or a farm.

By the time he was in his early twenties, in 1982, Wirtz had expanded his hog herd, deciding to stay on the farm and raise his animals rather than attend college. He married a local girl name Trela, whom he knew through church, and started a family on the same plot of land where he was raised with his two brothers.

As an adult, Wirtz had a manic temperament that made him perfectly suited to the seven-day workweek that hog farming required. He was up and fully dressed before sunrise most days, tending to his herd. By late at night his brain still raced with thoughts of how to improve his business by ordering the best genetic lines of sows or finding a new market in which to sell his hogs.

But Wirtz's skill and experience could carry him only so far. Any farmer will tell you that, at the end of the day, he lives or dies based on the markets. If there is not a profitable market in which farmers can sell their goods, all the hard work in the world can't save them. And as Wirtz worked six days a week or more in Iowa, the market for hogs was starting to shift fundamentally. And the transformation was being driven by farmers hundreds of miles away, in places like Holdenville, Oklahoma, where Tyson Foods was offering them the chance of a lifetime.

In the early 1990s, Bob Allen saw an advertisement in the local newspaper. A chicken company called Tyson Foods was looking for farmers around Allen's home of Holdenville. But the company didn't want the farmers to raise birds. It was looking for them to build hog barns.

Allen was intrigued. At the time, he leased some rocky pastureland around Holdenville where he raised about a hundred cattle. It was hard work, mending the fence lines and baling the hay necessary to feed his herd. The opportunity to build a hog farm for Tyson Foods meant he could consolidate his business onto one property, making it easier to manage. Like most farmers, Allen thought about his farm in terms of his children. He had four boys, and he wanted to leave them a business that would support them and keep them on their family's land. Plenty of farmers seemed to have the same idea.

Allen went to a crowded meeting in downtown Holdenville to hear what Tyson Foods had to offer him. Allen isn't anyone's idea of a pushover. It was hard to eke a living out of the grassy hill country around Holdenville, but hard men like Allen made it work. He had grown up accustomed to the seven-day workweek, and his only time away from farm work was his stint in the U.S. Army, when he fought in Vietnam. So he listened to the Tyson man's pitch with a skeptical ear. Allen wasn't looking to get rich quick or even make an easy living. He just wanted an operation he knew would pay his modest bills. He was pleased with what he heard from Tyson. The company said it would line up loans for anyone interested in building a hog house. It would offer farmers a series of three consecutive three-year contracts, which would last almost the entire life of the ten-year loan they would take on to build the farm. The work would be constant, but Allen was used to that. What worried him was whether the project would provide a viable enough cash flow to cover the amount of debt he would take on. Allen had heard about chicken farmers in neighboring states like Arkansas who had gotten too deep in debt when building their farms and were forced into bankruptcy when their contract payments came in lower than they expected. But those farmers operated on contracts that lasted only one year, or in some cases from month to month. With Tyson promising to provide a farm income for ten years, Allen felt more comfortable borrowing the $500,000 it would take to build two farrowing farms.

He talked the business proposition over with his neighbors and his wife. He thought about what it would mean for his boys. And in 1993 he took the plunge. He had a perfect piece of ground south of Holdenville that had been in his family for three generations where he planned to build his hog farm. With Tyson's support, he expected the land could stay in his family for at least another generation.

When he broke ground on his farm, he helped Tyson lay the foundation for its new industrial herds, which would eventually be shipped far beyond the hills of Oklahoma. Years later, the piglets would even be sent as far as 680 miles away, to farms outside little Iowa towns like Emmetsburg, West Bend, and Whittemore.

Chuck Wirtz had a simple theory: If someone was paying you money to raise hogs, he was doing it only because he could make more money than what he paid you. That concept rankled him. He, for one, wanted to make as much money as he could. If a company like Tyson or Smithfield Foods offered him a certain payment to raise pigs, Wirtz knew that it was making a certain percentage more than that. He wanted to capture that money himself rather than hand it over to an out-of-state corporation. So he decided to stay independent. He had every confidence he was smart enough to compete head to head with any pork producer in the country, even if it had hundreds of millions of dollars at its disposal.

In the 1990s the cash market for pigs had the critical fuel that keeps any market functioning: It had competition. Wirtz dealt with several buyers from different slaughterhouses in and around Iowa who were interested in buying his hogs.

On any given day, Wirtz was at his desk, a phone to his ear, calling around to local slaughterhouses and negotiating prices for loads of hogs. Wirtz ran his burgeoning hog business out of a small office in the feed store that his family owned in downtown Whittemore.

The feed store was in a small brick building with a couple of tall grain silos behind it, where trucks arrived to pick up loads of feed to deliver to local farmers. Inside the feed store's glass front door there was a wide-open area with a well-worn wooden floor where customers could stand at a counter and place their orders. Off to the side were two small candy machines and a coffeepot for the employees.

Wirtz's office was located through a side door behind the counter, and as customers waited out front he could sometimes be heard haggling with buyers for his hogs. He made the rounds on his phone, calling buyers one by one, trying to pit them against each other to gin up the highest price he could get.

Hog farmers, like cattle ranchers, are at a fundamental disadvantage when it comes time to sell their animals. When it comes time to sell, their window of opportunity is short. Once an animal reaches the right size for slaughter, it has to be sold quickly. Otherwise it starts getting too big to be desirable. While the selling window is small, a farmer's investment in the hogs is long term. He has money tied up in the land and hog barns, and he needs to pay those bills.

The slaughterhouses know that a farmer has a lot of money riding on each hog and just a short time in which to sell it. So the hog buyers try to wait out farmers until they're desperate to sell and willing to take a lower price.

Over the years, Wirtz developed tricks for getting them to sweeten their offers. He called buyers before he was really ready to sell his pigs. And he told them his pigs cost some outrageous price, well above market average. When the buyer scoffed, Wirtz thanked him for his time and hung up. Wirtz acted more confident than he really was. Then he called the buyer back a couple of days later. By this time, the shock of the ridiculously high price Wirtz was asking for might have worn off a little. Wirtz might come down a little, feigning a need to sell quickly. He often clinched a sale price that would have been unthinkable just a day or two earlier.

By staying independent, Wirtz took on greater risks but reaped bigger profits in the 1980s and 1990s, working a competitive market to his advantage. Wirtz couldn't see a reason in the world why he'd want to sign a contract and raise pigs for anyone else. As long as there was a free market, there was a lifeline for the independent hog farmer.

By the mid-1990s, Bob Allen and his neighbors were getting better at their jobs. They steadily increased the number of piglets they could get from each sow, creating a steady traffic of hogs to Tyson's nursery, where the animals were sorted and then shipped off to farms for fattening.

Though Allen and his neighbors could not see it, the pigs they were raising and sending out to contract farmers had an invisible effect on the entire national hog market. It was an effect that was poorly understood at the time it occurred, and it became visible only with the benefit of hindsight.

The hogs that were born in Oklahoma, raised in Arkansas, and slaughtered in Marshall, Missouri, never encountered an open, competitive cash market. They were moved through the supply chain under contract, owned the entire time by Tyson Foods. As contract hog farming became more prevalent, it meant that a smaller and smaller proportion of pigs were sold on open markets, at the kind of roadside sales barns where buyers and sellers haggled over an animal's price.

This caused a surprising shift within the hog market. Each 1 percent gain in the proportion of pigs sold under contract created a 0.88 percent drop in the price of hogs that were sold on the cash market. In other words, the rise of contract farming came at the direct expense of the independent cash market for pigs. Each hog that Bob Allen delivered to the Tyson nursery helped lower the overall price for pigs on the open market. Each contract a hog farmer signed sucked one more breath of oxygen out of the cash market upon which farmers like Chuck Wirtz depended.

This created a new center of gravity within the hog industry. Each new contract farm made it that much harder to survive as an independent farmer. This wasn't just a case of big farms driving out the little farms. Even if an independent farmer owned enormous hog barns and used the exact same high-tech methods to raise his pigs, he was at a disadvantage solely because he sold his pigs on the open market.

No one realized this was happening at the time, but people like Bob Allen might not have cared anyway. He had worries of his own.

Bob Allen's education in hog farming came fast. Every morning, Allen drove down a highway just west of Holdenville, pulling off at a small gravel driveway and then heading down a hill on the land his grandfather had farmed. Farther down the slope, there were two long, gleaming sheds with new metal roofs. They looked like chicken houses to the uninitiated, with curtained windows and big feed bins at each end. But as Allen walked in the front door of each house, he was greeted by the sight of hundreds of female pigs standing upright in two tight rows, wedged between metal bars that held them in place.

The first thing Allen learned about pigs is that they were sensitive to the Oklahoma heat. The air was more humid, more scorching in the summertime than in Arkansas. Conditions that worked on Bill Moeller's farm outside Springdale didn't seem to hold when they were transferred to Holdenville. Many summer mornings, Allen would enter the pig houses to find that sows had keeled over dead from the heat. More often, the pregnant sows miscarried their litters, a mess that Allen would get down on all fours to clean up. Each dead sow, and each lost piglet, ate into Allen's income.

Allen was paid through a tournament system. His performance was ranked against his neighbors', and Tyson docked his pay if he performed below the average. It didn't seem quite fair to Allen because his ranking was so dependent on the quality of the pigs Tyson delivered, but he wasn't one to complain.

Allen quickly learned who was in charge. Tyson sent field technicians to his farm, and initially Allen thought their job was to give him advice. But he soon came to see that the field techs arrived to dispense orders. They had the college education, and Allen was just a country rube. It wasn't smart for him to question their authority. Farmers like Allen were under strict protocols to clean themselves every time they left one hog barn before entering another. And they were told time and again to wear sterile rubber boots, and to step into a pan of disinfectant when they went in and out of each barn. These practices were critical, the farmers were told, to prevent the spread of disease. Allen watched with quiet anger as the college-educated field technicians marched into his houses without washing and tromped between barns without disinfecting their boots. They strode around his operation like they owned the place. Because, in a way, they did. Allen knew every day that Tyson could refuse to deliver him sows, and he'd be on his own to meet his debt payments.

When his first three-year contract with Tyson expired, Bob Allen drove to the company's corporate office just outside Holdenville. The building was the biggest industrial complex for miles around, its cylindrical, concrete feed towers rising far above the modest skyline of the city nearby.

Allen went into the offices and sat down across from John Thomas, who was the manager at the time of the Holdenville office.

Thomas had some bad news: Tyson wouldn't be able to offer Allen another three-year contract, as he expected. According to Allen, Tyson offered him a thirty-day contract, with another thirty-day contract available after that.

Allen was stunned. He owed well near half a million dollars on the buildings he'd erected on his family's land. He was being told now his economic security would be decided on a month-to-month basis.

— You can't do that, he stammered.

Thomas explained that Allen wasn't meeting Tyson's production goals. When Allen first built his farm, the company set a goal that each sow should produce an average of 16 piglets per year. Allen had met and exceeded that goal, along with other farmers in the area. Tyson then raised its goal to 19 piglets per year, a benchmark that Allen had also met. Now, Thomas explained, Tyson had set the bar at 20 pigs per year. Allen was producing an average of just 19.

— Your production has not reached the point that allows you to have a three-year contract, Thomas told him.

Allen was furious. He had mortgaged his family's land, borrowed half a million dollars, and become a Tyson farmer based on the company's promises. He vividly remembered having been told the company would provide contracts that would cover his debt payments for nearly a decade.

— You can't do that! That's not legal. We borrowed money on your say-so, on your idea that you were going to fulfill three, three-year contracts, he said.

Thomas seemed unmoved, and he appeared to be speaking from a tightly scripted statement. He told Allen there was no choice but to accept the shorter contract and that the change in plans was due to Allen's shortcomings as a farmer. Thomas repeated the same lines, regardless of Allen's protests.

— We have met the end of the three-year contract, and we will not be renewing it. You will be renewed on a thirty-day basis.

Allen left the office and began the drive back to his farm. He had walked into his meeting with Tyson as a man, and he left it as a chicken farmer.

Tyson Foods refused to comment on this incident or make John Thomas available for an interview. The company said in a statement: "We don't recall ever providing a contract hog farmer a month-to-month contract." Allen did not have copies of his contracts, having lost or disposed of them over the last decade.

By the late 1990s, it was impossible for smaller hog farms to survive in the shadow of farms like Wirtz's and Allen's. Even at that point, the Midwest was still populated with thousands of small- to midsize hog farms that appeared healthy and viable from the outside. In fact, they had already been driven out of business but didn't realize it yet. The reason behind their extinction was simple mathematics: Every pig raised on a small- to midsize farm was now a money loser.

It took 342 pounds of feed and 23 minutes of labor to raise 100 pounds of pork on small farms with only 500 to 2,000 hogs that were raised in older, low-tech barns. Big farms could do the same thing faster and cheaper. On average, it took about 247 pounds of feed and 7 minutes of labor to raise 100 pounds of pork on a farm with about 5,000 pigs.

Still, the smaller farms stayed in business despite this wide gap in economic efficiency. Even into the late 1990s, the business was profitable enough for almost everyone to make a buck. But all that would change in 1998, when the rise of industrial production led to an unprecedented crisis in the hog business. Like chicken farmers in the 1960s, America's hog producers were about to experience the first chickenlike bust of a market.

The hog market collapse of 1998 started slowly. No one really noticed. The year started out promising for the pork industry. Hog prices had risen in 1996 and 1997, and pork prices at U.S. grocery stores were standing firm. Smithfield Foods was looking to ramp up production at one of its biggest slaughterhouses in North Carolina, and hog farmers like Wirtz were borrowing money to build new, expensive hog barns to supply a growing market.

It only made sense that farmers should be prospering. They were feeding a population that had more money to spend. The late 1990s were a boom time, with unemployment hovering around 4.5 percent and the Internet fueling a stock market surge. Then a financial crisis swept across Asia, and consumers there quit buying pork from the United States. Suddenly slaughterhouses didn't need so many pigs because their export orders were drying up, even as more farmers were calling up with hogs for sale.

The global drop in demand was worsened by local hog plant closures in the United States. It went largely unnoticed when Iowa Beef Processors closed a slaughterhouse in Iowa. Then Smithfield shut down a plant in South Dakota. The plants were old and inefficient, and the industry didn't really miss them. But a subtle effect rippled out from the closures. When each plant was shut down, hog farmers had to look elsewhere to sell their animals. The remaining slaughterhouses suddenly had a glut of pigs at their front door.

The market price for live hogs started to fall. Historically, that wasn't unusual. Hog prices, like all commodities, rose and fell in waves that followed supply and demand. But when demand started to fall in 1998, it showed how radically the industry had been transformed in just one short decade. The old rules of supply and demand didn't work anymore.

When Wirtz was growing up, hog production was flexible. Farmers could get in and out of the market easily. When prices fell, farmers scaled back the size of their herds. They could do that easily because the hogs were just one part of a diversified farm. The hogs were the "mortgage lifter," but not the bread and butter. The roughly 700,000 hog farmers could read the market and respond adroitly by cutting back their supply. After time, the supply got low enough that prices bounced back, and farmers entered the business again.

By 1998, the business was dominated by operations like Wirtz's. Smaller hog farms were replaced by expensive, confinement operations holding several thousand pigs. The infrastructure was expensive, the costs were fixed, and producers didn't have the choice just to back out of the market when prices were low. They had big mortgage debts and utility bills to pay. Modern hog barns had to be filled, almost regardless of the price hogs commanded on the market. The scale of the industry demanded it. So when prices started to fall in 1998, the supply stayed rigidly high. The industrial machine couldn't slow down.

By the end of 1998, the price of hogs fell to 10 cents a pound, lower than they had been during the Depression. For the rest of America, the dot-com boom was in full swing, but in towns dominated by corporate hog production a deep recession had set in. The hog price collapse, unprecedented in American history, immediately began to wipe out farmers.

The pain wasn't shared equally. The downturn of 1998 disproportionately destroyed the smaller independent hog farms. Big industrial farms connected to meatpackers like Tyson and Smithfield had an advantage as they slogged through the downturn. Because they owned the slaughterhouses, companies like Smithfield reaped an enormous surge of profits from the crash of 1998. The companies bought hogs at Depression-era prices, then turned around and sold the pork at dot-com-era prices. The retail price of pork at grocery stores and restaurants remained relatively stable. The meatpackers sat in the middle and collected a surprise windfall worth millions. Their farms might be losing money, but the losses were more than recouped by the high prices consumers paid at the grocery store.

Smaller, independent farms reaped only the losses, and it drove them out of business. Between 1997 and 2000, the number of farms with 2,000 to 3,000 pigs fell by 18 percent. The number of farms even smaller than that, with fewer than 2,000 pigs, fell by 14 percent. At the same time, the number of farms with 10,000 to 50,000 hogs almost doubled. The number of megafarms with more than 500,000 animals grew by 11 percent.

Not only did the big operations survive, they multiplied during and after the downturn. This increased their market share and made it yet more difficult for the independent producers to compete.

The hog market started to recover in 1999, and eventually it returned to profitability. And the farms affiliated with the nation's biggest meat companies were the survivors who benefited from the upswing.

Bob Allen was on his knees. He was scrubbing the floor in one of his hog barns outside Holdenville, Oklahoma, and his head felt like it might split open. Sharp, rhythmic stabs of pain shot through his brain like lightning. But he labored on, scrubbing the floor after a mother sow aborted another litter of pigs. The work was unpleasant enough, but his labor was made all the more torturous by the headaches that now visited Allen every day.

Allen didn't let on how much pain he was in to the young men who worked on his farm. They were mostly Mexicans whom Allen could barely afford to pay. He needed the help, and it was nearly impossible to find anyone in Holdenville willing to put in an honest day's work at the hog barns. Only the Mexicans were willing to do the job. Over the years, Allen had developed a crew of men he could more or less depend on to show up every day. He hid his headaches because he didn't want them to know their boss was almost crippled by excruciating pain.

Eventually, Allen went to the doctor in town and told him about the headaches. The arc of pain neatly mirrored his career as a hog farmer. He hadn't suffered from headaches as a young man. The headaches started after he built the hog houses and spent seven days a week working inside them. Over time, they increased in intensity. It felt like there was a blade wedged into his forehead, and someone spent the day twisting it.

Allen underwent a series of tests, and his doctor told him he had an aneurysm. A blood vessel in his head was inflamed, and as it pulsed it pressed against a nerve. The doctor prescribed medication, and it helped. Allen took one or two pills every morning.

Then he took more. By 1999, he was taking a handful of pills every day, just to function. Still, he couldn't take off work. The sows needed tending every day, and their flow of piglets never stopped. So Allen did what he did well: He swallowed the pain and kept at it. Being on a month-to-month contract left him little choice. If he faltered for even a matter of weeks, Allen knew he might lose his farm. He worked through the pain, supplying Tyson with a steady flow of piglets to ship to its farms.

West Bend, Iowa, wasn't what it used to be. The town was struggling to hold on. In 1990, as the first big hog barns were being erected, West Bend boasted about 862 residents. It has shrunk steadily ever since. By 2000, about 830 people lived there and by 2009 there were 795. The towns around it shrank too, as the agricultural economy was shifted into fewer and fewer hands.

Chuck Wirtz often drove his farm truck into West Bend, where he attended church and had many friends. West Bend was one of the bigger towns near Whittemore, where Wirtz lived. Like many residents of rural America, Wirtz was growing accustomed to living in a place that was in decline. The landmarks were forever pointing backward, toward the glory days: the stores that used to be on Main Street, the homes where friends used to live before moving on.

There was a stubbornness to those who stayed behind, Wirtz included. He and his neighbors insisted on keeping the place alive. In other parts of Iowa, people were moving out only to have drugs and crime seep in. Vacant houses were rented and turned into methamphetamine labs, where improvisational chemists left behind toxic waste that made the structures uninhabitable. To fend off such decay, residents of West Bend pooled their money and bought empty houses, tearing them down rather than watching them go to seed.

Wirtz doubled down on his hog farm, even as the business became more volatile and subject to the power of a few big corporations. He expanded his herd after the crisis of 1998, even when conventional wisdom might have argued against it.

The crash of 1998 taught Wirtz two lessons. First, he had to get big to survive. Second, he was now too big to be wrong. With tens of thousands of hogs on his land at any given time, Wirtz had put his livelihood at risk. Another crash like 1998 and he might lose his entire farm.

To counter that risk, Wirtz signed futures contracts on the pigs he owned, or "hedging contracts," as they're more widely known. In essence, all of his pigs were sold before they ever arrived at his farm. This meant Wirtz could get a predictable price for those hogs even if the market crashed. It reduced risk but added layers of complexity to the business, entwining Wirtz in the futures markets for hogs and complicated agreements with derivatives traders.

His office in Whittemore was piled high with papers and contracts. The shelf behind him was lined with binder notebooks full of contracts for his hogs. Wirtz leaned forward and scanned the flickering numbers that rolled over his computer screen. He was watching the futures market for pork and for hogs, inspecting the flow of numbers as if his livelihood depended on it. But it wasn't just his livelihood. It was that of his sons, and even his neighbors. Wirtz's farm was a badly needed anchor for the economy around Whittemore and West Bend, and he knew it. He just had to figure out how to keep it going each day.

Bob Allen lost the fight. The pain was too great. He was taking pills by the fistful every day, and it did nothing to calm the stabbing pain behind his forehead. He relented, finally, and agreed to undergo a risky brain-surgery procedure. The doctors made an incision in his forehead and put a stent next to the bulging vein in his brain that was pressing against a nerve and causing him such pain.

Seven years into his hog production contract with Tyson, Allen was still heavily in debt. On paper, he was supposed to have paid off most of his loan, but the cash flow had never worked out as Tyson promised.

There were always expenses to be paid that weren't figured into the original plan: roads to be fixed, new equipment to purchase to make the hog houses more efficient.

Because his loan carried a 10 percent interest rate, Allen estimated he had paid nearly $1 million on his $500,000 loan by the time he sold the farm. Like many borrowers who would later be wiped out by subprime mortgages, Allen also discovered the painful realities behind attractive-sounding "balloon loans."

The seven-year term of his original loan expired in 2000, but Allen then had to pay an additional $160,000 one-time balloon payment. By pushing that balloon payment out to the end of the loan, the bankers had made the deal look more affordable. When Allen signed the contract with Tyson in 1993, he had assumed he'd have plenty of cash on hand to make that balloon payment.

Lying in his hospital bed, recovering from surgery, Allen realized he didn't have anything close to $160,000 to pay the bank. And even during the short period of time he was hospitalized, his hog farm started to fall apart. The operation was faltering. He got calls from neighbors saying his sows had escaped their pens and wandered onto adjacent property. Allen had to pay to have someone retrieve them.

Allen decided to sell his farm. After paying off his debt and losing the farmland that had been in his family for three generations, he was all but broke. But even years later, he was hesitant to complain about it. He had escaped his tenure as a Tyson hog farmer with his health.

Allen got out of the business, but his hog farm stayed in full production. Tyson's network of farms around Holdenville produces about one million piglets a year, which the company loads onto trucks and ships almost seven hundred miles north to Iowa. Tyson sells them to a middle man there who places them on contract farms, then sells them back to Tyson for slaughter. During their entire lifespan, the animals will never brush up against an open, competitive market.

Just west of Whittemore, Iowa, there is a lonely little white building next to the highway. The building used to be a sales station, where farmers brought market-ready hogs for sale. It sits behind a gravel driveway and parking lot where farmers can park trailer-loads of hogs. There is a scale where animals are weighed, and beyond that there is a maze of straw-covered pens where sows and boars can lie on their side and await the truck that will pick them up for their final ride to a slaughterhouse.

Over the last fifteen years, the vast majority of Iowa's sales stations have closed. They have been left empty to corrode in the elements or be bulldozed. The one outside Whittemore, just west of Chuck Wirtz's feed store, is one of the last in operation.

On a rainy afternoon in the summer of 2011, the front office was occupied only by Nancy, an employee of Lynch Livestock. Nancy sat behind a desk and looked through magazines. A small coffeepot on the table next to her was half full. In the pens behind the office, pigs wallowed and grunted as rain went pink-pink-pink on the roof above them. Lynch Livestock had bought the castaway pigs, the misfits no slaughterhouse would want. It had bought the overgrown and the underfed, the old breeding sows who had outlived their usefulness on the farm.

It's a niche business. Lynch sells some of the animals for luau-style pig roasts, barbecues, or other events. No self-respecting meatpacker still buys their hogs through a sales station. In fact, very few meatpackers buy pigs on the open market at all.

No one knows this better than Chuck Wirtz, foolish independent hog farmer that he is. Wirtz spends his days in the back office of his feed store, searching for the last vestiges of an open market.

As Nancy sat idly in her office at the sales station, Wirtz was in his rickety swivel chair in his cramped office. He was hunched over, as always, eyeing the blinking numbers of the futures market for hogs.

As he often did this time of day, Wirtz was struggling to figure out how much a hog was worth. It wasn't easy. The multibillion-dollar market in hogs had become a closed system over the last decade, run through confidential contracts where animals were never sold in a negotiated deal, let alone a transparent transaction.

Without an open, competitive cash market, there can be no such thing as an independent producer. Quite simply, they have nowhere to sell their animals.

By 2011, far less than 10 percent of all hogs were sold on the open market. On Christmas Eve 2010, the open market shrank to almost nothing, with just 2 percent of hogs sold through negotiated transaction. That was the lowest level in U.S. history. The remaining 98 percent of hogs were grown under contract for vertically integrated companies like Smithfield, or sold through the kind of long-term forward contracts favored by Tyson.

Wirtz was being boxed in. He looked at a USDA market website that tracked hog sales and tried to puzzle out what the tiny number of open market transactions told him. The sales were broken down by region, like the Eastern and Western Corn Belts, but there were paltry few transactions happening anywhere.

"This is a day when it's frustrating," Wirtz said. "You go to the Eastern Corn Belt, and there's nothing. We get no prices. We've got nothing to go on. In the Western Corn Belt, we do have a whopping 145 pigs traded. It's a meaningless number."

This death of the open hog market ends an era that started after World War II. The U.S. interstate highway system created a national market for hogs. They were traded in a vigorously competitive market, where the value of a pound of pork was discovered and rediscovered every minute at sales stations throughout the farm belt.

This system did more than put money in the pockets of people like Chuck Wirtz. The competitive market delivered ever-larger quantities of ever-better pork to consumers. In fact, the whole idea behind competitive markets is that they do the best job of allocating a society's resources. As a multitude of buyers and sellers hash out the price of a product, a weird thing happens: The product itself actually improves.

In the competitive market for hogs, for example, farmers like Chuck Wirtz had an incentive, every day, to give the market what it wanted. So farmers experimented with their herds. They developed the best pig that would fetch the best price from the highest bidder.

The competitive market stimulated innovation beyond the farm. Geneticists at universities and private companies strove to breed the best pigs. At 4H clubs, young farmers learned about the best hogs and cuts of pork, and back home they competed to keep up with the market by ordering the best genetic lines of pigs and raising them according to best practices.

Perhaps most important, the free market affixed its own price to a hog. This process is called "price discovery." Competitive markets wrestled a price down the precise nexus of supply and demand, helping to determine a product's real value.

In 2011, price discovery was happening in a different way.

It involves producers like Wirtz sitting behind desks with a phone cradled between their ear and their shoulder, trying to find someone to buy their hogs. Instead of a raucous market with hundreds of buyers to compete on price, Wirtz basically gets to choose between four.

Those buyers are Hormel, Cargill, JBS Swift, and Tyson. But really, not all four of them are in the market at the same time. Most of them have hogs locked up through forward contracts, and they enter the cash market only haltingly to buy last batches of pigs they need to keep their slaughterhouses running at full capacity.

On some days, farmers like Wirtz might try to stoke up competition between three or even two buyers. This wasn't the case even as recently as 1995. Back then, the top four meat companies controlled only about 46 percent of the total hog market. By 2006, the top four companies controlled 66 percent.

In a concentrated market like this, price discovery isn't just driven by supply and demand. A different force starts to creep into the equation, called "buyer power." Buyer power is the measure of desperation on the part of a seller like Wirtz, and power on behalf of the buyer, like Cargill or Tyson. Buyer power slowly pushes the price of a hog down past its natural point. This happens because Wirtz doesn't have enough competitive bidders to keep his price firm.

In a concentrated market, with just three bidders, a meatpacker faces little or no consequence for offering to pay less than a hog is really worth. After all, what's Wirtz going to do? Call Lynch's down the road and see if they want to buy 1,200 hogs?

When buyer power pushes hog prices downward, it gives more

money to companies like Tyson Foods. That's because the retail price doesn't change. Companies can extract a lower price from the farmer, without passing it on to the consumer.

The results have been stark in the hog industry. Consumers pay more, farmers make less, and corporations in the middle grab a windfall.

Back in 1980, hog farmers earned about 50 cents for every dollar a consumer spent on pork. But that share of the food dollar has steadily dwindled. By 2009, the hog farmer was only earning 24.5 cents for every dollar spent on pork.

At the same time, pork has become more expensive at the grocery store. Retail pork prices fell dramatically between 1976 and 2000, when adjusted for inflation. The cheaper meat was undoubtedly the result of the hog farm's industrialization, as Tyson and Smithfield came to dominate the market. But the decline in prices slowed down between 2000 and 2009. Since 2008, inflation-adjusted prices have slowly started to climb.

The divergence in fortunes is becoming more stark between rural America and the corporations that call it home. Hog prices are pushed lower on the farm, and pork prices climb higher in the grocery stores. And Tyson sits quietly in the middle, generating record profits by the year.

Chuck Wirtz came to an inescapable conclusion in the spring of 2011: He was finished building new hog houses and adding more pigs to his herd.

As he looked out into the future, he saw there simply wasn't money to be made in the business. At least, not by the farmers. People would always eat pork, and prices at the grocery store would probably continue to rise, perhaps even sharply. But meat companies like Tyson controlled the market for hogs. They controlled many of the farms themselves.

With no open market, the industry was going the way of the chicken business. All the farmer had was the physical buildings, the hog barns where he raised animals that someone else owned. Even if a corporation didn't own the animals outright, it would determine their value through contracts written by the company's lawyers.

The haggling, the open market, the room for an independent producer to squeeze a profit out of the business, it was all disappearing.

"When there is no opportunity to be an independent pork producer anymore, then the contractors have you where they want you. Because there is no other game in town. Then they'll start making the rules," Wirtz said, leaning back in the rickety chair in his office. On the computer behind him, the paltry numbers of a shrinking open market blinked across the screen. "It's not like the poultry industry is inherently evil. But they take advantage of the situation that they have. I just believe that the pork industry will eventually get to that point.

"I don't know the time frame that this is going to happen, but I don't want to be owning a whole bunch of hog buildings, with a whole lot of debt against them, when this happens. It's not like I'm grooming my kids to be in pork production."

CHAPTER 9

Pulling the Noose

(2011)

T HE COWBOYS were saddled up just after dawn. The wide Kansas sky above them was just turning light blue. Orange sunbeams slanted down through the clouds, washing over the rolling cornfields and green hills while the ranch hands rode their chestnut-colored horses.

There were three of them. Antonio rode in the middle, wearing a broad white cowboy hat. He looked like he was trying to imitate the Marlboro Man, riding ramrod straight in his saddle. Behind Antonio was a man named Christian and ahead of him was their boss, Cachu (pronounced *Ka-choo*). The men bounced along and held the leather reins in their hands, ready to start the morning's cattle drive. They were mostly silent, but they called out every now and then in their native Spanish tongue as they guided the horses through a narrow alleyway bordered by metal gates. The alleys led through a broad expanse of mud-floored pens that were home to 10,000 cows. The pens covered a broad hillside, which from a distance looked like some kind of third-world shanty town, populated by crowds of cattle. By late afternoon, a cloud of dust would hang over the maze of pens, making the brown, muddy hillside look hazy as the tawny-colored cattle paced slowly back and forth.

But it was still early, and the dust hadn't risen. The cattle groaned and mooed as the riders passed them, and some of the animals approached the sides of their pens as if expecting a bucket of grain.

Finally, the men reached their appointed pen. They opened the gate and a rider went inside to scare the cattle out into the alleyway, where the other two men waited. The cowboys yelled and whooped, the cattle ran down the narrow chute, and the cattle drive was under way.

Even a few decades ago, men like Antonio, Christian, and Cachu might have wrapped a tight little cylinder of clothing and bedding and strapped it to their saddle, ready to spend weeks out on the high prairies of Kansas, Oklahoma, or Texas. Cattle drives were long and sometimes arduous affairs, as cowboys drove their herds across state lines to new grazing lands or a stockyard.

In 2011, the cowboys are penned in. They might ride on horseback a few miles in a given day, but it will mostly be within the mazelike paths that run through the sprawling feedlot.

The modern U.S. cattle business itself is also increasingly confined, beleaguered on all sides by the rising tide of cheap chicken and cheap pork. While the cattle industry has gotten bigger, more complicated, and more expensive to operate than at any time in U.S. history, it has also entered an era of brutal and relentless downward pressure on profits. This has driven about 11,000 ranchers out of business every year since 1996, and wiped out 30 percent of all U.S. feedlots. The rise of cheap chicken has perhaps hurt no business more than the beef business. Consumers have spent less and less on beef, pushing red meat off their plate in favor of chicken patties.

The fight for survival within the beef industry is increasingly being fought between the fewer and bigger competitors that remain. The industry is divided into two broad sectors: There are the producers who raise the cattle, which are ranchers and big feedlot owners. Then there are the meatpackers that kill the animals and sell their beef, the companies like Tyson Foods or JBS Swift. Both of these sectors are more concentrated than they have been at any time in history. On the meatpacking side, there are now just four companies that buy 85 percent of the cattle sold in the country. Tyson is the biggest, followed by Cargill, JBS Swift, and National Beef. As meatpackers have become bigger, feedlots have tried to keep pace, expanding to meet the needs of their corporate buyers.

But the defining fight under way in the cattle industry isn't just a battle between big and small operators. It's a fight about control, a tug-of-war between the producers and the meatpackers. And the big meat-packers like Tyson Foods are clearly winning.

While Tyson and the other meatpackers have not been able to fully integrate the cattle business, they have been able to take control of the market by virtue of their size. When feedlot owners sell into a market of just four buyers, it's hard to reasonably call that market competitive. In the face of increasingly volatile prices and depressed profits, most cattle producers have opted to abandon the free market altogether. They have chosen, instead, to sell their animals under contract to companies like Tyson, with contracts that are modeled on those used for chicken and pork farmers. The remaining minority of cattle producers who sell their animals on the open market find that they must often take the price that is dictated to them by Tyson, Cargill, or JBS. It's hard to get a better price when the buyers refuse to bid against one another.

What has evolved is a kind of de facto vertical integration, with whole networks of feedlots tied to meatpackers under contract. The cattle market is technically an open one, but no one behaves that way, and it's an open secret that they don't. There is ample evidence that the big four meatpackers have chosen to divvy up the market, picking territories where they can buy all the cattle from a feedlot without facing a competing bid.

This arrangement means that Tyson has a steady supply of cattle to keep its plants running. And its contracts have allowed it to exert more control over the cattle business without owning the animals outright. When Tyson decides it wants to use a certain growth drug in its cattle, for example, all it needs to do is put the word out to its contract feedlots. There is no struggle to convince independent producers or advertise the need for it with open market purchases.

But a stubborn minority of feedlot owners and ranchers is still trying to maintain an open market for cattle by refusing to sign contracts with meatpackers. By doing so, they are trying to keep one last corner of the meat industry from being fully chickenized. There are economic reasons for these cattle producers to want to stay independent. But there are cultural reasons as well, reasons that trace back to the obstinate character of people like Gene Carson.

Gene Carson owns Maverick Feeders, LLC, outside of Dodge City, the feedlot where the cowboys Antonio, Christian, and Cachu were riding their circular cattle drive. There is something odious about the very word "contract" to a cattleman like Carson. He got into the business decades ago, straight out of college, and the first lesson he learned was that a cattle buyer's word is his bond. A cattle trade is built on ethics, not contracts. Contracts were for lawyers, and lawyers were for city slickers.

Carson started Maverick Feeders in the early 1990s, just south of his hometown in Dodge City, Kansas. The company was properly named, as Carson founded it promptly after quitting his job as a senior cattle buyer for National Beef, one of the country's four biggest meatpackers. Carson didn't like the corporate tone that was seeping into the culture of National Beef back in the 1990s, a culture that seeped into all the cattle business and seemed to have taken it over by 2011. It was a flaccid, spirit-killing culture defined by a single motto: "Father, may I?"

Something about asking "Father, may I?" rubbed Carson the wrong way. He didn't like getting orders from a corporate office and he dreaded the thought that one day he might be promoted to a place like Kansas City where he would sit in an office all day and where the only manual labor left for him would be mowing the lawn when he got back home. Carson couldn't picture himself mowing the lawn. That wasn't work. His idea of work was cutting horses and raising cattle. He worked as long as he was awake many days, and he didn't want to live his life any other way. So he quit his good-paying job at National Beef and rented a feedlot carved out of the isolated plains south of Dodge City. And over the years the feedlot expanded and expanded again until it reached its present size in 2011, covering the hillsides all around him.

By 2011, Carson belonged to a group of feedlot owners spread throughout the High Plains who have refused to abandon the cash market in favor of contracts. The benefit of doing this isn't immediately clear to an outsider. Every year, the independent feedlots seem just a little more isolated, a little more outside the favored circle of the big four meatpackers. The most influential trade groups and lobbyists increasingly deride the cash market as a throwback to the industry's history, just another manifestation of the cattle drives and cowboys that have been made obsolete by technology's onward march.

But for Carson, the decision is pretty simple. And it comes from a special insight. He spent about twenty years working as a cattle buyer himself for National and other companies. The thought of becoming a contract producer seems not only appalling but economically illogical. Meatpackers don't sign contracts to benefit feedlot owners. They sign contracts to benefit themselves.

"If you crawl in bed with a rattlesnake and think you ain't gonna get bit, then you're pretty stupid," Carson said.

The main strip in Dodge City is called Wyatt Earp Boulevard, named after the legendary gambler and lawman. Earp was one of the first people ever able to impose a measure of discipline on the American cattle business, and he did this in part by killing people. Earp famously gunned down three outlaw cowboys at the OK Corral in Arizona in 1881, setting the standard by which he would govern the cattle towns springing up around the migration routes that cowboys used to drive herds to the packing houses.

Things have mellowed since the OK Corral. Earp's six-shooter has become just another charming prop for Dodge City's healthy tourist industry. Now there is an Applebee's downtown next to Boot Hill, the plot of land where errant cowboys were once buried after they got shot. But there is still a fight that is centered here, albeit a much quieter one. It is a fight by companies like Tyson finally to subdue the Wild West, and to replace it with a predictability and corporate character that was unthinkable for most of the business's history.

This fight is waged from the giant compounds that embody modern beef production, like the National Beef plant that sits on the eastern edge of town. The National plant is a mini city, where semitrucks loaded with live cattle arrive around the clock and nose up to a chute where the cattle are led inside. About 6,000 cows can be killed and butchered within the plant each day. The sprawling parking lot is filled, at all hours, with the cars of 2,500 employees who report to their stations inside the factory.

Less than two miles east, there is a similar plant owned by Cargill. And sixty miles west is the Tyson plant outside Garden City.* This triumvirate of meatpackers has quieted the once rowdy competition that used to support a free market for cattle. Back in 1980, the four biggest meatpackers controlled just 36 percent of the cattle market. They faced daily competition from hundreds of smaller firms to buy the best cattle and to supply the best beef to grocery stores and restaurants at the best price.

With that competition wiped out, the meatpackers have more leeway to set the rules of the game. They have also gained the power to keep wages low in their slaughterhouses, giving rise to a more pliable workforce. Wyatt Earp would likely flee Dodge City out of boredom today. The street named after him is quiet most days. The small stores along Wyatt Earp Boulevard cater to the Hispanic, Asian, and West African immigrants who moved to town for steady jobs and a quiet life. La Jerezana Shoes sells the latest styles from Mexico and provides convenient money orders for shift workers who want to send their wages back to Latin and South America. Just down the sidewalk, the African Grocery sells carpets, juices, and cooking supplies for nostalgic immigrants who want the flavor of home. On a languid afternoon, two women in traditional Muslim headscarves sat on plastic chairs in the back of the store and watched daytime television, getting up to help the periodic customer. These immigrants from the developing world are willing to accept wages and benefits that the locals walked away from decades ago, a critical evolution that has helped the meatpackers keep their costs down.

Controlling the cattle producer has become a process of simple math. With only four giant meatpackers in the market today, the cash

---

* This was the original megaplant that was built by IBP in the early 1980s. The IBP plant outside Garden City was one of the first to make wide use of contracts to ensure a captive supply of cattle, a technique that is now standard for Tyson's competitors.

market for cattle has become competitive in name only. Just twenty-five or thirty years ago, a cattle producer like Carson might have had a dozen meatpackers to choose from. Fattened cattle were sold at auction barns where meatpackers bid aggressively for the best animals, one upping another in heated auctions. It was the best kind of price discovery, transparent and built on vigorous competition. Bad cattle fetched low prices, the best cattle fetched the highest price the market would bear. Those auctions for finished cattle have ended. The market, such as it is, is played out in a series of phone calls as meatpackers dial up the feedlots and tell them what they are willing to pay. The competition can be pallid. If two meatpackers don't want to buy cattle during any given week, for example, that leaves only two buyers to choose from: not the best scenario for igniting a bidding war. If three of the meatpackers aren't in the market, that would leave only one buyer, who could offer a take-it-or-leave-it price.

This gives meatpackers a chokehold over the independent feedlot owners and ranchers that supply them. If someone like Gene Carson can't get a fair price for the cattle he raises, if he can't hit that magical break-even point of $1.29 a pound, then all the expensive corn and the rental of his muddy pens will have been for nothing. Outside of Dodge City, getting a fair price for cattle isn't just dependent on the volatile swings of the futures market in Chicago. It's more dependent on simply finding someone willing to bid for his animals.

To understand how competition could have reached such a lowly point, it's helpful to see the market through the eyes of someone like Carson, who used to buy cattle for a big beef packer, until he got so disgusted that he quit.

Gene Carson used to go out into the cattle pens even when it was raining. He donned a poncho and got out of his truck, wading out into the muddy pens to inspect the cattle closely. He could gauge how much beef their frames would yield, guessing how many of them would win the USDA grade of "choice" beef that would be worth the most at a supermarket.

This was back in 1991, when cattle buyers like Carson fought one another for the best animals to deliver to the meatpackers that employed them. Millions of dollars in revenue and profits hung on the equations that raced through Carson's mind as he examined each pen. If he paid too much for the cattle, even by a few pennies per animal, a whole day's production could be unprofitable for his employer, National Beef in Dodge City.

Carson got his first job as a cattle buyer just out of college, working for the old-line beef company Armour. He was moved around the Midwest and eventually settled in Dodge City, where he got hired on by Hyplains. Small- to midsize companies like Hyplains still heavily populated the business into the 1980s, and they relied on their cattle buyers to make sure they beat the competition to the best pen of cattle. Carson was a shrewd buyer, but fair. The feedlot owners liked working with him, even if he was tough. Hyplains eventually made him head buyer.

Carson used a number of tricks to get Hyplains the best cattle without spending a penny more than he had to, a process called "putting the kill together." To assemble a good kill, Carson employed a team of buyers who visited the feedlots and reported back to him what they saw. Carson employed a strategy called "laying the noose." He gave each of his buyers a secret order to buy several pens of cattle at a given price. Then at an appointed time later in the afternoon, Carson instructed all of them to make the trade. That was called "pulling the noose." Within minutes, Hyplains locked up thousands of cattle before the competition could get at them. The competitors found out the next morning that the first cut of cattle was off the market.

Things started to change during the 1980s, as one meatpacker bought another and drove the smaller ones out of business. With fewer and fewer companies in the market, meatpackers needed fewer and fewer buyers. In 1990 Hyplains was purchased by National Beef, which took over the Dodge City plant and began to expand it into the megaplant it is today.

Gene Carson, the head cattle buyer at Hyplains, got a new boss. He also got an education in the new rules of cattle buying. Carson reported to Tim Klein, who oversaw operations at National Beef. Month by month, Klein made it clear to Carson that the rules of the industry were changing. As beef companies expanded, they centralized their operations. That meant that decision making shifted from the buyer in the field to a team of buyers at company headquarters.

Carson was too much of a cowboy to fit with National's buying program. He was used to operating by his instincts, feeling out the market and then striking when the opportunity was right. Under Klein, Carson needed to get the green light from corporate before he could make a move. He had to call headquarters before he could pull the noose.

Carson tried pulling the noose on his own a few times, and he was invariably chastised for it later by Klein. Eventually, Carson agreed not to make a trade unless he had permission from Klein.

Then Klein called Carson into his office to talk about a bigger problem.

— It looks like you have a reputation for paying too much, Klein told him.

National had evidence to back up the claim. It compared Carson's purchases with what other buyers were paying at other slaughterhouses. Carson was paying several cents more per every hundred pounds of cattle he bought.

This didn't surprise Carson. He often paid top dollar, because he got the best animals. He prided himself on getting the first cut of cattle, before the competition got to them. For all he knew, the other National buyers were settling for the second or third cuts of cattle.

Through Carson's career, he bid on cattle using one simple number, a metric he called "choice cost hanging in the cooler." What that metric represented was the value for a pound of "choice"-grade beef hanging in the cooler at a slaughterhouse. Choice-grade beef was the high-quality stuff. It's what made a good steak. That's what beef packers were aiming to get because that's what fetched the highest price. Select-grade beef, on the other hand, went into hamburger or other cheaper cuts.

In the old days, Carson figured out the choice cost hanging in the cooler and reverse-engineered that number to figure out what he would bid on any given pen of cattle. He could eyeball a pen of cattle and figure out instantly how many of them would grade choice, how many select, and how much meat they'd yield. It let him bid prices that were razor-sharp in their precision. This was at the heart of Carson's job, and the job of every cattle buyer.

Now Klein was telling Carson that it only mattered how his costs stacked up against those of a buyer several counties away.

— Are we going to compare choice cost hanging in the cooler? Carson asked.

— That's irrelevant, Klein told him.

And that was the end of Carson's career as a cattle buyer. In Carson's view, Klein was telling him that quality didn't matter anymore.* Carson was not supposed to start his calculations with the cost of choice beef in mind and then work backward. The modern cattle buyer was involved in a numbers game more than anything. He was looking to ensure a steady flow of cattle into the front door of the modern megaplant. This was how beef became more like chicken: more standardized, less specialized. There wasn't as much difference between the best steak and the lowest quality hamburger. The quality of meat was getting pushed toward the middle, toward the commoditized "good-enough" quality of poultry. Tim Klein disputed Carson's interpretation of his comment. Klein didn't mean to say that quality didn't matter. For him, the main point was that Carson was paying too much for cattle. National's analysis was showing that Carson's cattle weren't bringing enough extra value to justify the higher price he paid.

Carson said the final straw came when National promised him a raise and then recanted on that promise a few months later. Going back on your word wasn't something that was done in the cattle business.

"I just wanted plum out," Carson said. "I could see this corporate world was taking over."

So he founded Maverick Feeders. And only then, from the vantage

---

* Klein was later promoted to become CEO of National Beef, a title he still held in 2013.

point of the cattle producer, was it really clear just how complete the corporate takeover would become.

On Monday and Tuesday mornings, the cattle buyers fan out into the rolling hills and flat cornfields around Dodge City, looking to put the kills together for their bosses at Tyson, Cargill, National Beef, and JBS Swift.

The cattle buyers visit Maverick Feeders, and then some of them drive down Highway 400 back toward town. Just across the street from the Cargill plant, they take a right turn and head up the long gravel driveway into Winter Feed Yard. Up at the top of the gravel driveway is the head office, a small brick building that looks and feels like a corporate bank branch. The carpet inside is nice and new, the desks are made of burnished wood and adorned with new iMacs. The first thing that greets a cattle buyer when he enters the office is a friendly black German shepherd named Vicky.

But buyers seldom enter the Winter Feed Yard office. In fact, they rarely enter any feedlot offices. More often than not, Ken Winter, the feedlot owner, sees the cattle buyers only when he sits at his desk on Mondays and Tuesdays and looks out the window at the cattle pens. Winter can spot the buyers in their pickup trucks, driving the narrow lanes by the cattle. Sometimes they don't even slow down. It's all but inconceivable that a modern cattle buyer would put on a poncho and walk through the pens on a rainy day as Gene Carson used to do.

Modern cattle buying has become a kind of perfunctory dance, a spiritless stage play. All the actors fulfill their roles and read their lines, but no one seems really to believe the script anymore. The drama is gone.

Every Monday, feedlot owners like Ken Winter put out a show list that displays the cattle they have for sale. The buyers look over the show lists, visit the feedlots, and then offer their bids. But nobody's laying the noose anymore. The buyers don't seem as concerned about haggling over each penny. Ken Winter might entertain a few phone calls from buyers, but it's hardly a bidding war. It's a take-it-or-leave-it market.

Still, Winter insists on selling his cattle through the cash market. He can still remember the moment when Winter Feed Yard almost went the way of the contract producer. Ken Winter's dad, Ross Winter, was running the feed yard when Cargill approached the family and asked them to sell their cattle to the company exclusively, under contract. It made sense to do so for many reasons, not the least being the fact that Cargill was located across the street.

But Ross Winter had his doubts about backing out of the free market.

— I think this would make the Winter family a lot of money, but I don't think that it'd be good for the industry, Ross Winter told his son.

And so Ken Winter remains committed to selling his cattle through a shrinking cash market. The reasons for doing so seem based more on ideology than economics. Without the cash market, he reasons, there won't be an accurate way to figure out the value of a pound of beef. Without the cash market, cattle producers essentially must take the price that is offered to them by the meatpacker.

There are several derogatory terms that men like Ken Winter use to describe cattle sold under contract, one of the most common being "gimme cattle," a name that implies no one is bidding for them. Feed-lot owners deliver gimme cattle on demand, without negotiating for a price. They hand over their biggest asset to a meatpacker without even an idea of what their paycheck will be. Winter has resolved to negotiate for all his animals and to keep alive the last competitive market.

So Winter sits in his office and watches the cattle buyers drive their route around his cattle pens. He puts out his show list and he takes a few bids each week over the phone. And what ultimately happens at the end of the week only heightens the sense that the cash market for cattle has already died.

By the end of every week, the bidding for Ken Winter's cattle ends with the same verdict: Cargill wins the contest. More than 90 percent of the time, Cargill buys the cattle Winter is selling.

This doesn't make sense statistically. There are hypothetically four companies that bid on Winter's cattle. In a competitive market, the winning bids would normally be more evenly divided among the four major buyers.

What makes Cargill's dominance even more curious is the fact that this pattern plays out across the nation, with a single meatpacker somehow winning supposedly competitive bidding for cattle the vast majority of the time at feedlots. Down the road, Cargill somehow wins the bidding at Maverick Feeders more than 90 percent of the time. About seventy miles away, at Ranger Feeders in Dighton, Kansas, National Beef somehow wins the majority of bids and buys more than 80 percent of the cattle. In Ainsworth, Nebraska, JBS Swift wins the bidding for cattle at Ainsworth Feed Yard more than 75 percent of the time.

On paper, four meatpackers are supposedly competing to buy cattle from these feedlots. But on the ground level, the picture is far different. Feedlot owners say they are lucky to get two companies to bid on their animals. In many cases they have only one.

This picture is clear to Bruce Cobb, general manager of a company that sells cattle to meatpackers on behalf of feedlots. Cobb's company, Consolidated Beef Producer, keeps reams of data on the cattle market. The state of competition is the lifeblood of his firm because it negotiates its sales. Cobb kept a database of feedlot auctions and sales for a one-year period in 2010. The database covered sales in Texas, Oklahoma, and New Mexico. It showed that during the year, there were only two weeks when all four of the big meatpackers were bidding for cattle.

For eighteen weeks out of the year there was only one meatpacker bidding on the market. For a whole month there weren't any bidders (Cobb assumed they all had enough supply tied up through their contracts during those weeks). So for twenty-two weeks of the year, there was only one or no buyers on the cash market.

When asked why this happens, feedlot owners like Ken Winter just shrug. And then they smile a little bit. That smile seems to say: Come on, dummy. Why do you think it happens? The meatpackers quit competing. They divvy up feedlots so they can dominate buying at each location without having to bid up the price in an auction.

No one seems to think the meatpackers are dumb enough to have an actual sit-down meeting to divvy up territories where they won't compete against each other. But then again, they don't have to. With only two or three buyers in the market, each buyer can easily see where the other is active. Stable buying arrangements can solidify over time without any meatpacker engaging in the kind of explicit deal making that is illegal under U.S. antitrust law.

In the case of Winter Feed Yard, it might make sense that Cargill buys a majority of the cattle. The plant is located next door. But National Beef is just a negligible two miles down the road. Yet Winter says National Beef has not sent a buyer to his feed yard in about two years. He thinks it's because he refuses to sell them large numbers of cattle under contract. So he assumes National punishes him by not buying any negotiated cattle on the open market. Tim Klein, National Beef's CEO, said the company thinks Winter has a deal to sell his cattle across the street at Cargill. National quit sending cattle buyers to Winter's feedlot after not being able to find animals that met the company's specifications, Klein said. Winter has not called to ask a National buyer to return to his feedlot, according to Klein.

And then Ken Winter describes the buyer from Tyson Foods.

The Tyson buyer always shows up. The Tyson buyer is cordial and always wants to see the show list. The Tyson buyer almost never fails to drive by the pens and eyeball the animals. The Tyson buyer usually submits a bid for cattle, but he submits it after the other meatpackers have submitted theirs. And he almost always submits a bid that is lower.*

For all his activity and his constant presence, the Tyson buyer seems to do everything but buy. Feedlot owners allege that Tyson is just making the rounds to make it appear as if it's competing. When asked about specific instances where Tyson Foods passed up the chance to buy cattle at a certain feedlot, a company spokesman said the cattle weren't appealing to buy, and that the local feedlot owner wasn't willing to sell.

There is another possible reason why a Tyson buyer would take a pass on cattle at independent feedlots like Ken Winter's or Gene Car-

---

* Tyson Foods refused to discuss the behavior of its cattle buyers in Dodge City. The company said that it does "bid competitively on cattle we believe meet our requirements for high quality beef."

son's. To understand that reason, it is helpful to visit a different feedlot, called Ward Feed Yard, about forty miles away from Dodge City. The feed yard is part of a network of feedlots that are nominally independent but which deliver virtually all of their cattle to Tyson under contract. It is an operation that quite possibly reflects the future of cattle production.

Ward Feed Yard does not employ cowboys. Instead, the feed yard has an animal health department, whose employees ride on horseback. The animal health employees roam the massive feedlot grounds, looking for cattle that might be sick, then corralling them for a prescribed regimen of antibiotics or other drugs.

The feed yard also has a feeding department and a maintenance department. While Maverick Feeders employs eleven people, Ward Feed Yard employs fifty. It dwarfs both Maverick and Winter Feed Yard in its scale, covering several square miles of land on two nearby plots.

There weren't any cowboy hats to be seen in Ward Feed Yard's central office on an August afternoon. The boss is Chris Burris, a young man who looks like Matt Damon except a little taller and skinnier, and with the deep-set creases around his eyes that are the natural consequence of long days spent working in the sun. Chris Burris is a graduate of Kansas State University, where he studied animal science. His desk is as neat as a bank officer's, and pictures of his family line a small table near his chair. Burris doesn't talk about crawling into bed with rattlesnakes or putting kills together. He talks about the cattle business with the antiseptic language of an insurance broker. When Burris talks about selling cattle, he quickly slips into a discussion of value-based grids, base prices fixed upon the Kansas Practical Average Price, or top price, and the ongoing effort to capture premiums and maximize profits within a formula grid system.

All of this is a complicated way to describe the closed market that Ward Feed Yard uses to ship thousands of cattle each week to Tyson's slaughterhouses.

In the beginning, Ward Feed Yard aligned itself with Tyson just to survive. The idea was hatched by the company's manager in the late 1980s, a local banker and livestock producer named Lee Borck, a tall man with a booming voice. Borck doesn't favor cowboy hats, but he does wear the thick mustache of a small-town sheriff. Borck doesn't walk into his office with the cocky swagger of a cowboy but with the determined stride of a banker. When Borck saw radical changes were upending the cattle industry in the 1980s, he made sure he was at the front line to reap the benefits from those changes rather than being swept aside.

Borck recognized that as meatpackers consolidated, they needed bigger feed yards to meet their demand. Smaller operations like Ward Feed Yard were getting left behind, and they were getting paid several cents less for every pound of beef they delivered to the meatpackers. Those economics would eventually drive them all out of business.

So Borck pitched an idea to some of his competitors. They could form a partnership and leave the cash market, delivering all their cattle to IBP's new megaplants*. The feed yards agreed, and they formed a cooperative called the Beef Marketing Group. Together, the cooperative delivered the kind of tremendous volume that IBP, now Tyson, needed to stay profitable.

The Beef Marketing Group now includes fourteen feedlots, which operate as one entity in concert with Tyson Foods. The company pays them according to a grid system. Tyson ranks the cattle BMG delivers based on a grid that charts their qualities. A copy of one of Tyson's grid contracts shows the company pays premiums for cattle that are graded as choice beef and imposes discounts for cattle graded as select beef, for example. The grid also penalizes carcasses that weigh less than 500 pounds and more than 1,000 pounds.

The critical part of this grid contract is that it bases its final price on the cash market. If cattle is selling for $1.20 a pound, for example, Tyson will apply all the discounts and premiums of its grid against that price. This means that cattle prices on the shrinking cash market determine the prices for the millions of cattle sold under contract. So people like Ken Winter, who negotiate their cattle, are essentially working to

---

* This was prior to the IBP-Tyson merger.

help contract feeders like Lee Borck derive a price for their animals. But as Lee Borck sells more animals through a closed contract system, it takes that much more oxygen out of the cash market and makes it all the harder to negotiate a higher price.

Over the years, this reality has won Borck the loathing of independent cattle feeders throughout the High Plains. They call his BMG cooperative "the Cartel," and sometimes they call Borck far worse. Borck seems okay with that. He thinks men like Ken Winter are clinging sentimentally to an outdated business model. And Borck has the most powerful entities of the cattle and beef industry behind him. The farm state universities, the livestock and meatpacker lobbyists, the politicians from Kansas and Nebraska, they all point to Lee Borck as a visionary, holding up his contracting arrangement as the inevitable future of the cattle business.

While Borck has been called many things by many people, he cannot be accused of being sentimental. He knows exactly what his arrangement is doing to the industry. It is snuffing out free markets and some smaller producers. Borck thinks the cash market for cattle will eventually disappear altogether. Outside of some niche markets, everyone will align themselves with companies like Tyson and sell cattle under contract. Feedlots will become larger and fewer. Many independent companies will disappear. And Borck knows there will be a cost. Small towns like the one where he was raised near Ward Feed Yard will continue to shrink and disappear. The young residents of rural Kansas will continue to move away to find jobs.

Just because Borck sees the change as inevitable doesn't mean he thinks it's all good. Borck cherishes his upbringing in the town of Larned, Kansas. He thinks farm kids get an unparalleled education about nature, hard work, community, and God. But that way of life is disappearing along with the industries that supported it.

This presents rural Americans with a choice: They can raise food under the kind of system that Tyson embodies, or they can move away in search of a better job. Borck knows what most of them are likely to do: They are going to leave.

"Agriculture is a hard way of life. Nobody ever said it was easy," he said. "You'd be hard-pressed to find one in a thousand people who thinks our rural communities are going to come back and thrive again. People just don't want that.

"It's sad. But it's the truth."

The benefit of this arrangement to Tyson Foods is control over its cattle supply. The company is virtually guaranteed delivery of animals every week, without the hassle of negotiating prices.* And there are other arrangements that can be agreed upon without the hassle of public disclosure. One of those arrangements involved Tyson's little-known use of a growth drug called Zilmax.

Zilmax is a drug that can be mixed into cattle feed during the last month of the animal's life, after it has already been well fattened on corn. The results, by all accounts, are astounding. The animals blow up like muscled balloons. And Zilmax doesn't just make the cattle bigger, it makes them yield far more beef per animal than their peers. But the downsides of Zilmax are also beyond dispute: The amazing growth comes at a cost, and that cost is the quality of the meat, which is why most companies avoid using the drug.

Tyson quietly encouraged the feedlots aligned with it to use Zilmax on their cattle, juicing up the cattle's growth rate and maximizing the yield of beef at its slaughterhouses.

Because Tyson works directly with its contract producers in a closed system, the company could quietly and rapidly push the use of Zilmax into feed yards without worrying about the pushback that might emerge if it tried to do the same thing with independent cattle feeders. To get the same cooperation from independent feeders like Ken Winter or Gene Carson, Tyson would have to advertise publicly its use of Zilmax, at least by word of mouth to its buyers.

---

* Ward Feed Yard's contract allows the company to sell its cattle to meatpackers other than Tyson if Ward's managers are unhappy with the deal they get. But it appears that clause does not get used, and virtually all of the feed yard's cattle go to Tyson every week.

Zilmax seemed to be the perfect drug to bend cattle's physiology toward the needs of Tyson's grid contracts. The grids encourage high yields and maximize the amount of beef that Tyson can sell for each animal it kills. So does Zilmax. But there are reasons Zilmax isn't widely used. Zilmax-inflated steaks are less tender and it decreases the fat marbling that makes for a juicy steak. The meat is leaner and cheaper to produce. It's more like chicken, in other words.

Within the beef industry, there has been strong pushback against the use of Zilmax. Cattle ranchers have tried to distinguish beef from chicken by making it higher quality and stamping it with branded measures of flavor, like the Certified Angus brand. Zilmax undermines that trend and pushes beef toward the middle range of quality. In 2008, the man in charge of the Certified Angus Beef marketing campaign came out publicly against the use of Zilmax. As president of the Certified Angus Beef brand, it was John Stika's job to ensure that beef was produced at a certain level of quality. An industry group launched the Certified Angus Beef brand in 1978 to set beef apart from chicken and pork, making beef a premium product. Stika sent an open letter to the popular trade magazine *Beef*, warning about Zilmax's use. He said using the drug reflected "a 'pounds first' heap of indifference to quality."

For these reasons, meatpackers like Cargill backed away from Zilmax. But the drug was a perfect match for Tyson's needs. It helped the company deliver high volumes of consistent meat to big customers like Wal-Mart and McDonald's. Cheapness has become one of the most desired traits of beef in the age of fast-food dollar menus and Hamburger Helper.

Eventually, the use of Zilmax followed a familiar pattern: The business practices of Tyson Foods became the industry norm. Cargill finally caved in and decided to accept cattle treated with Zilmax in mid-2012. The company felt that with so many feedlots using Zilmax, it wasn't practical to refuse to accept cattle treated with it. By the time Cargill folded, the other two big meatpackers, JBS and National Beef, had also followed Tyson's lead.

Independent feedlot owners also felt increasing pressure to use Zilmax. Allan Sents, co-owner of McPherson County Feeders in Kansas, had resisted using the drug for years. But by the end of 2012, he felt like he had to. Sents sold a lot of his cattle to National Beef, and many of the animals were priced under a grid contract. A key part of that grid graded Sents's cattle based on how much meat was on each carcass when compared to the average carcass slaughtered at the plant. In other words, his cattle were put into a kind of tournament against other cattle at the slaughterhouse, with the winning price going to the cattle that had the most meat on their bones. As more feedlots beefed up their cattle with Zilmax, Sents felt pressure to do so as well. His cattle were being discounted because he wasn't using the growth drug. The rise of Zilmax was all but inevitable, thanks to the economic forces Tyson Foods helped unleash, and the industry is still dealing with the fallout. In August of 2013, Tyson Foods sent out a letter to feedlot operators saying it would not accept Zilmax-treated cattle "until further notice." The letter said Zilmax might be causing paralysis in some cattle, and rendering others unable to walk. Tyson didn't share the evidence on which it based these concerns, leaving feedlot owners and consumers to puzzle out how safe the drug might really be.

The age of the Zilmax sirloin points to the broader changes that contract cattle production has helped bring about. Tyson has finally managed to tame the cattle herd. And by doing so, it has largely completed its project of chickenizing the meat industry. There are still some holdouts in the cattle business, the Ken Winters and Gene Carsons of the world, but the tide of money is inexorably moving toward the contract operations like Lee Borck's.

While Tyson has been the architect of this system, the driving force behind it has been the American consumer. Americans have decided that meat must be cheap and plentiful. It must be consistent in its attributes and predictable in its taste. It takes factory farms to raise meat like that. It takes companies like Tyson. It takes networks of chicken farmers integrated tightly with big slaughterhouses like the one in Waldron. It takes a steady flow of genetically selected pigs from the nursery in Holdenville, Oklahoma, that are shipped to contract farms in Iowa for raising. It requires massive feedlots, controlled by contracts, that can guarantee a nonstop supply of cattle. The system also requires the rules that Tyson has imposed. This is what delivers the cheap pork chop, the Zilmax-infused hamburger patty, and the ever-ready supply of chicken McNuggets.

Billions of dollars flow into the industrial meat system each year, helping further entrench the system as the new way of doing business in rural America.

The changes already wrought by this system are seen as irreversible by many in the industry.

There doesn't seem to be any force powerful enough to stop this transformation. But some people have tried.

CHAPTER 10

The Food Dictatorship

(1994–2006)

U.S. ANTITRUST authorities mostly stood idle over the last forty years, as industrial meat producers like Tyson Foods extinguished open markets, bought up competitors, and replaced a vibrant livestock industry with a centrally controlled system dominated by a handful of meat companies. But that's not to say there hasn't been any resistance to the rise of the meat oligarchy.

There have been a few notable fights in which regulators have tried to slow the tide of vertical integration. These efforts show why it is so hard to stem the power of industrial meat producers. But they also show how even a single state regulator, if properly motivated, can foster competition and curb the worst abuses of big meat companies by simply taking action.

The biggest fight of all was waged out of Iowa, the nation's strongest farm state, the land of cheap corn and soybeans. In the mid-1990s, Iowa Attorney General Tom Miller launched a fight against vertically integrated meat production that ended up encompassing more than a dozen states and went all the way to Washington, D.C., and the halls of Congress.

But the legal and intellectual resistance to vertical integration didn't start with Tom Miller. Decades before Miller ever filed a legal challenge in Iowa, a small group of intellectuals started to sound warnings about what they saw happening in rural America, as companies like Tyson Foods began signing up farmers under contract. The warnings of these academics were summarily ignored by most experts and the broader public, but, looking back, the alarms seem remarkably prescient. While antitrust regulators in Washington were looking the other way, some people were closely studying the economic and social effects of industrial meat production as it became more powerful.

In the late 1960s, one of those people was a young researcher named Bill Heffernan. As a near-penniless graduate student, Heffernan logged an ungodly number of miles traveling the back roads of Louisiana. Heffernan was driving from chicken farm to chicken farm in the rural backcountry, laying the groundwork for a new research project. It was a study that he undertook in 1969, and it took him only about thiry-one years to complete. In the end, Heffernan and his colleagues produced a body of work that shows exactly why lawmakers should step in to correct a market that is no longer capable of correcting itself.

Heffernan's research was based in the rural area of Union Parish in Louisiana, where a booming poultry industry was expanding in the 1960s. Vertically integrated poultry production was still a radical concept back then, and Heffernan wanted to study it. So he undertook an effort that no one else seems to have duplicated. He went door to door, made phone calls, and drove hundreds of miles between farms. He surveyed farmers and documented their income and their debt. Crucially, he followed up with farmers in Union Parish every ten years until the turn of the century, building a dataset that was forty years deep.

But Heffernan did something more than ask about money. He did something most agricultural economists never thought of doing: He asked the farmers how they felt. He asked them, decade after decade, how much they trusted the companies they worked for and how well they were treated. In doing this, Heffernan assembled a picture that most economists missed. He tracked the relationship between the powerful and the powerless.

There was one reason that Heffernan asked these questions, when almost no one else was asking them. It was because he had read an arcane little book with an impenetrable title, called: *Individual Freedom and the Economic Organization of Agriculture.*

This book was written in 1965 by Harold F. Breimyer, a brilliant government economist who helped draft some of the earliest U.S. farm policies back in the 1930s. By the mid-1960s, Breimyer was starting to get worried about the American food system. For Breimyer, farms were more than just food factories. Like Thomas Jefferson, Breimyer saw farms as a way for families to own businesses and control their financial destiny. He considered the patchwork of independent farms to be the foundation of a democracy wherein people were free in both political and economic terms. By the mid-1960s, that patchwork was being torn apart as companies like Tyson Foods built networks of contract farms in the South.

Breimyer wrestled with questions that few others pondered: If farms became nothing more than food factories, would farmers become modern-era serfs? If the food industry consolidated, would rural economies become servants to big corporations that were funded by Wall Street capital? Would Americans have any say over how their food was produced?

Breimyer ended his book with a warning. He said vertical integration alone wasn't a problem, but it would become toxic if companies like Tyson were allowed to buy their competitors and gain broad market power. To use the language of an economist: he said the real danger lay in the convergence of vertical and horizontal integration.* His warning was almost quaint, in retrospect. He predicted that each region of the country might be dominated by an oligarchy of just four or five big poultry companies. Even Breimyer didn't imagine that just two companies would control almost half the national chicken market between them by 2011.

It would take more than thirty years, but Heffernan was able to document, in his decades-long study of Union Parish, Louisiana, what would happen when Breimyer's warning came to pass. Union Parish turned out to be a perfect microcosm of the national poultry industry. In 1969 four big poultry companies were doing business there. Two of them were locally owned. The companies competed for farmers, so the

---

* Horizontal integration happens when one company buys another and expands its reach across a market.

growers had a decent chance of signing on with a new company if one dropped them. These farmers responded to Heffernan's questionnaires with a marked enthusiasm about their business. A full 87 percent said the chicken company they did business with was either a good or very good business partner. A full 93 percent said they liked the people they met during work. Just 11 percent said they could find a better job.

Over the next thirty years, a wave of consolidation swept through Union Parish, just as it did in the rest of the country. Local companies went out of business or were bought. By the 1980s and 1990s, only one poultry company did business in Union Parish: ConAgra. By 1999, a company called Randall Foods built a second plant near the parish and gave some farmers a choice between two firms.

Heffernan documented the social and economic corrosion that this consolidation wrought. By 1999, just 47 percent of farmers said the company they did business with was good or very good. Now 40 percent said they could find a better job. Less than half said they would want their children to take over. Just 69 percent were happy with their success at work, down from 91 percent in 1981. Farmers reported that their contract terms got shorter with each passing year. In 1969 the contracts were often good for seven to ten years. By 1999 many of those contracts were extended only on a flock-to-flock basis.

In short, the Union Parish chicken farmers of 1969 sounded a lot like Iowa hog farmers in the 1990s. They gave up some independence to raise animals under contract, but they were generally treated well by the company with which they worked. They felt secure with their ten-year contracts. By 2000, things had changed. The Union Parish farmers sounded more like the Tyson Foods farmers around Waldron, Arkansas. They were frustrated and largely powerless. The difference between these two scenarios didn't seem to hinge upon economics alone but upon power. The chicken business became more profitable between 1969 and 2000, yet chicken farmers became worse off. It seemed to have more to do with the concentration of power than with the laws of supply and demand.

Perhaps more disturbing was the impact that consolidation had on the broader economy of Union Parish. Agricultural profits rose stratospherically over the decades, yet the county remained wracked by poverty. The money wasn't staying in the communities that earned it.

Heffernan became a professor of rural sociology at the University of Missouri. And during his career there he gained membership in a very small group of academics who spent their careers studying the concentration of power in agriculture. Heffernan, like many of these thinkers, spent about forty years publishing paper after paper warning about the effects of a rapidly consolidating food industry, and he was mostly ignored. Heffernan would get a little red in the face when people got him talking about the CR4, for example. The CR4 is a metric that shows how much of the marketplace is controlled by the top four companies in an industry. For decades, Heffernan carefully documented the uninterrupted rise of the CR4 in agriculture. When it came to the chicken business, Heffernan didn't even need the CR4. He could cite the CR2 (or the "CR-*Two!*" as Heffernan might exclaim in a typical exchange), which had reached nearly 50 percent with the rise of Tyson Foods and Pilgrim's Pride. But nobody seemed to care. Food was readily available and relatively cheap, and that seemed to be all that mattered.

Heffernan's forty-year-long study of Union Parish, though never published widely, was a blueprint for the new power structure of industrial meat production. And by the 1990s, many of Heffernan's and Breimyer's scariest predictions were coming to pass. Heffernan and Breimyer ultimately remained obscure figures, but as their predictions began to come true across rural America regulators started to notice and farmers started to fight back.

And the battle would be centered in the unlikely state of Iowa.

The Iowa Capitol Building in Des Moines is a magisterial edifice atop a hill facing downtown. It has broad marble columns and a gleaming dome gilded with 23-karat gold. The architecture reflects the quiet dignity of a state that for generations reaped a steady fortune from its fertile fields, built on the values of hard work and a strong civil society.

Then there's the Hoover Building next door. It looks like a giant cinder block that was carelessly dropped in the middle of a parking lot, with a few dark windows carved into its side. The architects must have been looking to evoke the spirit of heartless bureaucracy as they traced its harsh right angles and decided its hallways should be painted in drab, institutional beige and its floors lined with linoleum tile.

This is where Eric Tabor reported to work after he was hired at the state's attorney general's office in 1995. Tabor was born and raised on an Iowa farm, and he carried himself with the taciturn demeanor common to men who live off the land in isolated towns and measure their words carefully before speaking. Tall and rangy, Tabor kept his bright red hair close-cropped and wore subdued suits to the office. He wasn't a flamboyant attorney; he had a diligence and work ethic that came from helping his father mind cattle and raise crops. Still new on the job, Tabor walked toward the fortresslike Hoover Building, past the sand-filled cylinders where the state workers took regular smoke breaks, and pushed open the glass doors to walk inside. A series of framed political cartoons hangs along the hallway on the way to the elevators in the Hoover Building, drawn during the 1930s by one of Iowa's most famous political cartoonists. The pictures were rendered at a time when food politics were still a viscerally contentious issue in American life, particularly in Iowa, where farming provided most of the state's economic life. One cartoon shows President Herbert Hoover, an Iowa native, with a shotgun. The words "Food Dictatorship" are etched down the barrel of the gun. A weeping farmer is imploring Hoover to shoot the family dog, which is sitting there obliviously happy, with the title "American Habit of Extravagance" written on its furry back. Next to the dog is a dish with food scraps on it, titled: "Food Waste."

When Hoover was president, the concept of a "food dictatorship" was a contentious issue in the Midwest. The government was debating, and later passed, an unprecedented series of quotas and production guidelines to directly control the agricultural economy. The efforts were seen as a critical bailout to protect middle-class farmers who were still a considerable voting bloc in those days, and who relied on steady market prices to stay in business. The central planning of agriculture didn't end for nearly sixty years, and the government was still spending billions a year to prop up farms when Tabor took his job at the Iowa attorney general's office.

Food politics was still an emotional issue in Iowa in the 1990s, but it was dominated by worries over a different kind of dictatorship. Driven in part by government subsidies to big farms, the business of American food production became more consolidated than at any point in history. Just a few giant grain merchant corporations, like Archer Daniels Midland and Cargill, sat in the middle of the U.S. grain trade. The poultry industry was controlled by Tyson and a few of its smaller competitors, while the pork and cattle industries were moving in that direction. The biotechnology company Monsanto was quickly taking control of the seed industry through its patents on genetically modified crops, which were widely planted.

Nobody really seemed to care about this in America. Food was cheap, and that's all that mattered. But in Iowa, food politics still mattered. Farming was the last anchor of middle-class life throughout much of the state, and the state jealously guarded its food economy after the farm crisis and recession of the 1980s. Factories could close their doors and ship jobs overseas, but farming had to stay where the soil was. And the richest soil in the world was in Iowa. Farming supported more than just farmers. It paid for the schools, police, and Main Street businesses of Iowa's towns.

Tabor knew as well as anyone what farming meant to Iowans. Farm income had put him through college at the state university and paid for him to study law at Harvard. He returned from Harvard Law to help his father run the family's cattle operation, and eventually he earned his law degree from the University of Iowa. Farming wasn't just a way to raise food, in Tabor's eyes, but a way to keep money flowing to the middle class and to rural America.

It was only fitting that Tom Miller, Iowa's attorney general, hired Tabor to oversee the office's farm division. In Iowa, this was the equivalent of regulating Wall Street. Tabor would be one of the top regulators overseeing massive companies that now dominated the farm economy. When Tabor was still new on the job, Attorney General Miller told him he should look into a curious new practice that was becoming more common in Iowa: contract farming.

In 1980, only about 2 percent of Iowa's hogs were raised under contract. The rest were raised by independent farmers who sold their animals on an open cash market to the highest bidder. In 1995, the share of hogs grown under contract had grown tenfold, to 20 percent. By 1998 it would double again to 40 percent, and by 2011 well over 70 percent of all hogs would be raised under contract. But even in 1995, 20 percent of hogs being raised under contract seemed a breathtakingly high percentage to regulators and farmers in the state. More companies each month were entering the state and offering contract arrangements to farmers, promising steady income and less risk if they gave up their independence.

Bad stories were starting to spread from farm to farm about contract farming. Out-of-state companies often wrote agreements in complex language, with loopholes that left farmers powerless and shifted most of the farm profits to the companies. Miller explained that these contracts were apparently becoming common to raise turkeys, chickens, and even hogs.

— I want you to look into it, Miller said.

Tabor said he would assign some attorneys to explore the matter. Without knowing it, Miller had launched a battle that would last more than a decade, pitting the attorney general's office against the nation's biggest meat companies. The courtroom battle would center on Smithfield Foods, one of Tyson's biggest competitors. But the fight drew in Tyson and every other meat producer, and it was a battle that ranged from Iowa to North Dakota to Capitol Hill in Washington, D.C. Smithfield might have been the main target of Tom Miller's litigation, but it was clear that the effort could ultimately affect the entire national meat industry.

When Tabor looked for someone to investigate contract farming, his staff attorney Steve Moline was an obvious choice. Hogs had put Steve

Moline through college. Then, when he decided he didn't want to follow his father into farming, hogs had put Moline through law school.

Where Tabor was cautious and reserved, Moline was boisterous, blunt, and slightly profane. He also had a good relationship with several offices of attorneys general around the country. During the 1990s, Moline worked the phones, querying attorneys in the major farm states. What he heard created a disturbing picture of modern contract farming.

Moline heard from attorneys general throughout the South that contract farming completely dominated the chicken business. There wasn't an open market on which chicken farmers could sell their birds, so they were forced to enter contractual arrangements with big companies like Tyson to stay in business. Without an open market, and just a few "integrators" with which to do business, chicken farmers lost all bargaining power when they signed contracts. Complaints were pouring into state attorneys, who heard horror stories about farmers having their contracts canceled for nothing more than refusing to toe the company line.

When he reported back to Tabor, Moline's verdict on contract farming, at least in southern states, was unambiguous.

— It's just a titch over serfdom! Moline said. There's a sword right over your throat.

These contracts were similar to the ones being offered to Iowa's hog farmers. Perhaps more disturbing, Moline learned that companies were taking over ownership of the farrowing operations and contracting farmers to fatten the adult pigs at feeder farms. Having raised hogs ever since he was a kid, Moline knew that the industry's profits were locked up in the animal's genetics. To own the breeding herds was to own the most profitable part of the business, and corporations were rapidly taking them over. That would leave Iowa farmers with the lowest-yielding part of the business: fattening up the adult hogs. Farmers were basically becoming babysitters for outside companies.

It seemed far-fetched to think that hog farmers might one day be as powerless as chicken farmers in the South. But the number of contract operations in Iowa was growing by the day. And Moline had heard about what contract farming had done in the South.

— We don't want it here, he said.

The only thing that put Moline's mind at ease was the knowledge that Iowa farmers still had choices. There was competition. If a farmer didn't like the terms of a contract, he could walk away. In the chicken business, the independent cash market for chickens had effectively disappeared. But Iowa farmers could still sell their animals at the network of roadside sales stations. With a free market with which to compete, Moline didn't think companies could get too out of hand with the contract terms they imposed.

Things changed after the hog market crash of 1998, which wiped out so many independent farmers. And it was just around that time that Steve Moline started to entertain a series of unusual houseguests. When Moline came home from work as a staff attorney in the Iowa attorney general's office, he made sure his wife and kids were occupied, and then he waited for his guests to arrive.

They were hog producers, all of them, grown men with an independent streak who had decided to stick it out in an increasingly tough farming business. In spite of the grit they showed in other aspects of their life, the men approached Moline's house like furtive children, worried they might be spotted by authorities. They called Moline at his office and told him they wanted to talk but didn't want to meet at their farms. They were worried Moline might be spotted by one of the hog company field technicians who drove from farm to farm. The farmers were even too worried to arrive at Moline's office in Des Moines to meet with him, out of fear they might be seen there. Moline's solution was to invite them into his home. He sat with them at his kitchen table, or when the weather was nice they sat on his screened-in porch. Moline offered his guests hot coffee, and after a few sips they opened up, unburdening themselves.

Things had changed in the Iowa hog business. After the price collapse of 1998, big contractors had gained the upper hand. Farmers told him a variety of horror stories, recounting the ways big companies were driving them to the edge of bankruptcy now that the farmers had invested hundreds of thousands in their hog barns.

Big meat companies were shifting the risk of doing business down to the community level. They gave farmers new agreements called "ledger" contracts that kept a tally of whether the pigs were sold at a profit or at a loss. If the pigs were sold at a loss, the farmer still got paid. But the value of the meatpacker's loss was recorded on a ledger, and the farmer was obligated to pay it back. Some farmers racked up losses so high that they could never feasibly repay them. Companies were burying farmers in debt to cover their losses in the marketplace.

Other farmers told Moline that companies were paying them under a tournament system, ranking their performance against their neighbors'. They were convinced companies delivered them sick pigs, just to drive down their income because the farmer had been too argumentative.

Moline listened, but there was little more he could do. Being a farm boy himself, Moline knew how hard it was to prove whether one batch of pigs was healthier than another, especially after they had been sitting on a farm for a few weeks.

He tried to explain to his visitors, almost apologetically, that there was little the attorney general's office could do to help them. Suing big meat companies was never easy, and they would need near-airtight cases to do it.

— The proof problems are a monster, from a legal point of view, he told them.

But there were other means at Moline's disposal. He toured the state, visiting small towns and talking at meetings hosted by farming groups. Moline told his audiences that hog contracts were becoming more heavy-handed, even "egregious" and "unconscionable." He advised farmers not to enter into contracts with the kinds of provisions that were hurting those already in the business, and he publicized what he saw as the worst abuses in the industry.

At his office, Moline started getting angry calls from hog producers and field technicians who felt like he was interfering in their business. It didn't bother him. Moline knew Tabor and the attorney general supported what he was doing.

Moline also knew there was still one critical protection that kept companies like Tyson and Smithfield from gaining too much power. A 1975 law banned meatpackers in Iowa from owning their own animals. The old state statute broke the most critical link in a chain of vertical integration: If companies couldn't own both slaughterhouses and farms, they couldn't gain complete control over the marketplace.

Because of Iowa's corporate farming law, called a "packer ban," companies like Tyson and Smithfield could not sign up contract farmers in the state as long as they owned the slaughterhouses.

That left the field open to IBP, which bought its hogs under formula contracts; and to Murphy Farms, a smaller company based in North Carolina that copied the Tyson Foods playbook by building a network of contract hog farms in Iowa. By 1999, Murphy Farms was raising about 900,000 pigs under contract in Iowa.

But with the packer ban in place, the full circle of vertical integration was kept from closing. And the worst practices were kept at bay.

In September 1999, Moline was driving home when he heard the news on the radio: Smithfield Foods, the nation's biggest hog producer, had just purchased Murphy Farms. With the inking of one deal, a huge portion of Iowa's hog farming sector had been swallowed under Smithfield's control.

Moline couldn't believe what he'd heard. Smithfield had just blatantly violated Iowa's ban on vertical integration. The company knew full well the ban was in place and would prohibit it from buying Murphy Farms, yet it had gone ahead with the deal anyway.

Moline called Bob Malloy, a local lawyer who represented Murphy Farms, whom Moline had known for years.

— Bob, you're violating the law! Moline said.

Malloy was unmovable.

— I don't think we are, Malloy replied.

— We'll have to see about that, Moline said, before hanging up.

Iowa was about to wage the nation's biggest legal fight against vertically integrated meat production. That fight would eventually spill over and affect other companies, from Tyson to Cargill and Hormel.

The matter seemed clear-cut to Iowa Attorney General Tom Miller. Smithfield had simply ignored Iowa law when it bought Murphy Farms. The company was essentially saying that the state government had no role in writing the rules of the livestock industry. The ban on vertical integration was meaningless. If Smithfield had the money to close the deal, that's apparently all that mattered.

Moline and Tabor worked the phones and talked with Smithfield's attorneys. The company wasn't going to back down. It owned the biggest network of contract farms in Iowa, and it was going to run them how it wanted.

Tom Miller and his attorneys felt they almost had no choice. They sued Smithfield for violating Iowa's packer ban. The nation's biggest farming state sent a warning to all the major hog producers: Iowa's hog farmers weren't going to be sucked into a vertically integrated system. Not without a fight.

Joe Luter, the Smithfield Foods CEO, walked down the narrow path between office cubicles in Tom Miller's office in the Hoover Building. Luter was flanked by his well-paid attorneys, and he had come at the invitation of the attorney general.

Luter carried himself with the broad-shouldered air of someone who had just won a prizefight. And in many ways, he had. Luter joined Smithfield Foods just out of college and worked his way up through the company from his beginning in the sales department. Luter ushered Smithfield through a revolutionary period when it copied the model laid out by Tyson Foods, building a network of contract hog farms from scratch. By the time the company bought

Murphy Farms, Smithfield was big, rich, and seemingly too powerful to fight.

Miller greeted Luter and his lawyers and the men stepped inside Miller's office. They sat down at a small conference table and were joined by Eric Tabor and Steve Moline. If Luter was at all intimidated by the attorney general's lawsuit, he didn't show it. He sat down in his chair as if he owned the building. Miller sat across from him. With his white hair, thin face, and somewhat gaunt complexion, Miller could resemble an aging high-school principal more than a courtroom brawler. He tended to sit back and listen. That was good, because Luter didn't give him much time to talk.

Shortly after the meeting started, Luter interrupted his lawyers, looked at the attorney general, and began to school him in the realities of modern agriculture.

— You have to understand what's going on in this industry, Luter said.

Luter explained how vertically integrated chicken production had changed everything. The rise of cheap chicken put pressure on every other kind of meat, driving pork and beef off fast-food menus and the family dinner plate. That was reality, Luter said. If the pork industry didn't respond, it would shrink to obsolescence. The only way to compete with chicken was to imitate it. The evolution was unstoppable, and Iowa's ban on vertical integration was irrelevant. The transformation was going to happen regardless. The litigation, in other words, was pointless.

— We don't want the chickenization of the meat counter. We want to make sure hogs and cattle have a place, Luter said.

Luter was suggesting that Tom Miller should drop his lawsuit. It wasn't accomplishing anything but hurting Iowa's farmers. And it wasn't going to stop Smithfield, Tyson, or anyone else from taking over the hog industry.

— We've got to work together, Luter said.

Moline was stunned. He looked at Luter's attorneys, who seemed to be mortified by their client's lecture. Moline guessed they had advised Luter to stay quiet during the meeting but had failed to rein him in.

Attorney General Miller wasn't accustomed to corporate executives telling him how to interpret Iowa law, or which laws he ought to enforce.

After Luter left, Miller and his attorneys went over the meeting. It appeared to them the southern meat executives were accustomed to acting like bullies, whether dealing with farmers, regulators, or state officials.

In spite of Luter's bluster, they knew he didn't have leverage over them. His dire predictions about the collapse of the hog industry didn't hold water with Moline and Tabor. Iowa had the corn, and Smithfield needed it.

No matter how much money companies like Smithfield or Tyson saved by building farms in Oklahoma, Arkansas, or North Carolina, those savings were outweighed by the extra cost of shipping corn and soybeans there. In the race to win control of the hog market, the companies had no choice but to operate in Iowa.

Moline and Tabor returned to their offices, and they pressed ahead full steam on the case against Smithfield.

The lawsuit against Smithfield turned out to be far more complicated than just trying to enforce the packer ban. By prohibiting vertical integration, the attorney general's office was essentially suing Smithfield over the company's business model. So Smithfield just cleverly changed its business model, without really changing it, and let the lawsuit try to catch up to it.

At one point, Smithfield's new Murphy Farms division simply transferred the ownership of all its hogs to a man named Randall Stoecker.

Murphy sold all 900,000 of its pigs to Stoecker for about $79 million. Stoecker was hardly a millionaire, so Murphy loaned him the entire amount he needed. Stoecker didn't have to put a penny down. Then Murphy set up a company called Stoecker Farms Inc., and he was then able to argue in court that it did not in fact own any livestock in Iowa. So the state's ban on vertical integration didn't apply.

Attorney General Miller sued over the transaction, calling ?
sham. So Murphy shifted ownership again to a member of the
pany's board.

The whole case continued in this way. Steve Moline would sit in a conference room with Smithfield officials and question them about their company's operations.

He was convinced that after the questioning, the officials would huddle in the hallway with their attorneys and make calls back to headquarters, relaying orders on how to change the company to evade legal challenges.

All the while, Smithfield's business was running ahead full tilt in the state, with hundreds of thousands of hogs being raised for the company under contract.

Tom Miller and Eric Tabor felt they needed to do something bigger. A lawsuit wasn't enough. In September 2000, Miller unveiled a new law called the Producer Protection Act. It was by far the most stringent law ever proposed to constrain the power of companies like Tyson and Smithfield.

The act banned companies from making their contracts with farmers confidential. Miller wanted to post the contracts on his website, creating a transparent market for the rules of production. The act also banned companies from retaliating against farmers who complained or tried to join an organization like a growers' union. It protected farmers who talked back, in other words. The act also gave farmers the right to cancel any contract within three days of signing it, giving a lawyer plenty of time to look over the terms.

Miller enlisted fifteen other state attorneys general to support the Producer Protection Act. Not surprisingly, Tyson's home state of Arkansas did not join, but several important farm states supported the bill, from Nebraska to Missouri, Oklahoma, and Wisconsin.

By pushing vertical integration into Iowa, Smithfield had invited a fight that threatened to change the economic order of the meat industry throughout much of the Midwest.

Eric Tabor took the stage at a Marriott hotel in suburban Kansas City. was feeling good. This was his moment. There was broad momentum behind what he was doing, and Tabor decided to let loose and have some fun.

It was May 10, 2000. The hotel was packed with farmers from around the Midwest and regulators from Washington, D.C. Even the secretary of agriculture, Dan Glickman, was on hand. The U.S. Department of Agriculture was hosting the event, which carried the grandiose title "Visions for the Millennium." Perhaps more important, the conference was attended by senior leaders of a USDA agency called GIPSA*, the nation's top antitrust enforcer over meat companies.

For Tabor, the event signified that federal regulators had finally joined the campaign, started in Iowa, to curb meatpacker power.

Farm-state politicians and activists were berating the Democratic administration of President Bill Clinton to take action. The urgency of the issue was stoked by the upcoming presidential election. The Democratic candidate, Vice President Al Gore, faced a growing challenge from the longtime consumer advocate Ralph Nader. Nader was unequivocal in his opposition to industrial meat production and the rise of factory farms. Clinton's administration needed to look like it was doing something about it.

In this increasingly tense environment, Eric Tabor was given a rare public chance to be the good guy. Iowa had gone further than any other state in combating the rise of corporate agribusiness, and Tabor was invited to the Kansas City forum to outline what Iowa regulators were doing.

Tom Miller was attacking corporate meat production from two angles: through litigation and the creation of new laws. The lawsuit against Smithfield, filed just a few months earlier, threatened to upend the creeping vertical integration of the hog industry. At the same time, Miller was pressing for the passage of the Producer Protection Act in sixteen states, which would limit how much power companies like Tyson and Smithfield could wield over farmers.

Tabor was comfortable onstage at the Marriott hotel. He'd had a

---

* The Grain Inspection, Packers and Stockyards Administration, to be exact.

brief career in politics before joining the attorney general's office. He knew how to give a campaign speech. Tabor looked out over the crowd of upturned heads and realized these people were on his side. Rural Americans were counting on their government to do something, and Iowa was doing it.

Tabor started talking about the risks of contract farming and the power grab that was under way in Iowa's hog industry. Well-funded companies were taking over more of the market every day, driving out independent farmers and rewriting the rules of production. Some of the same companies already dominated the chicken business, where they kept farmers on the edge of bankruptcy. Now they wanted to impose that reality on cattle and hog producers. Tabor wound the crowd up with a series of rhetorical questions, in the best tradition of a pulse-quickening stump speech. He asked them: Why should these companies have the power to write the rules of rural America?

— What's wrong with growers having the right to organize? he asked incredulously. Regulators needed to step in, on both the state and federal level, to protect rural communities.

— Why shouldn't we do this?

The crowd was eating out of Tabor's hand by the end of his speech. Afterward, Tabor mingled with attorneys and officials from the USDA, and he met farmers who were hopeful the conference marked a turning point in the age of consolidation.

The wind was at Tabor's back, and the federal government was on his side. A new era of change seemed just around the corner.

Not everyone who heard Tabor's speech was moved. A man named James R. Baker sat quietly in the audience, taking it all in. Baker was the senior administrator of GIPSA, the antitrust regulator that was created before the Great Depression specifically to regulate U.S. meat companies. If anyone in the nation had authority to rein in the power of companies like Tyson, it was Baker.

Baker was sitting with Greg Page, a senior executive at Cargill Inc., the agribusiness conglomerate that was fast becoming one of the nation's most powerful meat companies. Page oversaw Cargill's beef division, and he was named the company's chief operating officer that year.*

Page was skeptical about Tabor's pitch for tougher regulations, and he told Baker as much.

— Who's it actually going to benefit? Page asked.

— I don't understand, Baker replied.

Page explained to Baker that tough rules in Iowa would hinder the industry. In Page's view, contract farming and vertical integration were essential pillars of the modern food business. The food system just wouldn't work without them. Page knew that Cargill had a team of salespeople roaming around Japan, looking to sell big shipments of American beef. Those salespeople needed to know that the supply of beef would be there when it came time to deliver, and signing long-term contracts was the best way to ensure a steady supply. The system also worked well for farmers, Page believed. How could a young farmer in Iowa get a big bank loan to build a factory farm if the farmer didn't have a contract to sell their animals? The contracts provided stability. Page thought that tough regulations on contract farming in Iowa could probably just end up pushing business across state lines into places that were friendlier to corporations.

— It kind of closes the door on wanting to go there and do business, Page explained.

Baker didn't need much convincing. He was a cattleman and banker from central Arkansas who favored wearing a cowboy hat even in Washington, D.C. He was familiar with the poultry industry and big meatpacking companies, and he tended to think they operated best when left alone. Government rules just impeded the natural functioning of the market. Tabor's efforts in Iowa, and the parallel efforts in Washington, D.C., and other states, were a bridge too far for Baker.

"Don't get away from the free enterprise system," Baker said later about Tabor's speech. "You start infringing on it with regulations like that."

---

* Page would later become CEO, in 2007. He still held that title in 2012.

Baker was nearing the end of his tenure as head of GIPSA. He served during an era in which the nation's top regulatory regime closely matched his fondness for an untrammeled free market. Big companies were allowed to merge with other big companies, creating an agribusiness industry that was almost unprecedented in its level of concentration.

IBP, for example, had been allowed to swallow its competitors at a rate that left just four beef companies controlling more than 80 percent of the market. Baker had no problem with this. To understand why, it is helpful to understand the origins of the antitrust agency he headed.

GIPSA gained its authority over meat companies from a law called the Packers and Stockyards Act, which was passed in 1921. The act was passed with the goal of breaking up the "meat trust," a collection of five companies that controlled about 85 percent of the market (a lesser degree of concentration than existed in 2000).

Back in the 1920s, meat production was a contentious political issue. A federal investigation found that the companies had gained so much power over the food system that they were defrauding consumers and farmers alike.

Meatpackers could do this because of their economically enviable position right in the center of the food business, buying cattle from the farmer and selling fresh meat to the consumer. By locking up control over this pressure point in the system, the meat trust was able to manipulate prices on both ends. They underpaid the farmer and overcharged the consumer. As a result, meat prices were climbing, and farm incomes were declining.

Corporations abused their power in a number of industries, such as oil and railroads, but the meat business raised problems that were all its own. Meat was seen as a necessity. People couldn't live without it. Many families felt that eating meat, and feeding it to their kids, was the best and cheapest way to get protein. And meat was a historical part of the American diet. People didn't feel that companies should be able to drive up prices at will and control the supply.

To combat the meat trust, Congress founded the Packers and Stockyards Administration, which based its authority on a very old body of regulations called antitrust laws, so named because they were passed to combat the power of "trusts," like John Rockefeller's Standard Oil Company. Perhaps more than any other body of U.S. law, antitrust regulations seek to limit corporate power. The animating idea behind the laws is that corporations can get so big that they start to distort, and ultimately destroy, the free market forces that support capitalism.

There's a lot of misunderstanding about what antitrust laws do. The laws don't necessarily ban being big. Antitrust laws recognize that, sometimes, concentration of power is a good thing. Having more companies running railroads doesn't necessarily provide better railroad service, for example. Businesses can get more efficient when they consolidate. Companies that get bigger can do things more cheaply because of economies of scale. And if companies can do things cheaply, they can pass those savings on to consumers.

What antitrust laws aimed to do was set down a list of rules to make sure big companies didn't choke out competition. For example, there's nothing wrong with four companies controlling the supply of beef in the United States. The problem comes if those four companies get together and make a deal among themselves to keep their prices high. The bigness itself isn't the problem. The anticompetitive behavior is the problem.

This is the rationale that James Baker deployed as head of the Packers and Stockyards Administration during the 1990s. It didn't alarm him that the industry was becoming more concentrated than ever. What mattered was the specific behavior of the few big companies that were left in control of meat production. As long as those companies didn't violate the specific rules that aimed to keep competition fair, there was nothing wrong with consolidation. The meat industry was expected to behave itself.

Meat industry lobbyists aren't brash. They aren't even that confrontational. Steve Moline knew he'd never get a threatening call from a meat lobbyist. They were too good for that. If people that powerful wanted to do something to you, you didn't see it coming. You woke up, and it was all over.

Tom Miller's Producer Protection Act initially got a warm reception in the Iowa legislature. It was one of those bills that seemed hard to argue against. It shifted power from out-of-state corporations to local communities. It stood up for independent farmers and the small businesses that supported them.

Then, quietly, the legislation started to die the slow death that visits most bills seeking to constrain big meat corporations. In lobbying-speak, the bill started to "carry water." Enthusiasm waned. Legislators suddenly had reservations. They didn't return phone calls. Previous supporters had to take a second look.

It seemed that calls were being made, from office to office. Lobbyists were paying visits to legislators. Leaders in the Iowa legislature weren't willing to bring the bill to the floor for debate. There were other priorities. Maybe next session, they said.

Many of the legislators seemed to be reading from one script. They said their big concern was that onerous legislation might drive the hog industry out of Iowa. The hog business was one of the last vibrant industries that called Iowa home. Better not to endanger it.

Miller's bill ultimately failed in his home state.

A similar story unfolded in Washington, D.C. The same concerns that sparked the Millennium Conference had stoked a genuine interest in passing laws to constrain the growing meat corporations. In March 2000, Senator Tom Daschle, a Democrat from South Dakota, was drafting a bill that would have required transparency, plain language, and disclosure in livestock contracts. It also would have barred companies from discriminating against producers. The discrimination clause alone might have opened the door for contract farmers to organize because they wouldn't be afraid that companies would cancel their contracts in retaliation.

The bill wasn't radical in the sense that it didn't ban contracts, didn't outlaw vertical integration, and didn't establish as many rights for farmers as Tom Miller proposed with his state-level proposal. But it was still too much for the meat companies to tolerate.

On March 8, 2000, as Daschle's bill was still being drafted, a meat industry lobbyist named Sara Lilygren sent out an e-mail. Lilygren worked for the American Meat Institute, the biggest and oldest lobbying firm for meatpackers. But her e-mail wasn't sent only to those in the meat business. The address list for this message was a broad cross-section of the industrial food system. It included lobbyists and employees of major food companies like ConAgra, Cargill, and Monsanto, along with lobbyists for industry groups like the National Chicken Council and The Turkey Federation. Lilygren included several of her coworkers at the American Meat Institute on the address list.*

The e-mail's goal was simple. All the corporate food lobbyists had to work together to stop Daschle's effort, which would rein in the market power of IBP, Tyson, and Smithfield.

The e-mail included a sample letter that was to be sent to U.S. senators, helpfully pre-addressed to "Senator xxxxxxx." This sample letter urged senators not to cosponsor Daschle's bill. In other words, it was urging lawmakers to back off from the measure before it was even proposed, winnowing away the number of lawmakers who might help bring it to the Senate for debate. The letter acknowledged that the bill wasn't even finished yet but still declared that it was an assault on the rural economy itself.

"We have only seen draft copies of the proposals at this point," the letter said. "These drafts represent sweeping changes in anti-trust laws. They include agricultural provisions that would force a radical restructuring of industry, would limit farmers' ability to partner with processors, and would establish an unprecedented invasion of privacy by the federal government into farmers' business practices."

The address list of Lilygren's e-mail was instructive. It was sent to every major meat lobbying group in Washington, even to companies that didn't seem to have a dog in the fight, like Monsanto. Industrial

---

* In 2002 Lilygren would leave the American Meat Institute to take a job as Tyson's chief lobbyist in Washington, D.C. In 2009 she graduated from that role to become Tyson's senior vice president over "external relations" (another term for lobbying).

food lobbyists know it's smart to stick together. A regulation over one of them could open the door to regulation over others. By pooling their money and time, they present a united wall against any legislation that might change the power structure of American agribusiness. They fight together, and they profit together. Meat lobbyists hold regular conference calls, sharing tips and news and planning future campaigns.

Even laws that seek to tighten food safety provisions tend to wither in front of this kind of resistance. Lawmakers have a hard time passing bills that aim to keep kids from being killed by tainted hamburger. More abstract laws dealing with market power and corporate control of the food economy, like the one Daschle was proposing, didn't stand a chance.

Daschle eventually introduced the bill, and he got thirteen cosponsors, all of them Democrats except for the Vermont independent James Jeffords. The bill went nowhere. It took on water. Lawmakers weren't ready to back it.

The same fate awaited a federal producer protection act that was modeled on Tom Miller's legislation. Iowa Democrat Tom Harkin proposed the federal Agricultural Producer Protection Act in October 2000. It didn't make it to the floor for a vote and never became law.

The fifteen state attorneys general who joined Tom Miller to pass a producer protection act didn't have better luck. When the act failed in Iowa, it took on the aura of a lost cause. It started carrying water in all fifteen states in which it was proposed.

In Oklahoma, the bill was pushed by state senator Paul Muegge. It gained momentum early on, as it did in Iowa, and passed the state senate by a wide margin. Then it stalled in the House Judiciary Committee.

Muegge released a statement in March 2001, fuming at the lobbying pressure to block the act.

"It's a shame that legislators can be bought and paid for by relentless companies," he said. The bill never reached a vote.

In all sixteen states in which it was proposed, the Producer Protection Act failed.

———

By 2004, it was beginning to look like Tom Miller's case against Smithfield was falling apart. Eric Tabor, Steve Moline, and a small group of attorneys met in a conference room to discuss the case, and a recent court decision in South Dakota had just blown a hole in the side of their sinking ship. It also spelled an end to the notion that states could fight the rise of vertical integration.

Rather than argue against Iowa's ban on packer ownership, Smithfield sued Tom Miller in federal court, arguing that Iowa had no right to ban vertical integration. Smithfield sued Iowa under Article 1, Section 8 of the U.S. Constitution, commonly known as the Commerce Clause. The Commerce Clause basically prohibits states from setting up their own trade barriers. It says that only Congress can pass laws that affect interstate commerce.

Smithfield argued that Iowa's packer ban was hindering interstate commerce. Vertical integration was embedded in the agricultural economies of the southern states. Banning it on a state-by-state basis violated the idea of an integrated, national economy.

Smithfield's fight against Tom Miller was part of a broader effort to tamp down state laws that banned corporate farming, including a similar case in South Dakota. In 2004 a federal appeals court in St. Louis ruled against South Dakota, saying the state's ban on corporate farming was unconstitutional.

Unfortunately for Moline and Tabor, they were scheduled to go before the very same federal court to try to argue that Iowa's ban on vertical integration was legal. It was a losing fight after the South Dakota ruling.

Moline didn't see the point in fighting. Smithfield would win and then have free rein to operate its Iowa contract farms as it wanted. It would only be a matter of time before Tyson, Cargill, and others rushed into the state to follow suit.

— This is the reality. We need to see if we can get something. Accomplish something, Moline said.

Moline and the attorneys on the case pondered their options, sometimes over beers after work. More than anything, they commiserated with each other. It was becoming clear that states wouldn't have significant power to regulate the economic power of meat companies. And Congress couldn't muster the political will to overcome the meat lobby.

The only cops left on the beat were the antitrust regulators in Washington.

———————

By 2005, GIPSA seemed to have drawn into a shell of nonenforcement. The reasons were partly due to the reorganization overseen by James Baker, the Stetson-wearing GIPSA chief who ran the agency during the Clinton era.

Baker's prime initiative as the antitrust regulator was to reshape the agency in the image of the highly concentrated meat industry that it oversaw. Baker closed the Packers and Stockyards branch offices that had been scattered around the county. Those offices once housed investigators who would fan out to farms and auction barns to hunt for wrongdoing. Baker moved them to centralized offices that focused on specific industries. An office in Atlanta focused on poultry companies, an office in Denver oversaw meatpackers, and an Iowa office focused on pork production.

When the Bush administration had taken over the agency in 2000, GIPSA personnel were cloistered in the central offices, like cops who had quit walking their beat. A government audit of GIPSA in 2000 found that the agency was broken. It was toothless in bringing cases against big meatpackers. GIPSA's staff of investigators was made up mostly of economists. They were good at tracking market prices, but they didn't have a good grasp of antitrust laws. They also didn't work with attorneys or investigators who knew the laws at other agencies like the U.S. Department of Justice or the Federal Trade Commission.

This lack of legal assistance crippled GIPSA. Its economists could look for theoretical violations of antitrust laws, but they didn't have the legal power to press cases.

Even the investigations that were launched tended to stagnate. GIPSA didn't have a formal tracking system to follow its own investigations. That meant there was virtually no accountability when a case was opened, no central way to see if it had been pushed to completion. Cases wandered along at the whim of scattered investigators at various GIPSA offices around the country.

GIPSA's leaders promised to solve the problems after the 2000 audit. They would set up a tracking system and forge partnerships with the Department of Justice. But strengthening antitrust enforcement was not a top priority for the Bush administration.

In 2006, a follow-up audit found none of the changes had been made. GIPSA was a ship without a rudder. Any meaningful regulations would have to be enforced on the state level. And not many states were interested in taking on big meat producers. There just wasn't much of an upside for politicians to pick a fight like that. Just a matter of months earlier, one of the biggest fights had already ended.

In late 2005, Eric Tabor and Steve Moline waited for the delegation of Smithfield lawyers to arrive at the attorney general's office. They had a meeting room ready, with piles of papers waiting to be signed. The state was prepared to drop its lawsuit against Smithfield, which had dragged on for years. The last stand against corporate hog farming was over.

The team of Smithfield lawyers arrived, but this time they didn't bring the hard-charging chairman, Joe Luter. The attorneys filed into the meeting room after exchanging pleasantries, and they sat down at opposing sides of the table, ready to begin the long parade of signatures.

The document they were ratifying that day was remarkable in its broad-reaching effects. It was no simple surrender on Tom Miller's part. Miller and Tabor had thought of one way they could escape the case with something in hand. When they crafted the settlement with Smithfield, they borrowed heavily from a piece of legislation that had been killed in sixteen states and Washington: the Producer Protection Act.

Miller agreed not to enforce the state's ban on vertical integration, but only for ten years. In return, Smithfield was required to voluntarily comply with a boiled-down version of the Producer Protection Act.

With the Smithfield settlement agreed to in 2005, Miller passed a kind of shadow legislation, enacting the strongest protections for contract farmers passed anywhere in the United States.

The settlement required that Smithfield allow its contract farmers to organize in any kind of association they wished, a right that had eluded Tyson's contract farmers in the South for decades.* The settlement also required that Smithfield allow its farmers to become "whistleblowers," taking concerns they had about the company to regulators or the media without fear of retaliation.

The settlement made it all but impossible for Smithfield to keep its contracts confidential. Farmers could discuss and share the documents with lawyers or regulators. The wall of secrecy around contract farming in Iowa was torn down. In Arkansas, by contrast, farmers still aren't even allowed to share the settlement sheets Tyson mails them to outline their performance in the tournament system. All documents are stamped "Confidential."

The settlement banned the use of a tournament system, which remains the pillar of Tyson's farms in the South. Smithfield is not allowed to dock a farmer's pay or cancel a contract based on his performance. The company is allowed to pay bonuses to good farmers but cannot use rankings as a financial punishment.

Farmers were also given the right to collect attorney fees from Smithfield if they sued the company and won. Without that right, most farmers were rendered legally helpless in the face of wrongdoing because they could not afford to pay an attorney out of pocket to sue the company.

Smithfield's attorneys signed a sweeping pact that day that could have saved countless Tyson farmers from bankruptcy in Arkansas

---

* It's true that in a few isolated cases, Tyson's contract farmers have met to discuss issues of shared importance, but they had no legal guarantees to protect their contracts if they publicly joined a farmers' union. The lack of that protection has kept a real farmers' association from ever forming. Even in 2011, Tyson farmers in states like Arkansas were terrified to be associated with any kind of effort that resembled a farmers' union, fearful the company would discover it and cancel their contracts.

and other states, had they been afforded the same rights and protection. With one document, a single regulator managed to tilt the scales of power in favor of rural communities and away from multibillion-dollar corporations.

The agreement, along with years of strong enforcement from Tom Miller's office, has provided concrete benefits for the state's farmers. Smithfield's hog farmers in the little town of Algona, for example, formed a growers' committee that met with Smithfield managers. The committee members pressed for benefits and aired grievances, and they exercised a bargaining power that was unimaginable for chicken farmers in Arkansas. The group pushed for Smithfield to stop using a tournament system to pay farmers, and the company complied.

Tyson, Cargill, and Hormel signed similar agreements to win the right to do business in Iowa. In spite of the legal limitations, they reap massive profits from their operations there.

The agreements didn't get much press when they were signed, and the companies didn't work to publicize them. Outside of Iowa, farmers labored under a different set of rules. In Arkansas, for example, Tyson's chicken farmers were still put out of business by a tournament system that was banned for Iowa hog farmers. Farmers throughout the South filed waves of lawsuits to recoup their losses, but their efforts never had the same impact as the settlement Miller imposed in Iowa.

The disparity in regulations between states showed that any really meaningful reforms for the meat industry would have to be passed on the federal level. And there was increasing pressure to do so. The fact that Tyson Foods kept chicken farmers on the verge of bankruptcy was gaining more attention with each lawsuit that was filed against the company. The lack of competition among meatpackers became the focus of a major class-action lawsuit that generated national headlines. Activist groups sprung up around these causes and lobbied lawmakers to pass reforms. By 2007, a window of possibility seemed to be opening. Academics like Bill Heffernan (who studied Louisiana chicken farmers back in the 1960s) and regulators like Tom Miller were finally being listened to.

One politician, in particular, seemed sympathetic to their cause. In

2007 a freshman senator named Barack Obama launched his presidential campaign with the promise of making big reforms. As he traveled through farm states during the Democratic primary campaign, farmers and activists pressed him to take up their cause. Once again, a regulatory fight over meat companies' market power would find its beginning in Iowa. This time, the seeds were planted on the campaign trail, as Obama heard farmer after farmer tell him the same disturbing story.

PART 3

TYSON'S PRIDE

"Under those conditions, integration is not primarily a means to efficiency, but an instrument of power."

—HAROLD BREIMYER, 1965

CHAPTER 11

The Transition Team

(2007–2011)

ARACK OBAMA looked tired. The Harvard-trained lawyer and
U.S. senator had been campaigning through rural Iowa, and the
relentless travel schedule seemed to be wearing on him. Obama could
be forgiven if he looked a little haggard. Every day was becoming an
uphill slog. By late 2007, the common political wisdom held that former first lady and U.S. senator Hillary Clinton had all but locked up
the Democratic Party's nomination for president, even before the primary voting had begun. Clinton had the type of political celebrity and
financial support that made her seem like an unbeatable candidate.
The national primary race was so lopsided that Obama's candidacy
looked like little more than a quixotic campaign, a catharsis for the liberal left. In Iowa, however, the race was tighter. It was an opportunity
Obama's campaign planned to exploit.

On the morning of November 10, 2007, Obama was determined to
woo one voting block that seemed estranged from Clinton's campaign.
Obama was going to win over white farmers.

Obama set himself apart from Clinton by staking out territory on
farm policy that Clinton had largely abandoned. As he traveled the
state, Obama heard stories about the rising power of corporations like
Tyson Foods, Monsanto, Smithfield, and ConAgra. He heard a narrative of frustration, and he appealed to it. Obama told farmers that his
administration would take a different approach to agriculture, and it
would take on the oligarchy of giant corporations that now dominated
U.S. food production.

So on that chilly morning in November, a road-weary Obama found himself at a small event called the Food and Family Farm Presidential Summit. The forum was sponsored by the Iowa Farmers Union, and it was Obama's chance to show the crowd that if they got behind his campaign, Washington might finally do something about the consolidation of corporate power in agriculture.

As Obama prepared to take the stage, Dave Murphy busily helped execute the final details of the presidential forum. Murphy was a political activist with the Iowa Farmers Union and a sixth-generation Iowan. Murphy called himself a Prairie Populist, and as such he had the ear of many farmers throughout the state. By November, he was telling them that Obama might be their man.

There was deep skepticism among farmers when it came to politicians who talked tough about big agribusiness. For decades, the Farmers Union watched an endlessly rotating stream of legislators promise they would take on the increasingly powerful agribusiness corporations, only to see them quietly abandon their fight once safely in office. But every campaign season, the Farmers Union still rallied its members to cast their votes, ever hopeful that the outcome might be different.

Murphy had been talking with the Obama campaign staff in Iowa for months, and he was impressed so far with what he had seen. It was clear to Murphy that Hillary Clinton had very little support in farm country. As an Arkansas native, Clinton's name was forever tied to Tyson Foods. Her husband, President Bill Clinton, was seen as Tyson's greatest political patron, who'd helped usher in the age of vertically integrated meat production—and had profited handsomely along the way from Tyson's campaign donations. Hillary Clinton's tenure on Wal-Mart's board of directors also didn't help. The world's biggest retailer left raw feelings throughout dilapidated small towns in Iowa, where Wal-Mart had single-handedly decimated the locally owned businesses that once thrived on the town square.

A few months prior to the presidential candidates' summit, Murphy was visiting the Obama campaign headquarters. A reporter came in and said she had just been to Clinton campaign headquarters, where the staff was certain they'd sweep the Iowa caucuses and put a quick end to the Obama candidacy. Murphy laughed out loud.

— You've got to be kidding me, Murphy said. She'll be lucky if she comes in third! I don't know a single farmer who would vote for her.

On the morning of the candidates' summit, Murphy was eager to hear what Senator Obama would say. It was Obama's chance to cement his role as the voice of rural communities. But Murphy thought Obama looked listless and worn out as he started his speech. The senator's delivery was short on the emotional cadence and passion that made Obama such a gifted orator. But the message was exactly what Murphy, and his constituents, wanted to hear.

"And it's about time that your voices were heard," Obama told the crowd. "Because for far too long, you've had to listen to politicians tell you one thing out on the campaign trail, and then close the door and do another thing in Washington when they make rural policy. You're sending your message, but sometimes you can't get through because there's a lobbyist who's already in line."

During the speech, Obama aligned himself with Iowa's longtime senator Tom Harkin, who sponsored the unsuccessful Producer Protection Act in Washington that was derailed by the meat lobbyists. Obama said he would give politicians like Harkin a new audience in the White House and a new lease on power. Obama would help them pass reforms that had been stalled for over a decade.

"When I'm president, you'll have a partner in the White House. Tom Harkin will have a partner in the White House," Obama told the farmers. "And we'll tell ConAgra that it's not the Department of Agribusiness, it's the Department of Agriculture!"

The crowd ate up that line, and it would echo in Murphy's memory for years to come.

Just a couple of short months later, Obama won the Democratic caucus in Iowa. Clinton came in third, as Murphy had predicted. The victory woke up American voters to the possibility that Senator Obama's campaign might be more than a liberal fantasy. Obama could win a state that was largely rural and white.

Obama won Iowa in part because he won over many of its farmers. And he did so with the promise that he would back their interests and take on the consolidated meat industry. It was a promise Obama wasn't going to forget.

When Donnie Smith arrived for work at Tyson Foods headquarters in mid-November 2008, it was like reporting for duty on a sinking ship. Smith had been working at the company for nearly thirty years, diligently climbing the corporate ladder and earning the rank of senior vice president over poultry and prepared foods. The CEO's office was finally in sight for Smith. Richard Bond, the former IBP executive who replaced Johnny Tyson as CEO, still ran the company. But there were grumblings about Bond's performance. Tyson Foods continued to drift, with no clear vision for where the next wave of growth would come. Don Tyson spent more time at the office, and he enlisted his two long-time friends Buddy Wray and Leland Tollett to come back as full-time "consultants" to help get the management team back on track. Even as Dick Bond tried to steer the company, he had Don Tyson, Buddy, and Leland looking over his shoulder. For an up-and-comer like Donnie Smith, the pathway to CEO looked clear.

But, Smith's luck being what it was, he was in line for the top job just as the chicken industry was entering one of the biggest train wrecks in modern history.

Smith walked toward the black steel-and-glass office building where he worked. In his position, he was responsible for all of Tyson's chicken operations. It was fast becoming the company's biggest money loser.

The economy was in a state of collapse that winter, with banks failing and the stock market crashing deeper each day. But even that broad chaos was just a distraction from deeper problems that had all but crippled Donnie Smith's business over the last couple of years. The cost of feed grains like corn had reached the highest levels in history due to new ethanol subsidies that President George Bush signed into law in late 2005. The ethanol mandate worked at direct cross-purposes with the USDA's multibillion-dollar crop subsidies, which had delivered cheap corn and soybeans to Tyson Foods since 1996.

Newly built ethanol plants were consuming more than a third of the entire U.S. corn harvest, wiping out grain supplies, boosting prices, and taking away the cushion of cheap grain that had helped keep Tyson profitable for more than a decade.

At the same time, consumer demand had fallen through the floor. Americans weren't eating at restaurants or buying Tyson's chicken nuggets at the grocery store. For the first time since World War II, per capita chicken consumption wasn't growing on a year-over-year basis. For fifty years, the economic underpinnings of the U.S. economy had been breaking in Tyson's favor. But now that Donnie was almost in charge, the tide of history was going the other way.

The story was told in stark terms in the numbers that ran across an electronic banner just inside the doorway of Tyson's front lobby. All day long, the banner ran a display of Tyson's stock price. That month, some of the most dismal numbers in all the company's history crawled across the display: . . . $7.02 . . . $7.12 . . . $7.19 . . . In between the stock quotes, the sign made little electronic fireworks bursts. The sign was probably installed as some kind of morale booster or incentive machine, but the numbers played like an unending insult to Tyson's current management team. A decade before, the stock had been worth $25 or more a share.

But none of this seemed to drag Smith down. Smith was a trim man, who still looked young and healthy at forty-nine years old. He was boyish almost, and his energy had driven him through the ranks since he joined Tyson in December 1980, just after graduating college with a degree in animal science. His career neatly mirrored the upward growth curve of the newly emerging chicken industry. Smith moved from the division that worked with farmers to the trading desk, where Tyson Foods bought billions of dollars worth of grain a year; then he moved on to oversee the company's transportation system. He was a natural company man, with a thick southern accent, a sharp business sense, and a self-deprecating manner that masked his ambition.

Smith walked past rows of cubicles, where workers tracked the company's supply chains and transportation systems. His office was at the far end of the floor, a corner spot with windows that overlooked hills that were bare in winter. Smith sat down at his desk and began to prepare for another long day.

The news scrolling across financial websites and CNBC was grimmer by the day. Tyson's biggest rival, Pilgrim's Pride, was facing possible bankruptcy, as the company tried to ward off angry creditors. Pilgrim's had been loaded up with too much debt, and it was buckling under the same pressures that were dragging Tyson's stock lower every day. Tyson could be next.

Don Tyson and his team of lieutenants had faced a similar crisis back in 1961, when chicken prices fell below the cost of production. But things were markedly different by 2008. Donnie Smith and his fellow executives were at the helm of a company that had an unprecedented level of power over the industry. In Don Tyson's day, low chicken prices drove inefficient companies out of business, leaving the survivors to compete. By 2008, Tyson and Pilgrim's Pride controlled more than 40 percent of the national chicken market between them. There weren't any scrappy upstarts that could go out of business and bring the chicken supply down, as there had been in the 1960s. So cutting the supply of chicken would be the job of the few titanic companies that ruled the industry.

To cut production, executives like Smith had an extraordinary array of tools at their disposal. From one office, Tyson could scale back the number of chickens placed on thousands of farms, the number of hogs shipped from its nursery in Oklahoma to farms in Iowa, and the number of cattle it purchased from feedlots in Kansas.

Modern American farming was run out of the central office. It was run out of meeting rooms, like the one where Smith was preparing to go that morning in November.

Every two weeks, Smith met with the group of Tyson's other top executives to get a real-time picture of the U.S. meat market, with data provided by Tyson's supply chain group. Smith didn't expect today's session would yield much good news. When Smith entered the meeting room, he sat down at a table with the vice presidents who ran

Tyson's separate divisions, like the beef and pork groups. Each vice president had a team of forecasters who collected raw numbers from the sales teams, showing how much meat big customers like McDonald's or Wal-Mart were buying. More important, the numbers predicted how much meat the clients would buy during the next 180 days. The forecasters ran the numbers through a software system that compared them against past orders and calculated what effect weather, unemployment, or inflation might have on future demand.

Getting the forecasts right, or nearly right, was critical for Tyson's profits. The company couldn't just crank up a factory line when orders increased. It needed to hatch chickens about twenty weeks before they were needed for slaughter. If the company overproduced, it would have tons of perishable meat on its hands. It was "sell 'em or smell 'em" in the modern era.

Tyson's forecasters had been accurate even into the late summer of 2008. But when the financial system unraveled in September, the models became worthless. The supply chain meetings showed that Tyson was dumping far too much fresh meat into the market. Inventories were building up, and the company was forced to sell chicken at a massive discount to traders, who turned around and unloaded the meat onto global commodity markets.

As Donnie Smith sat at the table that day in late November, the forecasters for each business division got up and relayed their findings. One after another, they made it clear that things were getting worse by the day. Orders were slowing, inventories of frozen meat were building up, and customers were cutting back on orders.

— Boy, that was rough, Donnie said after the presentations.

— In the first week of December, if this doesn't correct, we're going to have to make a production cut. This is a demand shift—we haven't seen this happen yet.

No one in the room was excited about the idea of a production cut. It was Tyson's nuclear option. It meant the company would intentionally scale back its business, cutting down its sales and profits. It also meant farmers would get fewer deliveries of chickens, reducing their income even as their debt payments stayed the same.

But by late November, Donnie Smith thought a cutback looked inevitable.

Around that time, Barack Obama was in Chicago, working with his transition team to build his new administration. By winning the presidential election that month, Obama inherited the management of the worst economic crisis since the Great Depression. Banks, auto companies, and even corporate giants like General Electric Co. were in financial peril.

Reforming agriculture wasn't top on anyone's mind. So Obama's selection for a new secretary of agriculture occurred largely out of the public eye. Most media outlets were focused on the administration's plans to salvage the economy. Away from the glare of television crews, Obama settled on a candidate who had the background, and the inclination, to implement sweeping changes over U.S. agribusiness. That candidate was Tom Vilsack, the former governor of Iowa.

In many ways, Vilsack was a safe choice. He was a moderate politician who had served as governor for nearly a decade before retiring in 2007. Vilsack seemed like a shoo-in to run a department that was best known for doling out massive subsidies every year, and for its close ties with the industry it supposedly regulated.

In another era, Vilsack might have simply joined the long procession of agriculture secretaries who did little in the job but cater to the needs of the nation's biggest agribusiness firms. Over the previous decade, the Democratic Party had become the party of industrial agriculture, and industrial meat production in particular. Between 2000 and 2010, the meat industry gave Democratic candidates for the U.S. House of Representatives $4.6 million in campaign donations, more than twice the $2.2 million the industry gave to Republicans in the House. Democratic legislators from the Farm Belt were among the strongest defenders of the industrialized meat system. Bill Clinton's first secretary of agriculture, Mike Espy, was so close with Tyson Foods that he ended up getting indicted on bribery charges for accepting plane rides, sports tickets, and lavish parties thrown by the company.

Outsiders might have been inclined to think that Vilsack would simply follow in the footsteps of previous agriculture secretaries like Espy. But from his earliest days on the job, Vilsack made it clear that he would focus on curbing the power of giant agribusiness companies.

By asking Vilsack to do so, Obama was doing more than just following up on a campaign promise. As corporations like Tyson Foods exercised their power to increase their profits, the resulting problems were becoming harder to ignore. The industrialization of the meat system had yielded a wave of lawsuits across the country over the previous twenty years. Chicken farmers were going to court because they had been turned away by the USDA's own antitrust authority: GIPSA. The agency didn't have the authority to file charges against poultry companies. Lawsuit after lawsuit documented the fact that companies like Tyson, ConAgra, and Pilgrim's Pride were manipulating scales at their slaughterhouses to underweigh loads of birds so they could underpay farmers. In Oklahoma, two Tyson Foods chicken farmers secretly taped a Tyson Foods employee while she described how Tyson plant managers were intentionally delivering lower-quality chicks to farmers the company considered to be troublemakers. In the cattle industry, a federal lawsuit, *Pickett* v. *Tyson Foods*, had revealed that the company was using its captive supplies of cattle to drive down the cash market price. When the cash price was high, Tyson could buy cattle under contract, which reduced demand on the open market and eventually brought the price down. A jury found that the tactic depressed prices Tyson paid to ranchers and feedlots by billions of dollars, even as the cost of beef in the grocery store continued to climb.

Obama wouldn't have the luxury of ignoring consolidation in the meat industry. And in this light, Vilsack proved to be a canny selection. While Vilsack appeared to be a pillar of the status quo, he was in some ways the person to institute sweeping changes. As Iowa's governor, Vilsack consistently stood behind Attorney General Tom Miller as Miller fought the rise of vertically integrated pork production. Vilsack knew about the rampant problems in the poultry industry and the concentration of power among big seed companies like Monsanto.

Perhaps more important, Vilsack had seen firsthand how just a few regulations could vastly change the balance of power in rural America. Attorney General Miller's settlement with Smithfield proved that regulators could constrain the worst abuses of meat companies. And Iowa's booming meat business showed that companies could still turn a profit, even in the face of new rules.

Vilsack made it clear to Obama's team: He was ready to take on the job.

In the winter of 2008, Tyson executives hatched a plan to react to the economic crisis. Specifically, they decided to cut production to boost chicken prices to consumers and salvage Tyson's profits. To execute this plan, Donnie Smith turned to a man named Donnie King. (King often worked closely with Donnie Smith, and the two of them were known as "the Two Donnies").

Donnie King was vice president over refrigerated and deli meat. So it was his job to carry out the production cuts when the order was given. Tyson's centralization allowed King and his team of employees to slowly pull back the levers of production. They cut back the number of egg-laying hens placed at breeding farms, thereby choking off the flow of eggs sent to Tyson's hatcheries. These factors were controlled by dozens of employees in Tyson's supply chain group, a unit of the company that was like the bridge of a giant warship. Employees there could monitor and control Tyson's vast network of farms and slaughterhouses.

The supply chain group was able to expand the footprint of "downtime" at the company's network of chicken farms by delaying the shipment of new chicks. Subtle tweaks made a big difference. By increasing the downtime from twelve days to thirteen days at each farm, for example, Tyson could throttle back the volume of chickens that were delivered to the slaughterhouses.

When Don Tyson ran the company with his father in 1961, this kind of central control was unimaginable. Each poultry plant had to figure out independently how much to scale back operations. Modern-day Tyson, by contrast, controlled a network of forty-one massive poultry complexes and could use its logistics network to ratchet back production at the plants. An act of such broad coordination could have been achieved only through illegal means back in 1961. It would have required poultry company executives to collude with one another, to plan and execute their production together and violate federal antitrust law. But by 2009, Tyson was bigger than the antitrust laws. The industry was so consolidated that collusion wasn't necessary. All it required was a series of orders from the supply chain group.

A similar set of orders from Pilgrim's Pride achieved production cuts for another 22 percent of the poultry business. Together, the companies could control almost half the U.S. chicken supply.*

For the poultry industry, the production cutbacks created a softer landing in the face of a cataclysmic drop in demand. For consumers, it meant that only two companies could cut their supply of chicken and raise prices. Tyson cut its production by 5 percent in December. Around that time, the industry as a whole was estimated to have cut back the placement of new eggs between 6 and 7 percent.

In a matter of weeks, the price of a boneless, skinless chicken breast rose by about 20 cents, according to an industry estimate. Within a short few months, Tyson's chicken business was profitable again.

Donnie Smith's star was rising.

If ever there was a time when an alternative model of meat production might arise to challenge Tyson's vertically integrated system, it was during the winter of 2009. The opportunity was born after Pilgrim's Pride declared bankruptcy in December 2008. But what unfolded after Pilgrim's Pride's bankruptcy showed why competition is becoming so limited in the meat industry, and why the free market alone won't likely be able to solve the problem. Even when given the chance, new competitors seem unlikely to arise to challenge the meat oligarchy.

---

* A federal judge later ruled that Pilgrim's Pride did indeed violate antitrust law when it closed plants with the explicit purpose of boosting chicken prices. That ruling only came about because chicken farmers had sued Pilgrim's Pride over the closures, a legal headache that Tyson escaped.

Pilgrim's Pride entered the crisis of 2008 saddled with heavy debt. That fall, creditors called in their loans and Pilgrim's didn't have the cash to meet its obligations. Pilgrim's Pride kept most of its plants running, even as it reorganized under Chapter 11. But to cut production and raise prices, Pilgrim's closed some plants and canceled contracts with hundreds of independent farmers. This chaos opened the door to fresh competition in the industry, and it did so in obscure little towns like Farmerville, Louisiana.

Farmerville was home to one of the chicken plants that Pilgrim's Pride planned to close. The facility was still open and running in 2009, but Pilgrim's Pride informed its farmers and employees that the plant would soon shut.

When Pilgrim's Pride said it was walking away from Farmerville, the company opened the door for a new kind of entity to do business in town. Around the country, some poultry producers were experimenting with a new kind of co-op system. They created locally owned "integrators" that gave farmers the chance to set their own rules of production while keeping the company's profits anchored in the community. This co-op model was rare, and its pied piper was a man named Sonny Meyerhoeffer.

Meyerhoeffer arrived in Farmerville, Louisiana, in March 2009 to tell his story. A group of local farmers paid his airfare and put him up in a local hotel. They wanted Meyerhoeffer to show them how, after Pilgrim's left, they might stay in business and take control of their economic destiny. After he arrived in town, Meyerhoeffer was escorted to a local meeting hall where several farmers had gathered. He got up on a stage in front of them, looked out over the rows of anxious faces, and proceeded to tell them how almost five years before, he had found himself in their very position. He had owned a turkey farm near Hinton, Virginia, where he raised breeding hens for Pilgrim's Pride. Meyerhoeffer was a third-generation turkey farmer, and like many of his neighbors he had staked his economic future on his poultry contract with Pilgrim's Pride. The company announced that year that it was getting out of the turkey business, shutting down its plant in Hinton and canceling its contracts with local farmers. Meyerhoeffer went to a meeting, very much like the gathering of nervous farmers in Farmerville, and listened as Pilgrim's Pride explained why they were putting him out of business. Meyerhoeffer turned to the person sitting next to him and said, just loud enough for everyone around him to hear:

— Heck. Let's just buy the dang thing.

That night, Meyerhoeffer started getting calls from farmers who'd overheard him. Did he really think it was possible? Could farmers buy the plant and run it themselves, without the backing of a corporation like Pilgrim's Pride?

The obstacles were immense, and they illustrate why Tyson and Pilgrim's Pride will likely never lose their stranglehold over the nation's poultry industry.

The costs for Meyerhoeffer and his neighbors to get into the poultry business were almost prohibitive. Doing some quick calculations, Meyerhoeffer realized the group would need somewhere in the neighborhood of $10 million just to take over the plant and keep it running. They would need to buy feed and eggs for the hatchery. They'd have to meet payroll at the slaughterhouse and the feed mill.*

Somehow, in a matter of six short months, Meyerhoeffer and his fellow farmers overcame these barriers and created the Virginia Poultry Growers Cooperative. The farmers pooled together their money and raised more than $2 million to invest. They got a rural development loan from the U.S. Department of Agriculture for $8 million to cover much of the remaining purchase price. To lock in a big customer, the co-op sold part of the new company to an outside food processor that made deli meat.

The farmers took over the turkey plant in Hinton and they rewrote the rules of production. The farmers retooled the tournament system to make the peaks and troughs less severe. Farmers also gave themselves the right to fire the plant's managers if they felt they were mistreated. The farmers formed an advisory committee to ensure they had

---

* This, by the way, was a best-case scenario. Meyerhoeffer and his neighbors would inherit an already functioning poultry plant. Building a new one from scratch, along with the farms to support it, could cost hundreds of millions of dollars.

a voice in decision making. The farmers didn't reap a windfall profit, but they regained power over their livelihoods.

"If nothing else, they had control over their destiny," Meyerhoeffer said. The co-op bought local supplies whenever possible, and its profits stayed in the hands of the people who owned the plant in Hinton.

As Pilgrim's Pride closed plants and canceled contracts across the country in 2008 and 2009, it created the chance for hundreds of farmers to follow the path of the Virginia Poultry Growers Cooperative. These farmers could have created a constellation of locally owned poultry producers to reignite competition with the very corporations that had built them.

Meyerhoeffer's pitch was inspiring. But local farmer Robin Mayo wasn't convinced. In fact, he was terrified. Mayo, like many farmers who worked for Pilgrim's Pride, was mired in debt. He thought forming a co-op would only force him to borrow more money, and he was convinced Tyson and Pilgrim's Pride would quickly destroy the new business.

The biggest obstacle for the Farmerville co-op would be finding a customer. Meyerhoeffer and his neighbors were lucky to be in the turkey business, where birds were still sold largely for deli meat or unprocessed parts. Chicken, on the other hand, was sold in a finely calibrated array of different products. Customers wanted chicken wings that measured within a range of a few ounces. They wanted precooked nuggets and processed patties. As Mayo and his neighbors held meetings to discuss Meyerhoeffer's plan, they realized that Tyson and Pilgrim's Pride could steal the co-op's potential customers by slashing their prices.

Robin Mayo and his neighbors wanted a safer option. So they were relieved when a California-based chicken company called Foster Farms offered to buy the Pilgrim's Pride plant. After it bought the facility, Foster Farms kept the same business practice and employees. Mayo's business changed very little, but he was deeply grateful to have a job. Other Pilgrim's plants closed down with no buyers, putting hundreds of plant workers and farmers out of work.

Meyerhoeffer's transformative tour basically ended at Farmerville. None of Pilgrim's facilities were transformed into co-ops. Meyerhoeffer learned that change wouldn't come easily to the chicken industry. Tyson and Pilgrim's Pride had a lock on the contracts with major customers like Wal-Mart and McDonald's. If the big companies didn't like a smaller competitor, they could simply cut their prices in certain regions and snuff out the competitor's chance of winning a contract.

"There's a lot of sharks out there, and they can starve you out if they want to," Meyerhoeffer said.

Big meat companies kept their hold on power through tightly coordinated integration. The government agencies that policed them were a different story.

In the winter of 2009, Tom Vilsack moved to Washington and started rearranging the furniture in his new office at the helm of the Department of Agriculture. When it came to regulating the world's biggest meat companies, Vilsack needed to do even more rearranging.

Vilsack inherited a regulatory system that was riven by bureaucratic divisions, miscommunication, and a lack of focus. The inefficiency and breakdown of coordination was breathtaking. While Tyson Foods could scale back national poultry production in a matter of weeks, it seemed antitrust regulators could barely get a memo from one office to another.

The most problematic agency was the one created almost one hundred years ago with the purpose of regulating giant meat companies, the Packers and Stockyards Administration. The PSA was drifting along, lost in a bureaucratic maze. The PSA was hobbled by a series of loopholes and oversights that had been layered upon the agency for decades through congressional action and heavy lobbying from the meat industry. The agency could investigate wrongdoing on the part of poultry companies, for example, but it did not have the legal authority to prosecute them. If the PSA wanted to bring a case against Tyson for fraudulently manipulating scales at its slaughterhouse to underpay farmers, the agency had to build a case and then hand it over to the Department of Justice for prosecution. This is even more difficult and cumbersome than it sounds, because complicated legal cases are like long novels. Passing a case off from one agency to the other, midstream, is like writing half a book and then giving it sight-unseen to another author and asking him to finish it. The Department of Justice had other things to worry about, like terrorism, narcotics trafficking, and white-collar fraud. Cases started by the PSA were referred to the Department of Justice but were notorious for languishing there.

To make matters worse, attorneys and economists within the PSA were barely *talking* with their counterparts at Justice, let alone sending them cases to be prosecuted. If an attorney inside PSA wanted to talk to an attorney at Justice, they were directed to go through the PSA's office of general counsel, creating a communications bottleneck that most people seemed to avoid by simply not picking up the phone.

It became clear, early on, that to accomplish anything, Vilsack needed a strong partner within the Department of Justice. Without that, the USDA would stay crippled in the face of a multibillion-dollar meat industry.

Christine Varney looked out over the crowd as she prepared to make her first speech as the Justice Department's new chief of antitrust enforcement. It was May 2009, just a few months into the new administration. Varney was beginning her tenure as Barack Obama's head of antitrust enforcement. Varney was preparing that Monday morning to address a friendly audience, which was a good thing, because Varney had a less than friendly message to deliver. She was about to send a shot across the bow to big business in America, saying in clear terms that a new cop was on the beat.

That message was a tough sell. The stock market had opened lower and fell throughout the morning Varney was to give her speech, with the Dow Jones Industrial Average hovering around 8,400 points. That was down almost 40 percent from its peak levels in late 2007. But even at that depressed level, the markets were rebounding from the terrifying lows of two months before. The unemployment rate was at its highest level in more than twenty years, and Americans were anxious every day that things might get worse: The market might fall further, companies might cut more jobs. Another depression seemed just one bad day away.

This anxiety played into the hands of big business. Companies argued that mergers, cost cutting, and market control were critical to staying profitable. Any government action to curb this behavior could be branded as a reckless act that could destroy jobs and send shockwaves of uncertainty through a fragile economy.

Varney had a different message to convey. She planned to deliver it in her speech that morning at a meeting of the Center for American Progress, a liberal think tank that had petitioned the Obama transition team for tougher antitrust enforcement. Varney seemed the ideal candidate to usher in such a change. She had been a member of the Federal Trade Commission* for three years during the Clinton administration. During the Bush years, she practiced antitrust law as a partner with Hogan & Hartson, a powerful Washington, D.C., firm. Varney had fought antitrust battles from both sides and she knew the law as well as anyone.

As Varney walked out onstage after a glowing introduction that dubbed her a "premier Washington superlawyer," she carried herself with characteristic composure. She didn't just look put together. She looked bulletproof. Varney had a smooth smile that was just polite enough, just strained enough, to telegraph that beneath it lay a resolve of steel.

When she began her speech, Varney wasted no time. She told the crowd that when she walked into her new office at the Department of Justice, she walked past the portraits of former heads of antitrust enforcement including Thurmond Arnold, who ramped up enforcement after the Great Depression. Varney said she admired Arnold and his rationale for tough enforcement. The U.S. economy enjoyed decades of prosperity after Arnold cracked the antitrust whip, ending a period of deep malaise dominated by cartels of companies that had government support.

"The lessons learned from history are twofold," Varney said. "First,

---

* The FTC enforces antitrust laws alongside the Department of Justice.

there is no adequate substitute for a competitive market, particularly during difficult economic times. Second, vigorous antitrust enforcement must play a significant role in government's response to economic downturns to ensure that markets remain competitive."

Varney said antitrust enforcement had been all "but abandoned" in recent years. Companies could get away with almost anything if they could prove there was an economic or "efficiency" rationale for their actions. Varney said this was harmful to consumers.

Corporate attorneys in offices around the country heard her message loud and clear: The old system would be getting a new look.

CHAPTER 12

Street Fight

(2010–2011)

INSIDE THE big auditorium, the crowd settled into their seats and began to quiet down when the dignitaries arrived. There was U.S. Attorney General Eric Holder, and next to him Secretary of Agriculture Tom Vilsack. The Republican senator Chuck Grassley stood nearby as Christine Varney, the head of antitrust enforcement at the Department of Justice, approached the stage. They were about to undertake the closest thing to a media circus that has ever happened in the world of agriculture policy.

It was a chilly morning in March 2010. More than a thousand politicians, farmers, lobbyists, and journalists had descended on the auditorium in Ankeny, Iowa, a nondescript little suburb of Des Moines. The auditorium was the site of an unprecedented public hearing that was jointly hosted by the U.S. Departments of Justice and Agriculture. About seven months into the Obama administration's tenure, the two agencies announced they would hold five hearings at locations around the country, beginning in Ankeny. The purpose was to examine the growing power of agribusiness corporations like Tyson Foods.

The dignitaries had flown in from Washington. And every major agribusiness lobbying group and company, from Monsanto to Tyson, had sent their public relations teams and lawyers to monitor what was spoken from the podium. Farmer activist groups brought in members from around the country who stood in long lines when it was time to deliver public comment.

Crews of security guards guided traffic outside the little auditorium, which was usually used for Future Farmers of America meetings. The parking lot was overwhelmed and groups of people walked down long sidewalks from auxiliary lots elsewhere, farmers in their denim next to lawyers in their high heels.

A few minutes before the hearing began, Attorney General Holder walked up a small set of stairs to a stage that overlooked the audience. He took his seat at a long table, with a microphone and nameplate placed in front of him as if this were some sort of Senate hearing. To his right sat Christine Varney. To his left sat Secretary Vilsack.

Just the sight of these people sitting at the same table was enough to cause palpitations for meat industry lawyers. For decades, attorneys at the Departments of Justice and Agriculture had played for different teams. They divvied up regulation of the meat industry between them in a system that was riddled with loopholes. The meat industry benefited tremendously from the dysfunction, which made regulators inefficient and aimless. The message being sent by the Obama administration was clear: These agencies would now be working in concert.

The meat lobbyists might have been even more concerned about the man who sat at the far end of the table, an individual whom most people in the crowd probably didn't recognize. It was Tom Miller, the slender white-haired attorney general of Iowa, who had spent more than a decade trying to roll back the vertical integration of the pork industry. Through his one-of-a-kind settlement with Smithfield Foods, Miller had laid out a template for regulating meat companies across the nation. If imposed on southern poultry producers, such rules could redraw the balance of power in many parts of rural America. For the first time, federal regulators were shining a spotlight on the patchwork system of rules that gave hog farmers in Iowa more rights than chicken farmers in Arkansas. Miller seemed eager to help level the playing field.

After the crowd settled into their seats, Vilsack opened the meeting.

"Let me start off by saying how deeply concerned I am about rural America," Vilsack said, hunching forward to speak directly into the little microphone set before him. He proceeded to run through the well-known litany of economic woes that characterized small-town

America. He described a farming system increasingly controlled by giant corporations, where four companies controlled 80 percent of the cattle market and four hog processors controlled 65 percent of the hog market. He described how the top-heavy (and remarkably efficient) food industry was punishing the very farmers who actually produced the food. Just 11 percent of a typical farming family's income came from the farm itself. The rest was earned through other means, like working a part-time job in town. This arrangement was systematically destroying midsize, independent farmers, with 80,000 of them disappearing in the last five years alone.

"And when we lose farms in the middle, it also impacts directly the entire rural economy. Today's rural America has a higher poverty rate than the rest of the country, a higher unemployment rate than the rest of the country, significantly less per capita income than the rest of the country, an aging population, a workforce that is less educated, and well over 50 percent of our rural counties have lost population since the last census," Vilsack said.

He then outlined a governing agenda that was characteristically ambitious for the newly minted Obama administration, which was just one year old. It wasn't enough to simply fix these problems by enforcing existing rules and regulations, Vilsack suggested.

"The president has instructed the Department of Agriculture to establish a framework for a new rural economy," he said. This statement played to the sense of hope and radical possibility that President Obama engendered with his campaign. For those in the crowd, from the farmers to the lawyers, bankers, and politicians, the prospect for fundamental reform was tangible. There could be a new framework, a new system of power in rural America.

In spite of its seemingly radical aims, the effort launched in Iowa would play out over the next two years largely under the public's radar. After the initial flurry of public attention paid to the hearing in Ankeny, the ensuing debates and regulatory actions that followed went largely unnoticed by most major media outlets.

That's partly because the debate didn't fit neatly into categories of red and blue, Republicans and Democrats. By trying to roll back the concentration of power among food companies, the Democratic Obama administration was aligning itself with deeply conservative small-town ranchers, like Chuck Wirtz and Ken Winter. By contrast, Republicans who opposed the administration's efforts found themselves defending an industrial meat system that was characterized by centralized control, the extinguishing of open and competitive markets, and bureaucratic decision making that replaced the collective wisdom of independent business owners.

Both parties also shared blame for what was happening. The consolidation of agriculture was a bipartisan affair, supported unwaveringly for decades by a revolving door of Republicans and Democrats.

But in Ankeny, as the hearing got under way, there was the palpable feeling that change was not only possible but imminent. And the feeling was justified. The government hearings were just the most visible part of a broader effort. Much of the real work was already being done away from the public eye.

In the months leading up to the hearing in Ankeny, Iowa, Tom Vilsack installed a team of regulators who would overhaul the Packers and Stockyards Administration, the antitrust agency set up to regulate meat companies before the Great Depression.

The PSA was housed under the bigger agency called GIPSA, which would now be overseen by a young man named John Ferrell, who was just thirty-three years old. Ferrell would directly supervise the PSA and that agency's new director: a gray-bearded trial attorney named J. Dudley Butler.

Ferrell and Butler were the consummate odd couple. Ferrell is a wispy guy who even in his midthirties looked like a freshly minted college graduate. At the public hearings held in Ankeny and elsewhere, Ferrell sat up on the stage and listened to public comments on behalf of the USDA. His gentle demeanor and fresh face made him look like an unlucky intern rather than an official at the USDA's antitrust division.

Butler, on the other hand, is brash and blunt-spoken. He had the reputation of being a man who was perpetually about to sue somebody. For decades, Butler represented poultry farmers who took companies like Tyson to court. Butler referred to contract farmers in the press as "sharecroppers," and he vowed at a public meeting in 2010 that he would help stop the "chickenization" of the beef industry. He was a meat lobbyist's nightmare, and he had just been given control over the levers of some of the nation's broadest and strongest antitrust laws.

While the Packers and Stockyards Act was a tough law, the agency that enforced it was weak and incompetent. Ferrell and Butler took over a Packers and Stockyards Administration in which the guiding doctrine for the previous decade seemed to be to sit on the sidelines and do nothing. There was still no internal system to track investigations, a problem that had been identified years before by the General Accounting Office and yet was never fixed. Staff members in the PSA seemed to have the mentality that it was best not to make waves and best not to antagonize the meat companies.

But the PSA had been given a rare opportunity to change the rules of the game. This opportunity came in the form of a mandate from Congress, passed years earlier in the 2008 farm bill. Congress included in the bill a provision that required the PSA to toughen its rules. The provision was a major victory for farmer advocacy groups, which had lobbied for years to pass the kind of protections that Iowa's attorney general had failed to achieve in 2000 when he promoted the Producer Protection Act. Some lawmakers, like Iowa senator Tom Harkin, had never given up the fight. As farmer bankruptcies and lawsuits mounted in rural America through the decade, Harkin and his allies gained momentum to push the reforms.

Ferrell had helped write the 2008 farm bill provision in his previous job, when he was a staff member with Senator Harkin. Now Ferrell and Butler planned to exploit to the fullest extent the chance to strengthen the PSA.

For example, the PSA was told to define the term "undue preference" as it appeared in the original Packers and Stockyards Act. The act banned meatpackers from giving one farmer or rancher an unfair preference over another. Defining which preferences were "undue" could instantly redraw the entrenched power arrangements in the cattle industry. It raised the question: Was Tyson's partnership with certain feedlots illegal? Was Tyson showing an undue preference to its contract feedlots, like Lee Borck's operation in Larned, Kansas, by paying him extra money to sign a contract with the company? If an independent feedlot owner down the road, like Ken Winters, could deliver the same number of cattle at the same price, why was Tyson paying Borck extra? Was it just to gain control over the market?

For several months during 2010, the policy makers inside GIPSA drafted a new rule that would carry out the changes required by the farm bill and take them much further. For example, the rule would ban any tournament system for chicken farmers that didn't guarantee the farmers a predictable base payment. Tyson could only offer incentives for good performance, in other words, rather than docking a farmer's income by adjusting the base pay rate through the tournament.

The rule also made one legal change that aimed to make the PSA more powerful than ever. The rule said that if a farmer or rancher wanted to sue a company like Tyson under the Packers and Stockyards Act, the farmer had only to prove that Tyson harmed the farmer himself, not the industry as a whole. This single provision rolled back a series of federal court decisions that had basically rendered the Packers and Stockyards Act toothless. The courts had ruled that to win a case under the act, a farmer had to prove that a company's actions amounted to an industrywide antitrust violation. If Tyson put Jerry Yandell out of business, for example, Yandell would have to prove that his termination harmed competition in the entire chicken industry to win a Packers and Stockyards case. Such a burden of proof was virtually impossible for most farmers and ranchers, so they didn't pursue cases. The new GIPSA rule changed that. It said the farmer had only to show a company was unfair or deceptive in its actions. That one change would open the courts to a deluge of litigation from farmers who felt they were wronged.

Policy makers inside GIPSA also considered more drastic measures. They discussed imposing an outright "packer ban" that would bar meatpackers from owning their own livestock, a measure long supported by opponents of vertical integration. If applied to the cattle industry, the ban would undoubtedly mean more cattle were bought and sold on the open market. If applied to the pork industry, the results would have been more radical, likely requiring companies like Tyson and Smithfield to divest their hog farming operations. GIPSA policy makers eventually backed off the idea of a packer ban. They thought it would have been hard to justify in court, so they decided not to draft a measure to enact it. The PSA would have to prove that meatpackers owned cattle or hogs with the express intent of driving down the price or limiting competition. It was a daunting standard to satisfy in court.

The GIPSA rule, then, was seen as a first step. It fulfilled the needs laid out by the 2008 farm bill, and it fulfilled some of the promises laid out by President Obama on the campaign trail.

The proposed GIPSA rule was released in June 2010, with Secretary Vilsack hailing it as a move that would hold "bad actors" to account when they tried to stifle competition.

"The reality is, the Packers and Stockyards Act has not kept pace with the marketplace," he said. "Our job is to make sure the playing field is level for producers."

Inside the American Meat Institute, there was shock the day the GIPSA rule was proposed. Mark Dopp, the lobbying group's director of regulatory affairs, didn't mince words about his opinion of it.

"We've had better days," Dopp moaned.

"This rule attempts, on many levels, to undercut all the progress that has been made. It will undercut innovation," he warned. "This isn't only going to affect bad actors, with all due respect to the secretary, I think that's a bit misleading."

What seemed most disturbing to the American Meat Institute (and its partner groups like the National Chicken Council and National Cattlemen's Beef Association) was the provision that lowered the bar to bringing lawsuits under the Packers and Stockyards Act.

"It's going to spawn all kinds of litigation," Dopp said. "I'm afraid

I think it will trigger a whole host of what I would consider specious lawsuits."

The meat lobbying groups began to gather their wits after the initial shock of seeing the new rule. The groups would follow their tried-and-true playbook and respond in unison.

By releasing the GIPSA rule, Vilsack kicked into motion one of the better-funded, better-coordinated lobbying machines in Washington. The meat companies themselves had tremendous resources at their disposal. The biggest meat companies—Tyson Foods, ConAgra Foods, Cargill, Smithfield, and JBS—spent a combined $5.94 million on lobbying during 2010 alone, according to an analysis of disclosure reports. Tyson had the biggest lobbying operation by far, spending $2.59 million.

The companies were joined in the effort by their industry front groups, including the American Meat Institute, the National Chicken Council, the National Cattlemen's Beef Association, and the National Pork Producers Council,* which together spent $1.85 million on lobbying during 2010.

Together, the trade groups and companies spent $7.79 million on lobbying in 2010. Influencing GIPSA directly wasn't going to be an option, and the White House had publicly cast its lot behind stronger enforcement. So the meat lobby turned to the governing body it knew could yield the best results: Congress.

Officials inside GIPSA heard about lobbyists working the halls of Congress, visiting legislators who were friendly to their cause and pressing them to oppose the new rule. The lobbyists made their case convincingly, warning of the jobs that could be lost and the higher meat prices that could result. Analysts inside GIPSA disagreed, but the agency was clumsy in making its case with lawmakers.

At the same time, regulators were getting an earful as they trav-

---

* The latter two groups, the NCBA and the NPCC, are strange entities in that they purport to represent "producers" in the broadest term, meaning both farmers and the big meat companies that buy their animals. Both groups came out against the GIPSA rule.

eled the country, attending the series of workshops that started in Ankeny. The job of reforming the meat industry was starting to look complicated.

Through the spring and summer of 2010, the U.S. Departments of Agriculture and Justice held their series of five public workshops, visiting out-of-the way towns like Normal, Alabama, and Fort Collins, Colorado.

John Ferrell, the boyish GIPSA official, sat through the long hours of public comment. He was often joined by another young regulator named Philip Weiser, who was Christine Varney's deputy of antitrust enforcement at the Department of Justice. Over a period of nine months Weiser learned far more about modern agriculture than he expected to when taking his job. And exactly what he learned showed why it is so difficult to reform the food system.

Big meat companies like Tyson had a critical advantage on their side in the argument over how to restructure the nation's food system. Their advantage was that they represented the status quo. It is far easier for a business to revolutionize an industry than it is for regulators to go back in and tinker with the gears of production, hoping to benefit the public.

Iowa attorney general Tom Miller and his lieutenant Eric Tabor were able to impose new ground rules on industrial hog production because they intervened when the industry was still evolving. They acted when farmers were building the first confinement hog houses and signing their first contracts with integrators.

The story was different for the entrenched southern poultry industry. It had been tightly integrated going back to the 1950s and 1960s. To impose similar rules on that business would mean destroying existing relationships and replacing them with a government-prescribed alternative. In the face of such actions, companies can argue convincingly that the government is experimenting in a field of worrisome unknowns. The actions can cost jobs, hurt productivity, and raise consumer prices. These arguments put a high burden of proof on regulators to show that their actions would improve life for more people than they hurt.

During the series of workshops, Obama administration officials saw just how powerful, and how difficult to change, the meat industry had become. Companies like Tyson had built massive supply chains across rural America, an economic circulatory system that connected industrial farms, high-tech slaughterhouses, distribution centers, warehouses, and trucking lines. The system shipped meat to grocery stores, restaurants, and refrigerated meat cases at Wal-Mart and Costco. This supply chain was enduring, profitable, and complicated. In many ways, the supply chain was also nonsensical and inefficient. A rancher in Colorado might sell cattle to a meatpacker in Austin, Texas, who then shipped the beef back to a Wal-Mart in Colorado. But escaping this supply chain, or changing it, seemed exceedingly difficult. Altering one part of the chain caused ripples downstream.

There were pockets of change growing in the shadows around this industrial system. Most of these alternatives were part of the burgeoning "localvore" movement, which connected consumers directly with nearby meat producers. It was increasingly common for suburbanites to buy "half a cow" from a local rancher, purchasing a big supply of beef they kept frozen in the basement. At local farmers' markets, shoppers were willing to pay several times the average price of the meat to buy chicken they knew was locally raised. These niche markets were growing. But the vast majority of meat was still sold through grocery store chains and fast-food restaurants. The localvore movement hadn't become a viable option for low- to middle-income Americans. And the quirky farmer next door wasn't able to supply these outlets with the volume of beef, chicken, and pork that they needed.

As it pressed its case to keep the status quo, the meat industry portrayed the current state of affairs as the natural, inevitable order of things. Lobbyists argued that regulators were backward looking in their efforts. Mark Dopp, with the American Meat Institute, put it succinctly in his opposition to the new GIPSA rule.

"This is an attempt to turn the clock back to 1950, on a whole host of levels," Dopp said. "Essentially, what this would do is undercut what

evolved over the last forty or fifty years that has made the U.S. probably the most effective and innovative meat processing system in the
world."

Ultimately, the USDA workshops and proposed regulations generated a big partisan street fight. The dispute ultimately boiled down to
predictable contours: Democrats trying to pass new regulations while
Republicans fought them on behalf of businesses.

Secretary Vilsack called a meeting to talk about the political pushback from meat industry lobbyists. The American Meat Institute and
its allies had been effective as they circulated Capitol Hill. Lawmakers
were starting to see the GIPSA rule as a job-killing act of regulatory
overreach that would send the meat industry back to the dark ages.

Officials inside GIPSA and Vilsack's office suspected that an upcoming congressional hearing was being arranged as a kind of showdown
over the rule, the meat industry's first volley in a fight to turn back
new regulations. The House Subcommittee on Agriculture was supposedly being convened to discuss the 2012 farm bill. But word was
spreading that legislators would grill the USDA about its proposed
GIPSA rule.

So Vilsack called the meeting with John Ferrell and other staff to lay
out the agency's strategy for the hearing. It was clear that the agency
wasn't going to let Dudley Butler, the veteran trial attorney, defend the
rule. He was considered to be a loose cannon. No one wanted a USDA
official dropping the word "chickenization" or "sharecropper."

GIPSA decided instead to send Deputy Director Edward Avalos,
a mild-mannered administrator who worked alongside John Ferrell.
Avalos had a tough job. He was supposed to defend the GIPSA rule, but
he was limited in what he could say. A federal law, called the Administrative Procedure Act, prohibits government officials from saying publicly how they plan to reshape rules in response to public comment.
Avalos had his hands tied in saying what GIPSA planned to keep, or
throw out, from its proposed rules. He couldn't even talk much about
the specific rationale for the rule.

Vilsack said he wanted Avalos to be forceful. He didn't have to get into specifics. He just needed to lay out why the rule was so important.

— This is about correcting a situation in which people were being treated unfairly, Vilsack said.

There was plenty of reason for Vilsack to worry about the upcoming hearing. By the summer of 2010, the Obama administration was losing the public argument over the wisdom of passing new regulations. The populist Tea Party movement had moved the public debate to the right, focusing initially on the administration's efforts to reform health care. Health care reform was derided as a socialist plot to set up "death panels" and determine if grandmothers got the medical care they needed. If GIPSA's efforts were painted in the same light, political support for the new rule would evaporate.

Vilsack warned his team that they couldn't let that happen.

— If we lose control of the public narrative, it's going to be hard to get it back, he said.

They lost it. After the hearing, the public narrative about the GIPSA rule would be defined by the squirming, stuttering, nervous demeanor of Edward Avalos.

During the agriculture subcommittee hearing on July 20, Avalos looked like a bank teller who had just gotten caught filching money out of his drawer. Both Democrats and Republicans alike lit into him, demanding that Avalos explain why GIPSA went far beyond the specific mandates of Congress to update the GIPSA rule.

David Scott, a Democrat from Georgia who chaired the subcommittee, was almost poetic in his anger as he stared down at Avalos.

"Mr. Undersecretary, I think what you have witnessed with this Committee today is a very passionate outpouring of very serious concern that the Agriculture Department, in proposing this new rule, has very seriously—seriously—overstepped their boundaries. This is especially true given the fact that parts of this new law's provisions were soundly rejected through the legislative process, every step—through the Committee, through the Senate, the House, and the farm bill considerations itself. And for you and the Department to arbitrarily go against the wishes and the intent of Congress is serious. It is what Shakespeare referred to when he said, 'Et tu, Brutus, yours was the meanest cut of all,'" Scott intoned.

In fact, officials at GIPSA were certain the agency didn't need approval from the farm bill, nor from Congress, to assert its authority. In the agency's view, it was just enforcing a Packers and Stockyards Act that had been sitting mostly idle for decades.

Avalos didn't summon the kind of emotional defense of the rule that Vilsack wanted. Avalos promised that GIPSA would carefully consider the public comments that were already flooding into the agency. He promised the agency would act appropriately and prudently.

It looked like GIPSA has been caught with its pants down.

To appease GIPSA's critics, Vilsack extended the public comment period for the new rule and promised that the USDA would conduct an economic study assessing the rule's impact on rural America. The study would take more than a year to complete. The extra time for comments and studies was a victory for the meat lobby. As the rule was delayed, it opened the door for a different narrative about the rules to emerge, and for opposition to grow.

To shape the debate, meat company lobbyists used an increasingly common tactic in the Washington influence industry. They stoked a "grassroots" movement of ordinary people who contacted lawmakers to voice complaints and make suggestions that perfectly mirror the wishes of big business. In the meat business, of course, there was no more effective group to enlist for such an effort than farmers themselves. If farmers opposed GIPSA's efforts, it was hard to justify them.

On August 4, 2010, the National Chicken Council sent out a confidential memo to poultry companies like Tyson Foods and Pilgrim's Pride. The memo urged the companies to contact their farmers and ask them to oppose the GIPSA rule by sending comments to the agency.

The memo, which was later leaked to the Agri-Pulse industry news service, focused specifically on the provision that would ban the modern tournament system. The National Chicken Council said this would ultimately wipe out all innovation in the industry. Paying farmers a bonus didn't seem to be incentive enough to get them to work hard or update their houses. There needed to be the threat of financial penalties as well.

It might seem like a tough sell for Tyson to persuade its farmers to fight against a rule that would stabilize their pay and remove the threat of bankruptcy through constant tournaments. The memo's author, lobbyist Richard Lobb, told the companies they should cherry-pick farmers that were most likely to support the companies' position:

"We assume that the above-average or more successful growers will be more likely than others to submit comments against the rule. We leave it to your judgment which growers you should contact," the memo read.

On October 21, GIPSA got an angry letter from Eunice Richardson, an elderly chicken farmer. Richardson raised birds for a small company called Wayne Poultry in Danville, Arkansas, not too far from Waldron.

For some reason, Richardson chose to write her letter in all capital letters. She told GIPSA:

I FURTHER BELIEVE THAT ALL GROWERS WILL BE THREATENED BECAUSE THE PROPOSED RULES WOULD DRIVE INNOVATION, COMPETITION AND HIGH PERFORMANCE OUT OF THE SYSTEM AND REDUCE THE EFFICIENCY AND COMPETITIVENESS OF THE DOMESTIC POULTRY INDUSTRY.

The language directly mirrored Richard Lobb's memo to the chicken companies, which said the rule would: "drive innovation, competition and high performance out of the system and reduce the efficiency of the domestic poultry industry."

Richardson said she sent the letter to GIPSA after "they" provided her a copy of the letter to sign. Richardson declined to say who "they" were. She said she didn't want to do anything that might get Wayne

Poultry in trouble. Even though she signed the letter at someone else's urging, Richardson said she truly believed the GIPSA rule was a horrible idea. She thought it would remove the incentive for farmers to work hard.

Besides, a new rule wouldn't help her anyway. Richardson declared bankruptcy and lost her farm about a year after she sent the letter. It had gotten harder over the years to pay the bills on her poultry farm. The utility costs kept rising, and her pay didn't keep up. The final straw came in 2011 when one of her power generators broke down and she couldn't afford to pay for repairs. After more than a decade in the poultry business, she declared bankruptcy.

But Richardson didn't complain. At age eighty, she collected social security. And she said she loved the Wayne Poultry employees like her own grandkids. The company had always treated her fairly, she said.

"I'll survive," she said. "That's life."

The public comment from Tyson Foods on the GIPSA rule didn't look like a letter. It looked like a lawsuit. The document was far more detailed than the messages farmers sent into GIPSA. Tyson submitted a legal brief that was 335 pages long, including exhibits. The cover page was presented in the format of a court filing, with the prominently displayed names of seven attorneys from Washington, D.C., and Tyson's headquarters in Springdale.

If GIPSA ever wondered what a legal challenge to the new rule would look like, they had their answer in Tyson's comment. The document argued against virtually every aspect of the rule and challenged GIPSA's very authority to enforce it.

The letter showed that Tyson was not ready to accept any of the rules. It wasn't ready to adopt the kind of tournament system that Smithfield used for its profitable hog farms in Iowa. Tyson's brief defended its tournament in different terms than were used in the letters that chicken farmers signed. Tyson's defense of the tournament was a little more honest. The company acknowledged that the tournament was basically a way to punish farmers who didn't upgrade their chicken houses. Without the tournament, Tyson wouldn't have a lever to force farmers to upgrade or build new structures.

The company also suggested it could not tolerate a tournament with a guaranteed base payment, in part because that would disrupt the "settled expectations" of farmers who invested in new chicken houses expecting premium payments. The company didn't mention the "settled expectations" of farmers with older housing, who didn't know their pay would be docked when neighbors built new farms.

The message to GIPSA was clear: If you finalize this rule, we'll see you in court.

The final hearing in the series of USDA/DOJ workshops was held in Washington, D.C., and it examined the growing gap between what consumers pay for food and what farmers earn for growing it. Between 1989 and 2009, the price that consumers paid for beef in the grocery store rose 60 percent. But the price of cattle rose only 12 percent. The price of pork in the grocery store rose 50 percent in that time, while the price of hogs on the farm actually *fell* 11.5 percent. The USDA couldn't determine the gap for chicken because there wasn't a good way to determine the price on the farm. In a vertically integrated system the company always owned the birds, and it kept the prices confidential.

David Murphy arrived at the hearing with some heavy boxes. Murphy was the liberal farm activist from Iowa who organized the presidential summit of 2007, where candidate Obama had laid down such a strong position on corporate agribusiness. Murphy had traveled the country during 2010 to attend the workshops that grew from this promise, and Murphy's hopes were high. Activists like Murphy had grown jaded over the years, watching such hearings. He called them "show trials," because they always seemed to end without any significant changes to public policy. But he thought this time might be different. The officials involved, from Tom Vilsack to Eric Holder to Christine Varney, seemed serious.

When he traveled to Washington for the final hearing, Murphy brought boxes full of petitions, signed by people who wanted the

Obama administration to take tough antitrust actions against Tyson and its peers. Murphy was granted a private meeting with Christine Varney and John Ferrell.

Murphy presented Varney with the petitions and told her the administration needed to act, now that it was finished with its nationwide listening tour.

Varney seemed sympathetic to his cause. But she also seemed hesitant.

— There are real problems out there. But we're having difficulty getting people to agree on how to move forward, she said.

During the course of 2011, the meat industry's intensified opposition to the GIPSA rule began to foster deep divisions within Secretary Vilsack's Department of Agriculture.

The GIPSA rule became a convenient scapegoat for Tyson Foods and its lobbyists to attack as the industry sought to push back efforts at reform. The rule came to represent everything the meat industry saw as wrong with the administration. It was portrayed as a job killer and the misguided work of bureaucrats who didn't understand how the real world worked. An information campaign spread through rural America, promoted by groups like the National Chicken Council and the National Cattlemen's Beef Association, which portrayed the GIPSA rule as the first step toward the economic ruin of the meat business.

This pressure fractured Secretary Vilsack's team into two camps: the pragmatists and the reformers.

To the pragmatists, the GIPSA rule was starting to look like a disaster. It was the worst of all worlds, in legislative terms. One single rule managed to infuriate all the major meat producers, from beef packers to chicken companies and industrial hog producers. By trying to regulate so many things at once, the rule managed to unite all the various meat companies against it. The pragmatists wanted to scale back the rule. They considered stripping some parts out, with the intention of pursuing them later. Some parts of the rule could be dropped altogether. The pragmatist camp had powerful advocates in Vilsack's office, including Krysta Harden, who became Vilsack's chief of staff in 2011. Harden had been Vilsack's liaison to Congress since 2009, and she was well attuned to the political horse trading that was necessary to get anything substantive done in Washington. John Ferrell, the young official at GIPSA and other agencies, had also spent years on the Hill, and he tended to lean toward the pragmatist camp.

Another pragmatist was Anne Cannon MacMillan, a senior advisor to Vilsack. MacMillan had spent years as a staffer and policy advisor to the Democratic congressman Dennis Cardoza. Cardoza worked closely with agribusiness firms, which did big business in his home state of California. Over the last decade, agribusiness was the single biggest industry that supported Cardoza with campaign contributions.

In the reformer camp, there was Dudley Butler. The Mississippi attorney had come to Washington with one thing in mind: reforming the meat industry. He didn't seem prepared to change course. During a series of meetings that year, staffers from Vilsack's office (people from "across the street," as they were referred to inside GIPSA, with just a note of derision) pressed Butler to compromise. Butler appeared to view this effort with growing contempt. It looked to him as if the political people around Vilsack were swapping provisions from the GIPSA rule as if they were just so many words on paper. But the impact the changes could have in rural America would be profound. Butler didn't have time for smoothing egos in Congress in order to do what he considered the right thing. He had expected a fight from the meat industry, and he was ready to engage it.

It seemed as if Anne MacMillan's job description became centered on one thing: babysitting Dudley Butler. Their exchanges sometimes grew contentious in meetings. MacMillan could point to the mountains of public comment against the GIPSA rule and the growing opposition in Congress.

— Nobody likes this rule! she said.

— There are hundreds of thousands of farmers that support this rule, Butler replied. At times he appeared to have difficulty disguising his disdain for MacMillan and other policy aides.

The two sides seemed at a stalemate. And as they argued, the meat industry enlisted more members of Congress to its side and told more ranchers and farmers how the rule could destroy their livelihoods.

Secretary Vilsack called a meeting in his office to discuss the GIPSA rule. He sat down at a conference table with Dudley Butler, Vilsack's top attorney Ramona Romero, and others. Vilsack laid out the situation in stark terms. The GIPSA rule was becoming a lightning rod for opposition, and they needed to figure out a way to move forward.

Vilsack turned to Butler.

— What do you think we should do? Vilsack asked.

— We can either be conciliatory, or we can do what we said we were going to do, Butler replied.

Ultimately, it would be up to Vilsack to decide which way to proceed.

On a chilly Thursday morning in October 2011, agriculture secretary Tom Vilsack walked into the NBC studios in Manhattan. He was set to appear on the popular cable news show *Morning Joe*, which was a rare bully pulpit for Vilsack to push his priorities. The show was a busy transit hub for presidential candidates, pundits, and politicians. It helped set the topic of discussion inside Washington, but it was also watched in households across America.

The U.S. Department of Agriculture was just months away from unveiling the final GIPSA rule, potentially the most sweeping antitrust measure since the Great Depression. But Vilsack never mentioned it during his appearance on the show that morning.

Barack Obama's reelection campaign was just beginning to get under way, and Vilsack seemed to have his campaign talking points ready. During his appearance, Vilsack used American agriculture as a kind of political prop to bolster Obama's campaign theme that things weren't all bad in the U.S. economy. It was a tough message to sell in light of the 9.1 percent unemployment rate.

"We're having a record year in agriculture," Vilsack told the panelists. "It's part of a story that's not told very often in the economy. Trade surpluses, job growth, record income levels."

Newspaper columnist Mike Barnicle, a frequent panelist on the show, asked Vilsack to elaborate.

"You know, we sit here in this urban cocoon," Barnicle said. "We have no frame of reference for that. What does it mean to have a record year in agriculture for the rest of the country?"

"Well, one out of twelve jobs in this country is connected to agriculture," Vilsack responded. "What it means is that farmers and ranchers are enjoying real success for the first time in a while."

Barnicle looked quizzically at Vilsack while the secretary enumerated the value of crop exports and the promise of free-trade agreements. Barnicle didn't seem to be buying it.

"Why is it that I still have this mental picture of the family farm disappearing, though, in spite of these record years?" Barnicle asked.

Vilsack had just been handed the ideal opportunity to mention the administration's efforts to curb the corporate abuses that were driving smaller farmers out of business.

"There's a lot of excitement and entrepreneurial activity going on in rural America," Vilsack replied. "There are large, production-sized agricultural firms, no question about that. But we saw in the ag. census that there were 100,000 new farming operations started in this country, very small operations. And these are folks who are connecting locally and regionally, at farmers' markets."

As he sat at the round table with the show's hosts and other guests, Vilsack painted a picture of the rural economy that was diametrically opposed to the one he had depicted a year and a half before in Ankeny, Iowa, when he launched the series of national hearings with Attorney General Eric Holder.

All the worries seemed to have vanished.

Inside GIPSA, it became clear that Dudley Butler had lost the fight. Butler himself realized this fact when he was no longer invited to critical meetings to finalize the GIPSA rule.

In the fall of 2011, officials from the Department of Agriculture met with their counterparts in the Office of Management and Budget, or

OMB. The meetings with OMB were part of the final process for getting the rule approved. OMB's job was to comb through the rule and evaluate its possible consequences and costs, advising the administration on what it found. It was the final hurdle to pass before the final GIPSA rule could be released.

Butler found out about the OMB meetings after they occurred. He heard secondhand about the concerns some OMB officials had about the rule, and he was frustrated that he couldn't sit in on the meetings to defend the measure.

Butler was told, for example, that OMB officials were worried that setting a base price for chicken farmers in the tournament system might violate antitrust laws. They thought that setting a base price could be considered a form of price fixing. Butler thought that idea was ridiculous. Hog farmers in Iowa were already guaranteed a base price for the hogs they raised. The base price was more akin to setting a kind of minimum wage than it was to fixing the price of a product. But Butler wasn't in the room to press his point. He suspected that that's why he wasn't invited.

The pragmatist camp was winning out. Parts of the rule were being abandoned, and other sections were going to be proposed again as temporary measures. In late 2011, Butler was presented with a final version of the GIPSA rule and given the choice to sign it or not.

Vilsack's team gutted the GIPSA rule's provision that would have reformed the poultry industry's tournament system for paying farmers. The final rule dropped the all-important measure that would have fixed a base price in the tournament system, which would have given farmers a guaranteed minimum payment rather than risking their financial ruin with each flock.

But the rule did keep one key protection for farmers: It would force companies like Tyson to restrict the tournament to farmers who owned similar chicken houses. That meant that farmers with older houses wouldn't compete against their neighbors with the newest, most expensive complexes. Such a rule seemed fair to Butler if the tournament was really meant to be an apples-to-apples contest that judged farming techniques rather than equipment.

The final rule over the tournament would be softened in another way. It was going to be presented as an "interim" measure, which would be enforced for just sixty days. That would give the meat industry more time to submit comment and ask for changes.

Vilsack's team also decided to delay enacting the GIPSA rule's most sweeping reform: the provision that would have made it easier to sue meat companies for unfair or deceptive practices. Vilsack himself had vehemently defended that provision when the rule was initially proposed, saying it was unreasonable to ask a single farmer to prove that a company's actions against him would harm the meat industry as a whole.

But the so-called "competitive injury" provision had become a political liability over the course of 2011. Kansas Republican senator Pat Roberts attacked the provision, and Dudley Butler, during a congressional hearing that summer. Roberts hinted that Butler was trying to expand the farmers' right to sue because, as a former trial attorney, Butler was looking forward to a big payday in court after leaving USDA.

As he sat behind the podium at the hearing, Roberts said he was disturbed by the USDA's "attack" on agriculture.

"I do not want to call into question anyone's motives. Let me make that clear," Roberts explained during the hearing. "But I must say that the actions of the USDA on this rule, and the past activities of GIPSA administrator J. Dudley Butler as a lawyer in the private sector, call into question the department's impartiality on the issue.

"It seems like the fox is guarding the hen house, and we're missing a few hens," Roberts said.

Roberts implied that Butler had misled Vilsack on Congress's intent regarding the GIPSA rule. He also read a direct quote that Dudley Butler had made in an earlier public appearance, in which he called the GIPSA rule "a plaintiff's lawyer's dream."

In fact, Butler had said during the appearance that it was the *previous* GIPSA regulations that were a trial lawyer's dream because they were so vague. Butler had said he wanted to better define vague terms in the law like "unfair" and "undue preference," while putting specific parameters around what was legal and what wasn't.

Senator Roberts's comments were inaccurate, but the damage had been done. The provision to help farmers sue under the Packers and Stockyards Act was increasingly seen as government overreach.

The USDA decided it would repropose the "competitive injury" rule rather than pass it as a final regulation, giving the industry more time to comment on it and request changes.

Butler decided to sign the interim GIPSA rule over poultry tournaments and support the reproposal of the competitive injury rule. Even stripped down, the rules would be the strongest regulation passed in decades to curtail the market power of big meat companies.

But Butler's decision to sign on to the plan would prove to be a moot point. Congress was about to make sure of that.

The meat industry had spent months, and millions of dollars, building opposition to the GIPSA rule in Congress. In late 2011, the investment paid off.

The House of Representatives passed a spending bill that summer that banned GIPSA from using any money to finalize its new antitrust rule. In essence, the "defunding" provision meant that the USDA couldn't enforce the GIPSA rule even if it was finalized. It was a classic case of Congress using its power of the purse to influence policy in the executive branch. But the House couldn't defund the rule by itself. The spending bill needed to be approved by the Democratic-controlled Senate as well.

Supporters of the GIPSA rule were encouraged when the Senate passed its own spending bill that kept funding for the rule. It appeared that the Democrats on the Hill were prepared to support President Obama's farm reforms. But in November, members of the House and Senate met in a closed-door session to iron out their different spending bills into a compromise measure. Inside that conference committee, the GIPSA rule was killed. Congress stripped funding for the GIPSA rule on a remarkably detailed level. The spending bill went through the proposed rule, naming specific paragraphs and provisions and barring the USDA from spending any money to enforce them.

After the bill was released, meat industry lobbyists gave a special public thanks to the senators who had helped them, including Pat Roberts from Kansas, who had publicly excoriated Dudley Butler in the Senate hearing. Missouri's newly elected Republican senator Roy Blunt was also singled out for thanks.

Between the Obama administration's own backpedaling and Congress's opposition, the GIPSA rule was dead. A final version of the rule was released in December. It enacted one reform, one that allowed poultry farmers the right to sue meat companies in court if they had a contract dispute. Most contracts had previously forced farmers into private arbitration hearings to settle disputes, keeping them away from unpredictable juries. The final rules also contained new guidelines suggesting when a poultry company could cut off a farmer or require a farmer to invest more money in his chicken houses. Those guidelines did not have the binding power of new rules, Vilsack admitted, but he hinted that the new measures would act as a deterrent for poultry companies.

A full year and a half after the joint workshops between the U.S. Departments of Agriculture and Justice were completed, no major new policy recommendations had been issued by either department. No major antitrust cases were filed. No joint report was issued.

The Department of Justice released its own small report on the workshops, with little fanfare, in May 2012. The twenty-four-page document enumerated all the problems and abuses the department learned about during the workshops, while outlining the unprecedented level of market concentration that existed after a wave of company mergers. But in its brief conclusion, the report mostly focused on why the Justice Department couldn't do much to solve the problems. Antitrust laws weren't made to solve many of the problems identified by the hearings, the report said.

The Justice Department pointed out that it had enhanced its cooperation with the USDA, helping that agency prosecute cases. It also said it would boost its efforts to block mergers that were anticompetitive. But the only major case the report could point to as an example of its efforts was one filed by the Bush administration in 2008, which blocked the merger of meatpackers JBS and National.

By the spring of 2012, the Obama administration had lost most of its key architects for a new agricultural policy. In May John Ferrell quit and went back home to Iowa, where he started studying for an advanced degree. Christine Varney quit later that summer and took a job with the elite law firm Cravath, Swaine & Moore. Varney assumed a prominent spot at the firm's antitrust practice, where she would help companies fight off challenges from the government. Ethics rules prohibited her from immediately protecting companies like Tyson Foods, which had been the focus of federal litigation under her watch. But even if Varney didn't directly take up Tyson's fight against stronger antitrust enforcement, the Obama administration had lost one of its toughest fighters.

Shortly after the GIPSA rule was defeated, Dudley Butler resigned. He returned to his family farm in Mississippi and started up a small law practice that represented farmers.

During the spring of 2012, the presidential campaign entered into full swing and Secretary Vilsack continued publicizing the campaign narrative that U.S. agriculture was an economic success story. Vilsack made public appearances extolling the job creation and income being generated in rural America, even as the broader job market remained tepid. It was clear that Barack Obama did not plan to campaign on his achievements as an industry reformer.

Vilsack was correct when he said that the agricultural sector, overall, was booking record profits, at least when it came to the industrial meat business. Billions in profits were being generated in meat producing towns like Waldron, Arkansas; Dodge City, Kansas; and Emmetsburg, Iowa.

But the existence of those profits told only half the story. The other half of the story was hidden and more complicated. And the other half of the story could be seen only after asking one simple question: If record profits were being made, who got to keep them?

CHAPTER 13

Don's Horizon

(2011–2012)

ONE OF Don Tyson's houses is a palatial estate in the countryside south of Springdale, with big windows and a commanding view of the Ozark hills and bluffs that surround it. The land it overlooks is rugged and remote. It is land where generations of settlers had failed to grow much of anything on the rocky soil, but it's where Don Tyson had built a multibillion-dollar empire whose tendrils reached from South Dakota to Mississippi, to Brazil, India, and China.

During the winter of early 2011, a lot of people stood and stared out those windows. They took in the view of barren trees and hard, cold ground. The emptiness of the vista reflected the sorrow of the moment. They had come to say goodbye to Don Tyson. His intimate circle of friends and family had learned he was dying.

Don Tyson had struggled for years with liver cancer, largely outside the public view. He visited clinics and doctors secretly, battling the disease. In 2010 his prognosis worsened, and the cancer progressed. By all logical predictions, it seemed he had just a few months to live.

Don Tyson quietly got his affairs in order. He structured Tyson Foods in a way that his leadership over the company would endure for years after his passing. With his approval, the company promoted Donnie Smith to the position of CEO. Smith, the vice president over poultry operations who had overseen the production cutbacks during 2008, seems a man cut from Don Tyson's own image. Smith has a pronounced southern twang, a kind of deceptive humbleness about him that resembled Don's. And Smith had learned the meat business at the feet of Don's lieutenants Leland Tollett and Buddy Wray. Don also structured his special class of voting stock in a way that passed control to his son, Johnny, and a trusted cadre of advisors and old friends like Tollett.

Even in the last years of his life, Don Tyson was pushing for visionary change and growth at the company that carried his name. His imagination was captured by the idea of taking Tyson Foods global. He kept color photos on his desk showing new poultry plants being built on the freshly cleared ground of Brazilian forests, and he watched over projects for new poultry plants in Asia.

Don Tyson saw the real opportunity in countries like Brazil, India, and China. Consumers there resemble U.S. shoppers back in 1960. The middle class is growing in places like Brazil, and it has more money to spend on meat and eggs. At the same time, people are getting busier. Fast-food chains are expanding in the developing world, with more drive-through windows opening every day. Tyson Foods planned to replicate its growth curve in the United States by catering to the growing middle class of the developing world.

In September 2008, Tyson Foods bought two poultry companies in Brazil, and it bought a majority ownership stake in a third. Tyson Foods announced three joint ventures in China, where it bought majority ownership in three big slaughterhouses. In India, Tyson bought a majority share of a poultry company based in Mumbai. These companies were Don Tyson's beachheads, the forward bases from which he would infiltrate the rural economies that represented billions in annual sales.

But it became clear in late 2010 that Tyson's global conquest would be left to others. Don Tyson made the final arrangements for his lieutenants to watch over the company, and he seemed ready to let go. He retreated to the place he loved best, his home in the Ozark hills of Arkansas. His wife, Jean, had died a few years before, the two of them estranged until the end. But Don was still surrounded by family. He presided over a big Christmas dinner, with Johnny and Johnny's now-grown children. Don seemed happy and energetic on Christmas night.

Over the next two weeks, a parade of visitors streamed through the house. Friends, children, and girlfriends, all of them saying their goodbyes.

One of the guests was a young woman who had just turned twenty-nine years old. Her name was J.J., and she lived in Texas most of the time but traveled a lot. She had an unmistakable roundness in her cheeks and a broad arch to her eyebrows. She also had a special kind of confidence, a loquaciousness and charisma. In short, she very closely resembled her father, Don Tyson. She looked a lot more like her dad than her half-brother, Johnny, who had been heir to Don's kingdom.

J.J. is decades younger than Johnny Tyson, the daughter of one of Don's girlfriends. Unlike Johnny, J.J. never worked for Don, and because of that she knew her father better in some ways. She saw the man outside of the corporate headquarters. The Don Tyson J.J. knew was a man who spent a lot of his time circumnavigating the globe on his yacht, and he often kept J.J. at his side.

J.J. Caldwell-Tyson was born in 1981 to Ramona Caldwell, an attractive blond woman from Fayetteville who was Don Tyson's long-time companion. Ramona Caldwell never became Don's wife, but she never became an exgirlfriend, either. Ramona and J.J. lived in a number of apartments over the years, in Little Rock and London, and Don Tyson often stayed with them when he traveled on business. He was always "Dad" to J.J.

Her childhood spanned the globe. In his later years, Don Tyson became dissatisfied with his yacht, *Tyson's Pride*, because it couldn't carry enough fuel for long, deep-sea voyages. So he bought a commercial tuna vessel and retrofitted it to be his home ship. He called it the *Horizon*.

J.J. spent a lot of time on the *Horizon*. She sailed it from Hawaii to Tahiti. Rather than regularly attending elementary school, J.J. traveled at Don's side to Tokyo, Tanzania, and Australia. They went on daytrips that Don called "cultural projects." Don hired drivers and guides and they toured different countries.

When Don was out on the open ocean, he woke up early to go fishing. He disembarked from the *Horizon* on smaller fishing vessels, like the *Tyson's Pride*, and headed out into deep waters. Out there on the back of the fishing boat, with whitecaps breaking against the hull and the world wide open around him, Don was in his own paradise.

Don Tyson often sat quietly, but J.J. knew there were jet streams of information swirling in his head. At a moment's notice, he could tell his daughter what the current cattle prices were, or how much soybeans were fetching on global markets. He chewed over business strategies and concocted new plans.

Even with a fishing line in the water, Don's life revolved around work. His bone-deep desire to make money never left him. He scheduled trips that also involved working stops, like visiting new sites for Tyson Foods plants in Brazil. There was never a moment when Don Tyson sat back and said: This is enough.

Don never pushed J.J. to join the business. This might have been born from hard-earned wisdom he gleaned at Johnny Tyson's expense. J.J. remembered the dark time when Don Tyson had to fire his son, and how much it seemed to hurt him.

— It's the hardest thing I've ever had to do. I'll always love Johnny, Don said. Don and Johnny seemed to overcome whatever hard feelings might have developed from their time at work together, and they still saw each other or talked on the phone almost every day.

J.J. hurried to Arkansas when she heard Don was losing ground against cancer.

She spent her days in the house as visitors came and went. She remembers her father reading a long letter he received from a perfect stranger, a woman who emigrated to the United States some twenty years before. Her first job in the country was at a Tyson Foods plant. Like so many who arrived here barely speaking the language and with few job skills to speak of, a job at Tyson Foods had been the first rung of this woman's American experience.

It was only then that it really sank in for J.J. how enormous her father's company had been, and how many lives he had touched.

Jim Blair drove down the lonely country roads, out to Don Tyson's secluded house. Blair was getting older. Years of vigorous exercise, some of it on the tennis courts behind his house, had taken their toll.

His hips bothered him some mornings, and he loosened up with long walks along the hillsides by his home. It wasn't easy, getting old, and it wasn't easy watching his best friend die. After Christmas, Don was weakening more by the day. He had trouble talking, and he seemed to be in pain.

Jim raided Don's wine cellar during one visit and brought up one of the finest bottles. He knew that Don loved a good drink.

— Does it taste good? Blair asked.

— Nothing tastes good, Don said.

Don Tyson didn't have any illusions about what was happening.

— You know, Don told Blair, I've been preparing for this for thirty years.

Blair tried to comfort him.

— Well, you've done everything you've wanted to do, you've seen everything you've wanted to see. You've slept with every woman you've wanted to sleep with.

Don groaned.

— Marilyn Monroe . . .

Blair smiled later at the memory of it. His old friend, dying, still had his eyes on the horizon, and the one woman he never took to bed.

On Sunday, January 4, 2011, Don Tyson watched the Arkansas Razorbacks play Ohio State in the Sugar Bowl with Ramona and J.J. Don Tyson usually paced during football games and hollered to support his team. He cheered on the Razorbacks that Sunday, and even though they lost, he seemed content.

Hours later, he went into shock. On Monday, the family came to sit by his bedside, though he couldn't speak.

Don's daughter Cheryl sat on the bed and held his hand. Seeing that J.J. was in the room, Cheryl patted the bed and gestured for her to sit down. Don's daughters, born decades apart and by different women, both held his hands.

In the early morning hours of January 6, Don Tyson passed away.

Don Tyson's funeral was a private affair. One old friend traveled many miles to attend it. President Bill Clinton was solemn as he walked to the front of the congregation to eulogize his old friend.

"I wasn't very important in Don Tyson's life, but he was quite important in mine," Clinton said.

Clinton recalled how Don Tyson supported Clinton's earliest campaign for Congress back in 1974, and how he later backed Clinton's run for the White House in 1991. Clinton recalled the time Don Tyson let him drive his Bentley.

"And it was like driving a big boat on a totally calm lake. I will never forget it," Clinton said. More than the fun they had together, Clinton remembered what he had learned from his early benefactor.

Don Tyson "had a realistic sense of what should and shouldn't be done. And he was always straight with me, and, I suspect, with all of you. I'll never forget when he came to the White House to see me once. He seemed a little bit awe-inspired, and yet, completely comfortable. . . . He was an astonishing man."

The people who mourned Don Tyson mourned the man. But many also mourned the loss not just of a specific person, but a kind of person. A man born in rural poverty in the depths of the Depression. A small-town kid who inexplicably dreamed on a global scale and saw a future for himself that was impossibly larger than the world he knew. And a man who also, somehow, managed to achieve that impossibly ambitious dream.

Don Tyson was buried that icy weekend in January, but his legacy was a restless thing that never quit moving. He left behind a company that was working and moving and growing around the clock, even as he lay dying. Tyson Foods was a kind of perpetual motion machine, an entity with its own interests and guiding principles. It was built to expand and to exert control wherever it could.

Don Tyson left behind a company that reaped $28.4 billion in annual sales. It controlled a network of more than 6,000 industrial chicken farms that grew about 2.1 billion birds every year. The company slaughtered 7.2 million cows annually, killing more than 19,700 every day. It killed 20.5 million pigs every year, many of them born at the company's contract farms in Oklahoma.

Tyson's meat was eaten by almost every American consumer, whether they realized it or not. The company had become the biggest U.S. supplier to fast-food restaurants, cafeterias, and grocery stores, producing about a fifth of all the meat eaten in the United States. This was the thing Don Tyson left behind. It wasn't just a company, but a new system of agriculture.

On February 4, 2011, Donnie Smith woke up early. He had a big morning ahead of him. Smith would be announcing, in the long-held tradition of the company's CEO, the latest financial results for Tyson Foods. Smith would sit at a table with other senior executives and talk into a speakerphone, telling investors and stock analysts just how well Tyson Foods had done with their money.

The previous year had been one of the worst for America's economy since the Great Depression. The unemployment rate was 9.7 percent at the beginning of 2010, and it hovered at that level through most of the year. The U.S. economy had shed millions of jobs during 2009 and there wasn't any sign that those jobs were coming back. In the aftershocks of the financial crisis, Americans were watching their incomes shrink and the cost of living rise.

In the midst of all this, Donnie Smith had some very good news to report to Tyson's investors. As he settled into his seat that morning and the speakerphone crackled to life, Smith sounded confident and upbeat. He spoke self-assuredly, almost cockily, the way that a quarterback might after winning the big game.

"Good morning everyone, and thanks for joining us," Smith said. "If you read our press release this morning you saw that we set a record in our first quarter of the fiscal year."

Tyson Foods had just reported an operating profit of $498 million for the previous three months. The company had sold $7.6 billion in products. And the record profits were part of a trend. Just a few months earlier, Donnie Smith had reported on a similar conference call that during the previous fiscal year, Tyson Foods earned $780 million in pure profit, breaking its own records. The company's total revenue had risen almost 7 percent to $28.43 billion in one year.

All this happened while more Americans were out of work than at any time since the 1930s and while household incomes were plunging. Tyson's results reflected the truth that even in hard times, people need to eat. And when people eat, Tyson's products were all but unavoidable. The only way to avoid them was to become a vegetarian.

When it came to controlling costs, Tyson was in an enviable position. The company was able to hold wages down at its processing plants without worrying that employees would jump to a competitor. In many towns, Tyson had no competitors. Farmers worked in the same economic isolation, willing to accept fewer shipments of birds when Tyson cut production because they were beholden to the company's contracts.

Labor had gotten so cheap in rural America that Tyson found that it was more profitable to hire more workers than buy expensive machines for its slaughterhouses. Smith told the investors that morning that Tyson had cut about $600 million in costs in its chicken division over the previous three years. Don Tyson's ethic of pushing costs down at every turn was alive and well inside his corporation.

Smith ended the conference call with an emotional mention of Don Tyson's recent death.

"He meant a lot to our team members. He meant a lot to me personally. We will miss him," Smith said.

"I think 2011 will be a year that would have made Don proud."

Smith's prediction turned out to be correct. Tyson Foods reported $750 million in profits for the fiscal year of 2011, just shy of the record $780 million it earned in 2010.*

While Don Tyson would surely have been proud of the profits, he might have been even more amazed with how Tyson earned them. The company was able to raise prices throughout the year, even as demand

---

* Tyson's fiscal year includes part of the previous calendar year, 2010.

and overall economic growth remained relatively weak. The company raised chicken prices 4.7 percent during its 2011 fiscal year. Tyson Foods raised its beef prices a remarkable 16.9 percent during the first nine months of the year even as beef sales volumes fell 1 percent. Tyson raised pork prices 15.2 percent.

Tyson Foods had come a long way from the volatile early days, when economic cycles could wipe out its profit margin and threaten its business. As the company demonstrated in late 2008, it was now big enough to help boost national meat prices through coordinated production cuts that squeezed supplies. Even in the wake of the biggest downturn since the Depression, Tyson managed to book a profit every quarter during 2011.

After 2011, price hikes and production cuts became central to Tyson's business model. Between 2006 and 2012, Tyson Foods would raise chicken prices five out of the six years. It raised pork prices four out of the six years and beef prices five out of the six years. Tyson and its competitors raised prices in part to offset higher grain costs, but the price hikes clearly helped these companies turn bigger profits. The operating profit margins of the nation's top four meat companies doubled between 2008 and 2009, even in the face of an economic crisis. The top four meat companies more than doubled their profit margins again to 4.5 percent between 2009 and 2010.

In early 2012, Donnie Smith was able to deliver a string of good numbers to the company's investors, as Tyson delivered profits quarter after quarter. The company forecasted that overall U.S. meat supplies would fall between 2 and 3 percent during the year, which would help it raise prices. The executives at Tyson Foods seemed almost to be bragging about the company's ability to cut production and raise prices.

By the middle of 2012, the plan was working well. During the first six months of the year, Tyson Foods raised chicken prices 9.6 percent, beef prices 16 percent, and pork prices 7.3 percent. The $322 million in profits it earned halfway through the year wasn't as high as the same time in 2011, but Donnie Smith predicted the company's profits during all of 2012 would stay near the record levels of 2011 and 2010.

While Tyson did well for itself, it is less clear how well the company did by the communities that made it rich. Remarkably little research has been done to measure the economic impact of vertically integrated meat production on the nation's economy. Instead, the massive fire-power of public research dollars has been aimed at a different question: how to accelerate the industrialization of agriculture. At the University of Arkansas in Fayetteville, for example, researchers study, on the molecular level, how chickens can more efficiently convert feed into meat, helping companies like Tyson to further compress their cost margins. At Kansas State University, researchers are finding new ways to keep cattle from getting open sores on their feet during the months they stand in manure-covered feedlot pens.

But an extensive analysis of publicly available data shows the impact of Tyson's rise has been, at best, a mixed blessing for the communities where the company operates.

Tyson's income gains are an open book, advertised each quarter when the company releases its earnings results to Wall Street investors. The company is reaping record profits of hundreds of millions of dollars every year.

The income patterns of rural America, where Tyson makes its money, are a little more difficult to discern. But it is possible, using government data, to build a map of Tyson's economic footprint.

By 2011, Tyson had slaughterhouses and production plants in seventy-nine counties across the United States, with an additional four offices and plants located in big cities like Chicago and Houston. Federal data shows per-capita income levels in all of these counties, going back to 1969.

The forty years between 1969 and 2009 is a good period to measure Tyson's economic impact. During the 1960s, Tyson was just becoming the company it is today, expanding its network of contract farms and buying up competitors. Over the next forty years, Tyson came to dominate the economic life of towns in rural Arkansas, Iowa, Oklahoma, and elsewhere. Tyson had an unquestionable influence on the per-capita income in those places. In towns like Waldron and Berryville, Arkansas, for example, Tyson is the predominant economic force. Without Tyson, there is no local economy.

The verdict on Tyson's economic impact is stark.

In 68 percent of the counties where Tyson operates, per-capita income has grown more slowly than the state average over the last forty years. Tyson counties, in other words, were worse off in terms of income growth than their neighbors, even as Tyson's profits increased. That analysis excludes the four major metro areas where Tyson has facilities (Chicago, Dallas, Fort Worth, and Houston) because the multitude of other businesses there makes Tyson's impact harder to detect. But even if those four cities are included, the analysis does not significantly change: In that case, 65 percent of the Tyson counties fared worse that their state's average.

Tyson's defenders might refute this data by pointing out that the company often operates in impoverished rural areas, which should not be expected to outperform the state average.

But the analysis does not compare the overall per-capita income in Tyson counties to the state averages. What this analysis measures is the *rate* of income growth in Tyson's counties, compared to the rate of income growth in surrounding counties.

It is not unreasonable to expect that the economic dynamo of Tyson Foods, which has created billions of dollars of income for investors over the years, might help boost the income growth rate in the towns that produce the company's actual value: the animals, the feed, and the meat. If Tyson is the economic anchor of a town, it could be expected to improve the economic lot of residents there.

But the data suggests that Tyson is a suffocating economic force on the communities from which it derives its wealth. Without question, the company provides thousands of jobs and steady paychecks. But its cost-cutting ethos and the lack of competition restrains income growth in rural America. The company has expanded in economically marginal areas, and it has kept those areas economically marginal. Tyson

Foods is feeding off the lowly economic position of rural America, not improving it.

This analysis has its limits. Measuring per-capita income on the county level is a broad metric. It takes into account a lot of economic activity that isn't attributable to Tyson Foods, while some activity outside the county's borders (like some of Tyson's more far-flung farms) would not be reflected in that county's income figures. But by any standard, Tyson is a major economic force in the rural counties where its slaughterhouses, feed mills, and farms employ thousands of people. County-level income data might not be perfect, but it is the best picture of Tyson's economic shadow that is publicly available.

Interestingly, the situation is worst in the one state where Tyson has the most power. In Arkansas, fully 89 percent of the counties in which Tyson operates are worse off than the state as a whole. This is the state where Tyson has by far the most employees and the state where Tyson has laid its deepest roots.

That 89 percent figure even gives Tyson the benefit of the doubt. The two counties that beat the state average that were also home to Tyson's plants were located in the metro area of North Little Rock and the town of Rogers, which sits in the same county as Wal-Mart's global headquarters (which has spawned gated communities and upscale retail centers in its orbit).

This finding suggests that Harold Breimyer's warning back in the 1960s has come to pass. The income pattern drawn by Tyson's system doesn't reflect productivity; it reflects power. When one company owns the machinery of production in a town, it can keep the lion's share of the profits. When one company buys the vast majority of its competitors it doesn't have to compete with higher wages to retain workers or farmers.

This means many parts of rural America can look to Arkansas if they want to see their future. As hog farmers in Iowa and feedlot owners in Kansas sign their first contract with Tyson, the state of Arkansas can show them the logical conclusion of Tyson's path.

It's unclear if anything will change this pattern. The likelihood that change will be driven from the ground up, from the communities where Tyson operates, is slim. To understand why this is, it is helpful to visit the Tyson town of Berryville, Arkansas, in rural Carroll County. The big, concrete expanse of the Tyson complex sits at Berryville's core. Just south of that is a grotto of trailer homes that is home to many of Tyson's immigrant plant workers.

Berryville's First National Bank sits on a corner at the town square. From his perch in the president's office there, Robert West had been able to observe Berryville's economy for decades. West was born in Berryville, and he still remembers the time when the city had mostly dirt roads.

Now in his seventies, West has retired as bank president but still sits on the board of directors. West knows his place when he talks about Tyson. The First National Bank of Arkansas is sort of like a wild mushroom at the foot of a giant oak tree. The bank survives off the nutrients cast off by the giant above it. During West's career, the bank extended mortgages and car loans to the lower-income workers at Tyson's plant. It provided farm loans to the company's chicken farmers. The plant workers never really jumped an income bracket. The farmers never really left their cycle of indebtedness. People might complain, but there really wasn't an alternative.

Berryville had the Tyson plant, and in the eyes of most of its residents that's all that the town would ever have. Berryville was remote. Berryville was left behind. Berryville was lucky to have Tyson.

"They're gonna pay what they think they can afford. If they pay more, well, that'd be good for the town," West said. "But it might not be good for the company."

And Berryville would make do.

"I don't know what we'd have if it wasn't for them," West said.

Of course, discontent with Tyson's system has gained momentum across the country, culminating in lawsuits and a push for tougher regulations. A ragtag coalition of interest groups representing small farmers, with alphabet-soup names like R-CALF USA and RAFI-USA, have spent years lobbying Congress and they continue to lobby the White

House to impose new regulations on Tyson and other meat giants. When President Obama visited North Carolina in late 2011, RAFI-USA took out a full-page newspaper ad, urging passage of the so-called GIPSA rule.

But by 2012, farmers had joined consumer advocacy groups like Food and Water Watch, which are concerned that meat prices have risen much faster than many other staples of modern life. Tyson's expansion has left little consumer choice for middle- and low-income shoppers when it comes to buying meat. While niche localvore farmers are increasing in numbers, consumer advocates still worry that most middle- to low-income Americans rely on industrially produced meat for nutrition.

These new coalitions of interest groups appear to have been out-matched and outmaneuvered by meat industry lobbyists in Washington during the Obama years. The White House has backed off its initially aggressive stance on the issue, and the odds of Congress passing new legislation seem increasingly remote.

And the debate over these issues has not slowed Tyson's growth. The company's entrenched power is increasing and its control over rural economies is increasing. Every day, Tyson evolves, grows, and renews itself.

Tyson Foods used to recruit new contract farmers by placing ads in local newspapers. Now Tyson has a website to advertise its opportunities, extolling the virtues of modern meat production to rural entrepreneurs.

The website's pitch isn't much different than the one Buddy Wray made back in the 1960s, when he toured small towns and signed up farmers to supply Tyson's expanding slaughterhouses.

"Tyson supplies the birds, feed and technical advice, while the poultry producer provides the labor, housing and utilities," the website says. "In other words, growers are ensured of a consistent price for their efforts, no matter what the feed or grocery markets are doing."

Interested parties are given a list of phone numbers to call if they want to join Tyson's ranks. Residents of Scott County, Arkansas, are provided the phone number of a production manager in the town of Waldron. For a lot of people in rural America, opportunities like this are about the best for which they can hope.

Tyson is waiting to take their call, and ready to shape their future.

ACKNOWLEDGMENTS

A lot of people inside Tyson Foods talked to me for this book, and many of them did so at great financial risk to themselves. I am deeply grateful that they entrusted me with their stories. I am particularly grateful to the farmers who talked to me in spite of their fears.

I am grateful to former senior executives at Tyson who spoke to me for this book. I think they talked to me because they knew the history of Tyson Foods was much bigger than most people understood. Many of them were appropriately proud of what they accomplished. I am grateful to all of them, and I apologize if they disagree with the conclusions I have drawn. I did my level best to tell the truth with this book, even though that truth is bound to make many people mad.

I am grateful that Don Tyson gave me his time and shared his stories and insights, even though he had no need to do so. I had the opportunity to interview him twice at great length for this book. I consider those discussions to be among the few times I have sat in the same room with a genius.

This project would not have existed if it were not for the talents and decisive leadership of my editor, Priscilla Painton, at Simon & Schuster. Priscilla is an editor's editor, in the finest tradition of the business. Priscilla began asking incisive questions about this project from the first moment she encountered it. Each question pushed the book forward and made it better, and I am lucky to have been part of the process. Priscilla's ethics, her hard work, and her dedication to great journalism are an inspiration. I am so grateful for Jonathan Karp's support for this project.

Editor Michael Szczerban was indefatigable in his support for the book, providing me with many an hour on the phone as I hashed through ideas and tried to figure out a way forward. I am grateful that Sydney Tanigawa swooped in to carry the book through to the end. Thanks to Phil Metcalf for shepherding the manuscript through production, and to Robert Castillo for his sharp-eyed edit and suggestions. Thanks so much to Nina Pajak, Meg Cassidy, and Larry Hughes for helping get the word out.

I am indebted to my agent for this book, Diana Finch, who never gives up. Diana is both a sprinter and a marathon runner, which is handy in a business where the finish line is always moving.

I am so lucky that Lucy Shackelford decided to go below her pay grade and work with me on this project. Researcher extraordinaire, Lucy has combed this manuscript with the sharp eye of an auditor, removing embarrassing errors. I am indebted to her for both her research skills and her rock-solid advice and guidance. Thank you. It goes without saying that all the mistakes left are my own.

I am deeply grateful to everyone at the New America Foundation. I am lucky to walk through the door every day, and I never let myself forget it. I would especially like to thank Steve Coll for giving me the chance to come to New America and for his advice along the way; there is no better role model for a journalist than Steve. Andres Martinez has been an invaluable mentor and supporter, and I am forever grateful for his help. Rachel White has been a remarkable leader during my time here. I am thrilled that Anne-Marie Slaughter has decided to pick up the torch; the future is bright. Barry Lynn has been patient and wise in his guidance and his lessons about power. I am so grateful to learn every day from Becky Shafer, Konstantin Kakaes, Steve LeVine, Lina Kahn, Louie Palu, Susan Gwaltney, John Williams, Faith Smith, Alex Holt, Stephanie Gunter, Fuzz Hogan, Elizabeth Weingarten, Adam Sneed, Josh Freedman, Michael Lind, Patrick Doherty, Reid Cramer, Kevin Carey, Torie Bosch, Kirsten Berg, Victoria Collins, Clara Hogan, Patrick Lucey, Cyrus Nemati, and Nick McCllelan.

Bill Bullard at R-CALF USA has been a remarkable source over many years. He is a straight shooter who always has incredible graphs and spreadsheets at the ready, and I am indebted to his help. Becky Ceartas at RAFI was invaluable for her insight into the legal ins-and-outs of chicken farming.

My great friend Whitney Lane was kind enough to donate her time to edit early versions of this book. It wouldn't have been the same without her sharp eye and hard work, and I don't know what I would have done without her help. Deanna Benjamin helped me edit the first chapter and my book proposal, and I benefitted greatly from her wonderful feedback and encouragement. Casey Smith was an incredible whiz with using government data, and I am grateful for her help and creative thinking to build and analyze data sets for this book.

I have been very lucky to spend most of my career in a series of newspaper and wire-service jobs, where I worked with a group of extraordinary editors who showed me the way. At the *Columbia Daily Tribune*, I thank the incredible duo of Scott Swafford and John Schneller; I am glad you caught me when I was still young enough to learn. Managing editor Jim Robertson broke protocol in 1999 and let my first story on Tyson Foods go past the jump, for which I am still grateful (but still too intimidated to say anything about it). At the *Arkansas Democrat-Gazette,* I was lucky to work with John Magsam, Serenah McKay, Roger Hedges, David Bailey, and Griffin Smith.

I am so lucky to have fallen in with the team I did at the Associated Press. I learned more than I can say from the outstanding examples of Jim Salter, Chris Clark, Randy Picht, Paul Stevens, and Kia Breaux. Jim Salter was not just a great boss but a wonderful role model.

I am eternally indebted to the wise guidance of the Reverend Lowell Grisham in Arkansas and the Reverend Andrew Archie in Saint Louis. Neither man knew the specifics of the project I was working on, but both were generous enough to give me guidance as I navigated the thorny business of investigative journalism. Thank you.

At the University of Missouri, I was lucky to have Mary Kay Blakely as a tireless defender, mentor, and guide—thanks so much for all the help over the years. Steve Weinberg always had time to give advice. Thanks to everyone at Mizzou for showing me what journalism is. Thanks, Leigh Lockhart, for my first job out of college.

To the Ponca gang: Thanks for making this a fun business to be in; I look forward to many more years of it. To the Blue Planet Posse: Thanks for helping me figure out who I was going to be when I grew up. To the Andreses, the Riches, the Higdons, the Diekempers, the

Lanes, the Wolfs, the Dobsons, and the Berzons: Saturday nights just aren't the same without having you all over for dinner. To Mary Ann: You believed in this first.

John and Joan Miller are the most supportive parents-in-law that a guy could ever dream of having. It must have been dispiriting for them to learn that their daughter was going to marry a writer, but they have never been anything except my greatest champions. Their support is more than I deserve.

I am lucky to have grown up in Kansas City, surrounded by people who are good in the deepest sense of the word. Uncle Ron Spradley is the best godfather that there could be; thanks for being a wonderful role model and just an all-around great friend. Thanks to Aunt Blythe and Uncle Dave Launder, and to David, Betsy, Andrew, and Victoria. What's life without Launders? Thanks to Hotchy Kiene, Hunter Wolbach, Andrew Moore, Stuart Wolferman, Sarah Eckles, Matthew Wood, and too many great, lifelong friends to name here. Thanks to John Eckles for being a great friend to the family, and a free lawyer when I needed one. Thanks to Julie Zimmer for coaching me on the important things since before I can remember. Thanks to Larry Ward and everyone at Shughart, Thompson & Kilroy.

Victoria Leonard, Mom, where would I be without you? You have shown me my whole life what it means to have a moral compass, to be compassionate, and to think of other people first. You have shaped how I see the world, and I don't trust anyone's advice like I trust yours. Thanks for always picking up the phone when I need you, which is more often than I can count.

David, thanks for teaching me how cool reading and writing can be. Blythe, thanks for the guidance and undying support over the years. And thanks to both of you for teaching me how to hold my own during dinner-table debates.

Of course, nothing in my life is possible without my wife, Josie Leonard. She is my sounding board and my foundation. She had the courage to pay for trips to Arkansas with the family credit card before anyone believed in this project. I owe it all to you, Josie.

And to the rug rats: I love you.

NOTES

A NOTE ON SOURCES

Some sources agreed to speak to me for this book only on the condition that the interviews were on "background," meaning that I could use the information from the interviews but not attribute it to those sources. There were two classes of sources to whom I granted this privilege: Tyson Foods employees (both current and former) and officials inside the U.S. Departments of Agriculture and Justice. I think granting these sources anonymity was worth the trade-off of getting their candid observations of what transpired. When information was obtained under such ground rules, it is cited below as "Background interviews by author."

Also, some of the information in this book comes from knowledge I derived after spending more than ten years writing about U.S. corporate agribusiness. Some background facts, such as the advent of the U.S. ethanol industry, for example, come from my personal reporting over the years. These end notes do not list every article I wrote to substantiate that reporting.

STATEMENT FROM TYSON FOODS:

In final preparation for this book, I submitted two memos to Tyson Foods with a total of 63 detailed questions for the company to respond to. The questions outlined key allegations laid forth in the book, and the memos also provided an overview of key points in the narrative. The company was given months to respond to the reporting in the book. Eventually, Tyson Foods spokesman Gary Mickelson replied with a statement from the company. The company refused to answer the majority of the questions I posed.

Here is the statement from Tyson Foods, in whole:

Chris -

It appears some of the primary sources for your book are disgruntled farmers and former employees who have told you about a handful of conversations or incidents that allegedly happened years ago. We have not initiated a detailed investigation into each of their claims, but we can tell you that most of them make no sense and simply lack credibility.

We encourage you to dig deeper into the motives of these sources and press them to provide proof of their claims before incorporating them into your book. We also suggest you compare their claims to the stories of farmers and livestock producers who have enjoyed a positive working relationship with our company over the years.

Tyson Foods has been working on a contractual basis with farmers since the late 1940s. During this 70 year period, we've worked successfully with tens of thousands of farmers and livestock producers. We want and need each of them to succeed. We depend upon them to supply livestock and raise our chickens so we can efficiently operate our plants. On the poultry side of our business, there are contract farmers who have successfully raised chickens for us for decades. In addition, we receive inquiries, almost weekly, from people that have interest in growing chickens for us.

With these comments in mind, we've chosen to provide specific responses to some of the questions we can answer without starting a time-consuming investigation into dated, uncorroborated claims from disgruntled sources."

Where Tyson Foods addressed questions with information that was relevant, that information was incorporated into the text where appropriate.

PROLOGUE: THE HIDDEN KING

1 *Nobody ever visits the stranded little community of Waldron, Arkansas:* Notes from reporting in Waldron, Arkansas, 2004, 2008, 2010, 2011.

2 *This illusory appearance cloaks Tyson's existence:* Notes from reporting in Waldron, Springdale, Arkansas, 2004–2011.

2 *The Tyson brand name wouldn't necessarily stand out:* Tyson Foods brands, company website: http://www.tyson.com/Products/Our-Products.aspx.

3 *Just a handful of companies produce nearly all the meat consumed in the United States:* 2011 P&SP Annual Report, Packers and Stockyards Program, U.S. Department of Agriculture Grain Inspection, Packers and Stockyards Administration (March 2012), 31; William Heffernan and Mary Hendrickson, "Concentration of Agricultural Markets," Department of Rural Sociology, University of Missouri, 2007.

3 *While Tyson's operations are remote, the company's business practices affect virtually everyone:* Thomson Reuters-NPR Health Poll, Meat Consumption, March 2012.

4 *The first barrier to change is the fact that everything about Tyson Foods seems hidden:* Notes from reporting, Springdale, Arkansas.

4 *At the core of Tyson's strategy is an economic principle called vertical integration:* James Blair, Joe Fred Starr, Don Tyson, Buddy Wray, interviews by author, 2010 and 2011; background interviews by author.

5 *Tyson first pioneered this model in the poultry business:* Don Tyson, interviews by author, 2008, 200;. James Blair, interviews by author; Stephen F. Strausberg, *From Hills and Hollers: Rise of the Poultry Industry in Arkansas* (Fayetteville: Arkansas Agricultural Experiment Station, 1995); Marvin Schwartz, *Tyson: From Farm to Market* (Fayetteville: University of Arkansas Press, 1991).

5 *From the 1960s through the 1990s, this industrial meat machine provided tremendous benefit to American consumers:* James M. MacDonald and William D. McBride, "The Transformation of U.S. Livestock Agriculture; Scale, Efficiency, and Risks," U.S. Department of Agriculture Economic Information Bulletin Number 43 (January 2009); data on meat prices provided by Food and Agricultural Policy Research Institute, University of Missouri.

5 *Between 1955 and 1982, the amount of time it took to raise a full-grown chicken fell:* Facts on chickens getting bigger derived from USDA report on transformation of livestock industry, and chicken breeding reports;

Tomislav Vukina, "Vertical Integration and Contracting in the U.S. Poultry Sector. *Journal of Food Distribution Research* (July 2011), 33.

6 *After realizing the huge boost of savings that came from raising animals in factories, the growth curve started to flatten in the 1990s:* Data on meat prices provided by Food and Agricultural Policy Research Institute, University of Missouri.

7 *In 2008, food prices jumped 6.4 percent:* USDA report on food inflation found at: http://www.ers.usda.gov/data-products/food-price-outlook.aspx.

7 *Not only does Tyson have control over how meat is priced, it also sets the rules for how meat is produced:* Christopher Leonard, "Why Beef Is Becoming More Like Chicken: Cheap, Uniform and Bland," *Slate Magazine,* February 14, 2013; Andrew Martin, "U.S. Withdraws Approval for Tyson's Antibiotic-Free Label," *New York Times,* November 20, 2007.

9 *The power is etched into the fretful face of men like Edwin:* Edwin, interviews by author, 2004, 2011.

9 *Tyson's power could be felt several miles down winding country roads from Edwin's farm:* Notes from reporting in Waldron and rural Missouri.

10 *In 2010 alone Tyson Foods sold $28.43 billion worth of meat and cleared $780 million in pure profit:* Tyson Foods Annual Report for fiscal year 2010, SEC Form 10-K.

10 *On Saturday night, Waldron's Main Street is quiet to the point of abandonment:* Notes from reporting in Waldron, 2010.

11 *The average per capita income in Waldron and surrounding Scott County has stagnated in Tyson's shadow:* Per capita income data by county, U.S. Bureau of Economic Analysis.

12 *During that time, Tyson's annual income rose 245 percent:* Tyson Foods annual reports.

12 *But the economic malaise of rural America caught the attention of a young presidential candidate:* U.S. Secretary of Agriculture Tom Vilsack, interviewed by author, 2010, 2011; Dave Murphy, interview by author, 2011; background interviews by author, 2011.

CHAPTER 1: HOW JERRY YANDELL LOST THE FARM

17 *Kanita Yandell was waiting for the men to come:* Kanita and Jerry Yandell, interviews by author, 2004, 2010, 2011; Christopher Leonard, "Poultry Chicken Deaths Baffle Growers, Tyson Foods," *Arkansas Democrat-Gazette,* March 28, 2004.

18 *About every eight weeks, a Tyson truck delivered birds to the Yandell farm:* Jerry and Kanita Yandell, interviews by author; notes from reporting at Yandell farm, 2004.

19 *Around Christmas, Kanita and Jerry realized it didn't matter:* Jerry and Kanita Yandell, interviews by author.

20 *The struggles on Jerry Yandell's farm could be observed on blinking computer screens inside the offices of Tyson Foods:* Donnie Smith, Donnie King, interviews by author 2009; background interviews by author.

21 *The Tyson plant is a self-contained rural economy:* Notes from reporting in Waldron.

22 *The reason for this is simple, even if it has been kept secret:* James Blair, interview by author, 2010.

25 *Jerry Yandell knew how to work:* Yandells, interviews by author.

26 *The chicken business in Waldron picked up in the mid-1980s:* Don Tyson, interview by author, 2008; interviews in Waldron, Arkansas, with Tyson Foods chicken farmers and residents, 2004, 2008, 2010, 2011.

26 *Jerry and Kanita signed contracts with Tyson:* Yandells, interviews by author.

27 *The Yandells received their first flock of diseased chickens in the winter of 2003:* Yandells, interviews by author.

27 *By the time the Tyson trucks arrived at Jerry Yandell's farm to pick up the first flock of sick chickens, just about half of the birds were still alive:* Yandells, interviews by author.

29 *One of Jerry Yandell's field technicians over the years:* Tommy Brown, interviews by author, 2010, 2011.

32 *By December of 2003, Jerry and Kanita Yandell were sinking:* Yandells, interviews by author.

32 *Perry Edwards arrived for work before dawn:* Perry Edwards, interviews by author. "Perry Edwards" is a pseudonym used to protect a source who wanted to remain confidential. Please see Author's Note.

37 *Tyson Foods insists that such accusations are the stuff of "urban myth":* Statement from Tyson Foods, May 2013; Perry Edwards, interviews by author; "Plaintiffs present admissions of a Tyson 'insider,'" *McCurtain Daily Gazette,* March 17, 2010; Cynthia Johnson, interviews by author, 2011.

38 *After New Year's Day of 2004, Jerry Yandell sat in the office:* Yandells, interviews by author

40 *Shortly after signing the papers, Kanita took out an advertisement:* Personal Ad, "Auction, Personal Property," *Waldron News,* March 2004.

40 *The Saturday auction was busy:* Yandells, interviews by author.

43 *Jerry Yandell wasn't the only farmer to receive batches of sick birds:* Doug Elmore, Edwin, several anonymous Tyson Foods chicken farmers, interviews by author, 2004, 2008, 2010, 2011.

44 *Even years later, many farmers affected by the problem:* Christopher Leonard, *Arkansas Democrat-Gazette*, March 28, 2004.

44 *Eventually, Jerry and Kanita drove up to the federal courthouse:* Yandells, interviews by author, date.

45 *The company found a new crop of farmers:* Christopher Leonard, "State Becomes Fertile Ground for Laotian Immigrants Eager to Own Poultry Farms in Arkansas," *Arkansas Democrat-Gazette*, May 30, 2004.

CHAPTER 2: THE EDEN CRASH

47 *In 1930, a twenty-five-year-old man named John Tyson was exiled:* Don Tyson, interview by author, 2009.

49 *The ruination of a family farm was more than just a business failure:* Harold F. Breimyer, *Individual Freedom and the Economic Organization of Agriculture* (Urbana: University of Illinois Press, 1965).

51 *In 1931 Springdale was a tiny crosshatch of streets:* Brooks Blevins, *Hill Folks: A History of Arkansas, Ozarkers and Their Image* (Chapel Hill: University of North Carolina Press, 2002); Shiloh Museum of Ozark History, Springdale, Arkansas.

51 *Don's earliest memories were of strange men sleeping in a room:* Don Tyson, interview by author, 2009.

51 *The orchards outside Springdale had been profitable for decades:* Stephen F. Strausberg, *From Hills and Hollers: Rise of the Poultry Industry in Arkansas* (Fayetteville: Arkansas Agricultural Experiment Station, 1995), 92; Shiloh Museum of Ozark History, Springdale, Arkansas.

52 *But John Tyson noticed a new opportunity growing in the shadow of the orchards:* Don Tyson, interview by author, 2009; Strausberg, *Hills and Hollers*, 61.

55 *In the 1930s and 1940s, they worked a thin layer of soil:* Blevins, *Hill Folks*, 147-169.

56 *Cash-poor farmers rented land:* Strausberg, *From Hills and Hollers*, 33-34; Blevins, *Hill Folks*, 147-169.

56 *John Tyson took it a step further:* Don Tyson, interview by author, 2009.

57 *During the Great Depression, farmers raised bountiful crops:* Christopher

Leonard, "1919 Farm Crisis Shows Some Bailouts Hard to Undo," Associated Press, October 19, 2008.

57 *A federal law called the Agricultural Adjustment Act:* Bruce L. Gardner, *American Agriculture in the Twentieth Century* (Cambridge: Harvard University Press, 2002), 216.

58 *When he was twenty-three years old, in 1953, Don Tyson took a trip:* Don Tyson, interview by author, 2009.

CHAPTER 3: EXPAND OR EXPIRE

63 *Haskell Jackson, a college-trained accountant:* Haskell Jackson, interview by author, 2011.

63 *The Tyson Feed and Hatchery offices:* Marvin Schwartz, *Tyson: From Farm to Market* (Fayetteville: University of Arkansas Press, 1991), 10.

63 *It was an odd place for Jackson to end up:* Haskell Jackson, interview by author.

65 *By the early 1960s, Americans were in a hurry:* Steve Striffler, *Chicken: The Dangerous Transformation of America's Favorite Food* (New Haven: Yale University Press, 2005), 16.

65 *Don Tyson saw the changes clearly:* Joe Fred Starr and Blair, interviews by author, 2010, 2011.

67 *Don discovered a new source of credit:* Joe Fred Starr, interview by author, 2011.

68 *As Haskell Jackson was organizing Tyson's financial ledgers:* Haskell Jackson, interview by author.

73 *While Tyson couldn't escape paying taxes altogether:* Carol D. Petersen, William Shear, and Charles L. Vehorn, "Cash Accounting Rules for Farmers: Differential Benefits and Federal Costs," *Journal of Economic Issues,* June 1987; Haskell Jackson, interview by author.

74 *On Monday mornings at six o'clock:* Haskell Jackson, Joe Fred Starr, and Buddy Wray, interviews by author, 2011.

76 *Just a year after he joined the company:* Haskell Jackson, interview by author.

79 *Tyson's contract farmers were largely shielded:* Arkansas Valley Industries v. Freeman. 415 F.2d.713. United States Court of Appeals Eighth Circuit. 1969, https://bulk.resource.org/courts.gov/c/F2/415/415.F2d.713.19204 _1.html, accessed April 20, 2013.

79 *As Don Tyson had predicted:* Haskell Jackson, interview by author.

80 *A photograph from 1963 shows a young Don Tyson:* Strausberg, *From Hills and Hollers*, 108.

81 *Garrett owned Garrett Poultry in Rogers:* Haskell Jackson and Buddy Wray, interviews by author; Schwartz, *Tyson: From Farm to Market*, 57.

82 *Nobody in the courtroom ever expected mercy:* Jim Blair, interview by author; Attorney Mark Henry, interview by author, 2011.

84 *New members of the Northwest Poultry Growers Association: Arkansas Valley Industries* v. *Freeman.* 415 F.2d.713. United States Court of Appeals Eighth Circuit, 1969,. https://bulk.resource.org/courts.gov/c/F2/415/415.F2d.713.19204_1.html, accessed April 20, 2013: Strausberg, *From Hills and Hollers*, 104; Jim Blair, interview by author.

85 *By 1966, Don Tyson was eyeing his company's next acquisition:* Haskell Jackson and Buddy Wray, interviews by author; Schwartz, *Tyson: From Farm to Market*, 15.

87 *Haskell Jackson noticed that as the company grew:* Haskell Jackson, interview by author.

88 *In 1967, John Tyson and his wife, Helen:* Don Tyson, interview by author.

CHAPTER 4: THE INDUSTRIAL ANIMAL

91 *Don Tyson became a billionaire:* Haskell Jackson, Buddy Wray, Joe Fred Starr, interviews by author; background interviews by author.

91 *Between 1970 and 1978 alone:* Data provided by Food and Agricultural Policy Research Institute, University of Missouri.

92 *By the early 1970s, Tyson Foods had moved out of its offices:* Haskell Jackson, interview by author; background interviews by author.

93 *Don Tyson's obsession with fast food made him:* Jim Blair and Joe Fred Starr, interviews by author; background interviews by author.

94 *Look, we'll dedicate a whole plant to your production:* Jim Blair, interview by author.

95 *Although he didn't know it, Haskell Jackson hired his replacement:* Haskell Jackson, interview by author; Gerald Johnston, interview by author, 2011.

97 *Haskell Jackson liked to play basketball:* Haskell Jackson, interview by author.

97 *After Haskell Jackson's departure Gerald Johnston rose through the ranks:* Gerald Johnston, interview by author.

98 *Jim Blair didn't want to raise unnecessary attention:* Jim Blair, interview by author.

100 *When Lane refused to sell to Don Tyson in 1982:* Jim Blair, interview by author; *SEC News Digest,* July 15, 1983.

102 *Among Gerald Johnston's more unpleasant tasks:* Gerald Johnston, interview by author.

102 *One of the slaughterhouses that Tyson bought:* Jerry Skeen, interview by author, 2011; Tommy Brown, interview by author.

104 *When Tyson bought Valmac:* Background interviews by author, 2011.

107 *In 1969 the average American ate:* Data from the National Chicken Council, http://www.nationalchickencouncil.org/about-the-industry/statistics/per-capita-consumption-of-poultry-and-livestock-1965-to-estimated-2012-in-pounds/, accessed April 23, 2013.

108 *In 1994 Tyson Foods made an acquisition:* Tyson Foods Inc., *Fiscal 2012 Fact Book,* 26.

108 *In 1925, it took fifteen weeks to raise:* N.B. Anthony, "A Review of Genetic Practices in Poultry: Efforts to Improve Meat Quality," *Journal of Muscle Foods* 9 (1998), 27.

109 *Tyson's wave of acquisitions wasn't easy:* Jim Blair, interview by author.

110 *Between 1962 and 1997, Tyson Foods bought at least thirty-three companies:* Tyson Foods Inc., *Fiscal 2012 Fact Book,* 24-28; Paul Whitley, *I Refuse to Have a Bad Day* (PBWinSights, LLC, 2008), 218-220.

110 *In 1979 Tyson's annual sales were $382.2 million:* Tyson Foods, annual reports.

110 *By 1992, 88 percent of all chicken in the United States was produced:* Michael Ollinger, James MacDonald, and Milton Madison, "Structural Change in U.S. Chicken and Turkey Slaughter," Economic Research Service, U.S. Department of Agriculture (September 2000), 7.

110 *Jim Blair didn't have much time to think:* Jim Blair, interview by author.

CHAPTER 5: CAGE MATCH

113 *During 2004, it was common to see groups of Laotian immigrants:* Christopher Leonard, *Arkansas Democrat-Gazette,* May 30, 2004.

113 *And so it happened that in 2004:* Boonau Phouthavong, interviews by author, 2008, 2010, 2011, 2012.

115 *At the end of any given week, a series of letters is mailed out from the Tyson*

complex: Various farmers in Waldron, interviews by author, 2004, 2008, 2010, 2011.

116 *If a farmer ranks near the top, he might earn 5 cents a pound for his labor:* Tyson tournament settlement sheets, 2009.

116 *The differences in pay are severe:* Tyson tournament settlement sheets, 2009.

117 *Around 2008, longtime farmers who raised chickens for Tyson Foods in Waldron noticed a change in their paychecks:* Coy Butler and Richard Moore, interviews by author, 2008.

120 *Tyson and its defenders say the tournament price incentivizes farmers to work hard:* C. Robert Taylor, interview by author, 2011; C. Robert Taylor, e-mail message to author, April 18, 2011.

123 *Boonau Phouthavong's background made him an ideal chicken farmer:* Boonau Phouthavong, interviews by author.

125 *Greg and Donna Owens had done well in Tyson's tournament system for nearly a decade:* Greg and Donna Owens, interview by author, 2008.

127 *The tournament system isn't built to produce enduring winners:* Boonau Phouthavong, interview by author.

128 *The chicken houses on N&N Farm:* Nouk and Nue Yang, interviews by author, 2008, 2010, 2011.

130 *In 2009 Boonau Phouthavong discovered he was a failure as a chicken farmer:* Boonau Phouthavong, interviews by author; documents obtained by author.

132 *C. Robert Taylor, the Auburn economist, has seen the trend clearly in the data he reviewed:* C. Robert Taylor, interview by author; C. Robert Taylor, e-mail message to author, April 18, 2011.

132 *On Valentine's Day, 2010, only the children were home at N&N Farm:* Nouk and Nue Yang, interview by author, 2010; personal reporting by author.

133 *The Tyson trucks had delivered 39,000 chickens to each of the Yangs' seven houses:* Delivery log documents viewed by author.

133 *By the end of the second week, they had taken between 2,000 and 5,000 dead birds from each house:* Mortality sheet documents viewed by author.

134 *The Yangs had no idea what kind of disease was burning through the birds:* Nouk and Nue Yang, interview by author.

135 *By the time N&N Farm got up and running, Jerry and Kanita Yandell were well ensconced in their new life:* Jerry and Kanita Yandell, interview by author.

135 *Nouk Yang spent his long weekend days alone on N&N farm:* Nouk Yang, interview by author.

137 *On a hilltop south of Waldron, an old farmhouse has been painted in wild tropical colors:* Personal reporting, photographs by author.

138 *With his own farm on the edge of failure, Boonau was at a loss:* Boonau Phouthavong, interview by author.

138 He had just signed a contract with the company: Tyson's Broiler Production Contract, 2009, obtained by author.

138 *After a long Saturday morning of work in 2011, Boonau Phouthavong sat on the front porch:* Boonau Phouthavong, interviews by author.

139 *The tournament system is kept afloat by an obscure federal organization called the Farm Service Agency:* Personal reporting; Farm Service Agency website, http://www.fsa.usda.gov; Jim Radintz, interview by author, 2010.

139 *Ron Burnett is a loan officer in Arkansas:* Ron Burnett, interview by author, 2011.

140 *The Farmers Home Administration (FHMA) was created in the 1940s because private banks had backed out of the business of extending farm loans:* A Brief History of Farmers Home Administration, U.S. Department of Agriculture, 1989, http://www.rurdev.usda.gov/rd/70th/history%20of%20farmers%20home.pdf, accessed April 23, 2013; Jim Radintz, Ron Burnett, interviews by author.

140 *The FMHA extended some loans to chicken farmers, but that was a small part of the agency's business:* Jim Radintz, Ron Burnett, interviews by author.

140 *Burnett and other loan officers noticed a change in the mid-1990s, when the FMHA got wrapped into a large agency:* Ron Burnett, interview by author.

140 *Under the guaranteed loan program, the FSA would pay back the bank more than 90 percent of the loan value if a farmer defaulted:* A Brief History of Farmers Home Administration, U.S. Department of Agriculture, 1989; Farm Service Agency website, http://www.fsa.usda.gov.

141 *The FSA became a pipeline of credit for chicken farmers:* Documents provided by the Farm Service Agency (FSA) in response to author's Freedom of Information Act request.

141 *As more Laotians moved south to buy up poultry farms:* Documents provided by the Farm Service Agency (FSA) in response to author's Freedom of Information Act request.

142 *The paperwork for these loans reflected the same sort of hazy math and willful blindness:* Mark Henry, interview by author, 2011.

142 *A review of the Farm and Home Plans submitted by a single loan officer in Arkansas:* Farm and Home Plans obtained from Mark Henry.

143 *One reason it's difficult to put an exact dollar amount on this subsidy is that the government itself does not know:* Jim Radintz, interview by author.

143 *According to one internal FSA audit, the agency guaranteed more than $568.9 million in new loans:* Documents provided by the Farm Service Agency (FSA) in response to author's Freedom of Information Act request.

144 *But a series of open records requests sent to the nation's biggest poultry-producing states met with mixed results:* Documents provided by the Farm Service Agency (FSA) in response to author's Freedom of Information Act request.

145 *Jim Blair, Don Tyson's top attorney, repeatedly reminded his boss that U.S. antitrust laws prohibited Tyson Foods from taking over the entire market:* Jim Blair, interview by author.

CHAPTER 6: PIG CITIES

149 *In the early days, Don Tyson's hog farms:* Bill Moeller, interview by author, 2011; *The Tyson Swine Story,* Tyson Foods corporate history of farming operations, March 1994; Schwartz, *Tyson: From Farm to Market,* 89.

149 *The takeover started in 1973, on a nondescript farm in northwestern Arkansas:* Bill Moeller, interview by author, 2011; Schwartz, *Tyson: From Farm to Market,* 89.

152 *In 1973 there were about 736,000 hog farms in the United States, which collectively made about $7.7 billion a year:* "Meat Animals, Farm Production Disposition Income, 1972–1973," U.S. Department of Agriculture, April 1974.

152 *Luckily for Tyson Foods, the livestock industry was becoming more vulnerable to a takeover in the 1970s and 1980s:* Striffler, *Chicken: The Dangerous Transformation of America's Favorite Food,* 18; data from the National Chicken Council at http://www.nationalchickencouncil.org/about-the-industry/statistics/per-capita-consumption-of-poultry-and-livestock-1965-to-estimated-2012-in-pounds/, accessed April 23, 2013.

153 *Moeller's business plan was almost thwarted by piglets:* Bill Moeller, interview by author.

155 *By the late 1980s, Tyson had built a small network of hog farms based on Moeller's system:* Bill Moeller, interview by author; *The Tyson Swine Story,* Tyson Foods corporate history of farming operations, March 1994.

155 *Downtown Holdenville, Oklahoma, is like a ragged grid of inner-city ghetto, inexplicably dropped down into the middle of desolate prairie:* Personal reporting and notes from Holdenville, May, 2011.

156 *When Bill Moeller saw Holdenville, he knew it was perfect:* Bill Moeller, interview by author.

157 *Throughout the 1990s, industrial hog farms began sprouting up across rural America:* Personal reporting over the years in Missouri and Arkansas.

CHAPTER 7: THE NEXT GENERATION

159 *There was a sense of grandeur, by the mid-1990s, at the Tyson Foods complex:* Gerald Johnston and Donald Wray, interview by author; background interviews by author.

159 *Tyson Foods even made a $243 million bet that it could control the seafood industry with its purchase of Arctic Alaska Fisheries:* Helen Jung, "King of Poultry Decides to Bail on Fish Business," *The Seattle Times,* June 20, 1999; Tyson Foods Annual Report, SEC, December 12, 1992.

159 *The 1990s was the age of dominance for corporate agribusiness:* Tyson Foods Annual Report 1996, Form 10-K, 57.

159 *Having built this empire, Don Tyson finally decided it was time to step aside:* Patricia May, "Tyson Names Tollett CEO, Don Tyson Remains Chairman," *Arkansas Democrat-Gazette,* April 2, 1991; background interviews by author.

160 *Don Tyson's lieutenants had vied for decades:* Jim Blair, interview by author; background interviews by author.

160 *He was always "Johnny":* Jim Blair, Joe Fred Starr, and Gerald Johnston, interviews by author; background interviews by author.

160 *The name was his childhood name, and it stuck:* Jim Blair, interview by author; background interviews by author.

162 *Johnny Tyson later admitted to heavy drug and alcohol abuse:* David Barboza, "John Tyson Kicked Drug Habit; Takes Leadership Chal-

lenge," *New York Times*, March 11, 2001, http://www.nytimes.com /2001/03/04/business/business-why-is-he-on-top-he-s-a-tyson-for-one.html?pagewanted=all&src=pm; Scott A. Johnson, "John Howard Tyson from Chicken to Beef and Pork," *Arkansas Democrat-Gazette*, December 1, 2002.

162 *By 1991, John Tyson wasn't ready for the top job:* "Tyson Names Leland Tollett CEO," *Business Wire*, April 1, 1991; background interviews by author.

162 *Even when Don gave Leland the title of CEO in 1991:* Tyson Foods Proxy Statement, 1999.

162 *Under these circumstances, Leland Tollett exercised what authority he could:* Gerald Johnston and Donald Wray, interviews by author; background interviews by author.

163 *Investors weren't impressed:* Historic stock prices for Tyson Foods provided by Yahoo!Finance.

163 *Leland Tollett quit in 1998:* "Tyson Chairman Leland Tollett to Retire; John Tyson Elected Chairman of Board; Wayne Britt Chosen CEO," PR Newswire, September 25, 1998.

163 *In September 1998, Tyson's senior managers were called to the company's auditorium:* Background interviews by author.

164 *But Johnny Tyson had made at least one change:* Barboza, *New York Times*, March 11, 2001, http://www.nytimes.com/2001/03/04/business/business-why-is-he-on-top-he-s-a-tyson-for-one.html?pagewanted=all&src=pm.

164 *The company's Seafood Group:* Tyson Foods Inc. Annual Report, 2001, http://media.corporate-ir.net/media_files/irol/65/65476/reports /2001AR_2.pdf.

164 *Tyson's stock price sank steeply:* Tyson Foods historic stock prices provided by Yahoo!Finance.

164 *Wayne Britt left the company in April 2000:* "Britt Announces His Departure as Tyson CEO; Grandson of Founder to Take Post as Poultry Producer Tries to Rebound," *Arkansas Democrat-Gazette*, April 13, 2000; background interviews by author.

165 *By 1994, taxpayers were spending $7.9 billion every year:* "Agricultural Income and Finance Situation and Outlook. Rural Economy Division, Economic Research Service," U.S. Department of Agriculture, September 1995, http://usda.mannlib.cornell.edu/usda/ers/AIS/1990s/1995/ AIS-09-25-1995.asc.

192 *Bob Allen's education in hog farming came fast:* Bob Allen, interview by author; background interviews by author.

193 *When his first three-year contract with Tyson expired, Bob Allen drove:* Bob Allen, interview by author.

194 *By the late 1990s, it was impossible for smaller hog farms to survive:* James M. MacDonald and William D. McBride, "The Transformation of U.S. Livestock Agriculture; Scale, Efficiency, and Risks," U.S. Department of Agriculture Economic Information Bulletin Number 43 (January 2009), 17.

196 *Smaller, independent farms reaped only the losses, and it drove them out of business:* John D. Lawrence and Glenn Grimes, "Production and Marketing Characteristics of U.S. Pork Producers," U.S. Department of Agriculture Economic Information Bulletin Number 43 (January 2009), 17.

197 *Bob Allen was on his knees:* Bob Allen, interview by author.

198 *Chuck Wirtz often drove his farm truck:* Chuck Wirtz, interview by author; notes from reporting in West Bend, Iowa, 2011; population data from U.S. Census Bureau.

199 *Bob Allen lost the fight:* Bob Allen, interview by author.

200 *Just west of Whittemore, Iowa:* Chuck Wirtz, interview by author; notes from reporting in Whittemore, Iowa, 2011.

202 *By 2011, far less than 10 percent of all hogs were sold on the open market:* 2011 P&SP Annual Report, Packers and Stockyards Program, U.S. Department of Agriculture Grain Inspection, Packers and Stockyards Administration (March 2012), 47; Chuck Wirtz, interview by author.

202 *Wirtz was being boxed in:* Chuck Wirtz, interview by author.

203 *In 2011, price discovery was happening in a different way:* Chuck Wirtz, interview by author; notes from tour of Tyson Foods hog-processing plant in Storm Lake, Iowa, 2011; background interviews by author.

204 *Back in 1980, hog farmers earned about 50 cents for every dollar a consumer spent on pork:* "USDA Announces Proposed Rule to Increase Fairness in the Marketing of Livestock and Poultry," U.S. Department of Agriculture press release, June 18, 2010.

204 *At the same time, pork has become more expensive at the grocery store:* Data provided by Food and Agricultural Policy Research Institute, University of Missouri.

204 *Chuck Wirtz came to an inescapable conclusion:* Chuck Wirtz, interview by author.

CHAPTER 9: PULLING THE NOOSE

207 *The cowboys were saddled up just after dawn:* Notes from reporting outside Dodge City, Kansas, 2011; Gene Carson, interview by author, 2011.

208 *The modern U.S. cattle business itself is also increasingly confined:* R-CALF USA analysis of data from U.S. Department of Agriculture, provided by Bill Bullard.

208 *On the meatpacking side, there are now just four companies that buy 85 percent of the cattle:* 2011 P&SP Annual Report, Packers and Stockyards Program, U.S. Department of Agriculture Grain Inspection, Packers and Stockyards Administration (March 2012), 31.

210 *Gene Carson owns Maverick Feeders, LLC:* Gene Carson, interview by author, 2011.

211 *The main strip in Dodge City is called Wyatt Earp Boulevard:* Notes from reporting, Dodge City, Kansas, 2011.

213 *Gene Carson used to go out into the cattle pens:* Gene Carson, interview by author.

215 *Carson was too much of a cowboy to fit with National's buying program:* Gene Carson, interview by author; Tim Klein, e-mail correspondence with author, 2013.

215 *National had evidence to back up the claim:* Tim Klein, e-mail correspondence with author, 2013.

217 *On Monday and Tuesday mornings, the cattle buyers fan out:* Gene Carson, interview by author; Ken Winter, interview by author, 2011; Bob Sears, interview by author, 2010.

217 *But buyers seldom enter the Winter Feed Yard office:* Ken Winter, interviews by author.

219 *What makes Cargill's dominance even more curious is the fact that this pattern plays out across the nation:* Christopher Leonard, "AP IMPACT: Beef Industry Woes May Mean Poorer Meat," Associated Press, October 19, 2010.

219 *This picture is clear to Bruce Cobb, general manager of a company that sells cattle to meatpackers on behalf of feedlots:* Bruce Cobb, transcript of testimony, U.S. Departments of Justice and Agriculture, Public Workshops Exploring Competition Issues in Agriculture; Livestock Workshop, August 27, 2010, 214, http://www.justice.gov/atr/public/workshops/ag2010/colorado-agworkshop-transcript.txt.

219 *When asked why this happens, feedlot owners like Ken Winter just shrug:* Ken Winter, interview by author.

221 *Ward Feed Yard does not employ cowboys:* Chris Burris, interview by author, 2011; notes from reporting at Ward Feed Yard.

222 *The idea was hatched by the company's manager:* Lee Borck, interview by author, 2011.

224 *One of those arrangements involved Tyson's little-known use of a growth drug called Zilmax:* Christopher Leonard, "Why Beef Is Becoming More Like Chicken: Cheap, Uniform and Bland," *Slate Magazine*, February 14, 2013.

224 *Tyson has quietly encouraged the feedlots aligned with it to use Zilmax on their cattle:* Background interview by author, 2011.

225 *The grids encourage high yields and maximize the amount of beef:* Copy of Tyson Foods grid contract for cattle purchases, obtained by author.

CHAPTER 10: THE FOOD DICTATORSHIP

230 *Heffernan's research was based in the rural area of Union Parish in Louisiana:* William D. Heffernan and David H. Lind, "Union Parish, Louisiana: The Third Phase of a Thirty Year Longitudinal Study," 2000. Report at http://www.justice.gov/atr/public/workshops/ag2010/001/AGW-00067-a.pdf.

230 *There was one reason that Heffernan asked these questions:* Harold F. Breimyer, interviews by author, circa 1999 and 2000; William Heffernan, interviews by author, 2010, 2011, 2012; Breimyer, *Individual Freedom and the Economic Organization of Agriculture.*

235 *Tabor knew as well as anyone what farming meant to Iowans:* Eric Tabor, interviews by author, 2010, 2011.

236 *In 1980, only about 2 percent of Iowa's hogs were raised under contract:* Contract Feeding Facility Operators Lien, Background Paper on Proposed Legislation, by the Attorney General's Farm Division, Tuesday, December 8, 1998, Iowa Attorney General Tom Miller's Office, 1998; Starmer and Wise, "Living High on the Hog: Factory Farms, Federal Policy, and the Structural Transformation of Swine Production."

236 *Bad stories were starting to spread from farm to farm:* Eric Tabor, Steve Moline, interviews by author, 2010, 2011.

236 *When Tabor looked for someone to investigate contract farming, his staff*

attorney Steve Moline was an obvious choice: Steve Moline, Eric Tabor interviews by author.

240 *Smithfield Foods, the nation's biggest hog producer, had just purchased Murphy Farms:* "Smithfield Foods Reaches Agreement in Principle to Acquire Murphy Family Farms," http://investors.smithfieldfoods.com/releasedetail.cfm?releaseid=297154, September 2, 1999.

240 *Moline couldn't believe what he'd heard:* Steve Moline, interview by author.

241 *The matter seemed clear-cut to Iowa Attorney General Tom Miller:* Eric Tabor, Steve Moline, interviews by author.

241 *They sued Smithfield for violating Iowa's packer ban:* "Miller Sues Smithfield Foods to Block Acquisition of Murphy Farms in Iowa," http://www.state.ia.us/government/ag/consumer/press_releases/smithfield.html, January 24, 2000.

241 *Joe Luter, the Smithfield Foods CEO, walked down the narrow path:* Eric Tabor, Steve Moline, interviews by author.

243 *The lawsuit against Smithfield turned out to be far more complicated:* State of Iowa, ex re *Miller* v. *Smithfield*; Eric Tabor, Steve Moline, interviews by author.

244 *In September 2000, Miller unveiled a new law called the Producer Protection Act:* "Iowa Leads States Pushing 'Producer Protection Act,'" http://www.state.ia.us/government/ag/latest_news/releases/producer_act.html, September 13, 2000; Eric Tabor, Steve Moline, interviews by author.

244 *Eric Tabor took the stage at a Marriott hotel in suburban Kansas City:* Eric Tabor, interview by author; speech notes and event agenda, obtained by author.

246 *Not everyone who heard Tabor's speech was moved:* James Baker, interview by author, 2011; Greg Page, interview by author, 2013.

249 *This is the rationale that James Baker deployed:* James Baker, interview by author.

249 *Meat industry lobbyists aren't brash:* Steve Moline, interview by author; background interviews by author.

250 *Then, quietly, the legislation started to die the slow death that visits most bills:* Background interviews by author.

250 *A similar story unfolded in Washington, D.C.:* "Bill Summary & Status, 106th Congress (1999 - 2000), S.2411," Thomas, Library of Congress, accessed April 2013, http://thomas.loc.gov/cgi-bin/bdquery/z?d106:s.02411.

251 *On March 8, 2000, as Daschle's bill was still being drafted:* E-mail from Sara Lilygren, "Update on Signatures to Senate Letter on Daschle Antitrust Bills," March 8, 2000, obtained by author.

252 *Daschle eventually introduced the bill:* "Bill Summary & Status, 106th Congress (1999 - 2000), S.2411," Thomas, Library of Congress, accessed April 2013, http://thomas.loc.gov/cgi-bin/bdquery/z?d106:s.02411.

252 *The same fate awaited a federal producer protection act:* "Bill Summary & Status, 106th Congress (1999 - 2000), S.3243," Thomas, Library of Congress, accessed April 2013, http://thomas.loc.gov/cgi-bin/bdquery /z?d106:s.03243.

252 *In Oklahoma, the bill was pushed by state senator Paul Muegge:* John Greiner, "Bill Meant to Protect Farmers Sidelined," *Daily Oklahoman,* March 29, 2001; Paul Muegge, interview by author, 2012.

CHAPTER 11: THE TRANSITION TEAM

261 *On the morning of November 10, 2007:* Dave Murphy, interview by author, 2011.

263 *"When I'm president, you'll have a partner in the White House":* Speech transcript, provided to author by Dave Murphy.

264 *When Donnie Smith arrived for work at Tyson Foods headquarters:* Donnie Smith, interview by author, 2009; personal reporting and notes from Tyson Foods headquarters, 2008, 2009.

268 *Around that time, Barack Obama was in Chicago:* Tom Vilsack, interviews by author, 2010, 2011; background interviews by author and personal reporting.

268 *Between 2000 and 2010, the meat industry gave Democratic candidates:* Meat & Poultry Industry PAC Contributions to U.S. House of Representatives 2000 – 2010 Election Cycles. Food & Water Watch analysis of Center for Responsive Politics Data.

269 *In Oklahoma, two Tyson Foods chicken farmers secretly taped a Tyson Foods employee:* "Plaintiffs Present Admissions of a Tyson 'Insider,'" *McCurtain Daily Gazette,* March 17, 2010.

269 *In the cattle industry, a federal lawsuit, Pickett v. Tyson Foods:* C. Robert Taylor, "Buyer Power Litigation in Agriculture: *Pickett v. Tyson Fresh Meats Inc.*," *Antitrust Bulletin* Vol. 53, No. 2/Summer (2008).

270 *In the winter of 2008, Tyson executives hatched a plan:* Donnie Smith, Donnie King, interviews by author, 2009.

271 *A similar set of orders from Pilgrim's Pride achieved production cuts:* Greg Hilburn, "Pilgrim's Pride May Appeal Court Ruling" *News-Star*, October 5, 2011; personal reporting by author.

271 *Tyson cut its production by 5 percent in December:* Tyson Foods, Earnings Call Transcript discussing Q1 2009 results, January 27, 2009.

272 *Pilgrim's Pride entered the crisis of 2008 saddled with heavy debt:* Emily Fredrix, "Pilgrim's Pride Loses Nearly $1 Billion in Fiscal 2008," Associated Press, December 11, 2008.

272 *Around the country, some poultry producers were experimenting:* Sonny Meyerhoeffer, interview by author, 2011.

272 *Meyerhoeffer arrived in Famerville, Louisiana, in March 2009 to tell his story:* Sonny Meyerhoeffer, interview by author.

273 *The farmers took over the turkey plant in Hinton and they rewrote the rules:* Sonny Meyerhoeffer, interview by author.

275 *Vilsack inherited a regulatory system that was riven by bureaucratic divisions, miscommunication, and a lack of focus:* Background interviews by author.

276 *Christine Varney looked out over the crowed as she prepared to make her first speech:* Remarks by Christine Varney to the Center for American Progress, Washington, D.C., May 11, 2009, video available at http://www.youtube.com/watch?v=Ig2U9oYX2To.

CHAPTER 12: STREET FIGHT

279 *Inside the big auditorium, the crowd settled into their seats:* Personal reporting, notes from event, 2010; "Agriculture and Antitrust Enforcement Issues in Our 21st Century Economy," http://www.justice.gov/atr/public/workshops/ag2010/ (transcript at "Public Workshops Exploring Competition Issues in Agriculture, A Dialogue on Competition Issues Facing Farmers in Today's Agricultural Marketplace," http://www.justice.gov/atr/public/workshops/ag2010/iowa-agworkshop-transcript.pdf, March 12, 2010; video at http://www.justice.gov/atr/video/iowa-agworkshop-video.php).

282 *In the months leading up to the hearing:* "Press Release, Agriculture Secretary Vilsack Names John Ferrell as Deputy Under Secretary for Marketing and Regulatory Programs," http://www.usda.gov/wps/portal/usda/usdamediafb?contentid=2009/06/0209.xml&printable=true&contentidonly=true, accessed April 19, 2013.

282 *a gray-bearded trial attorney named J. Dudley Butler:* "Press Release, Agriculture Secretary Vilsack Names J. Dudley Butler to Serve as Administrator of Grain Inspection, Packers and Stockyards Administration," http://www.gipsa.usda.gov/Newrelease/2009/05-06-09.pdf, accessed April 19, 2013.

282 *Ferrell and Butler were the consummate odd couple:* J. Dudley Butler, interview by author, 2012; background interviews by author.

283 *While the Packers and Stockyards Act was a tough law:* "Packers and Stockyards Programs: Actions Needed to Improve Investigations of Competitive Practices," http://www.gao.gov/new.items/rc00242.pdf. September 2000.

284 *For several months during 2010, the policy makers inside GIPSA drafted a new rule:* "USDA Announces Proposed Rule to Increase Fairness in the Marketing of Livestock and Poultry," http://www.usda.gov/wps/portal/usda/usdamediafb?contentid=2010/06/0326.xml&printable=true&contentidonly=true, accessed June 18, 2010.

284 *Policy makers inside GIPSA also considered more drastic measures:* Background interviews by author.

285 *The proposed GIPSA rule was released in June 2010:* Christopher Leonard, "USDA Touts Tighter Meat Industry Antitrust Rules," Associated Press, June 18, 2010.

285 *Inside the American Meat Institute, there was shock:* Mark Dopp, Janet Riley, interviews by author, 2010.

286 *The meat lobbying groups began to gather their wits:* Personal reporting, background interviews by author.

286 *The meat companies themselves had tremendous resources at their disposal:* Lobbying disclosure reports obtained by author from the Office of the Clerk, U.S. House of Representatives.

286 *Together, the trade groups and companies spent $7.79 million on lobbying in 2010:* Lobbying disclosure reports obtained by author from the Office of the Clerk, U.S. House of Representatives.

286 *Officials inside GIPSA heard about lobbyists working the halls of Congress:* Background interviews by author.

287 *Through the spring and summer of 2010, the U.S. Departments of Agriculture and Justice held their series of five public workshops:* Reporting and author's notes from USDA/DOJ workshops in Ankeny, Iowa, and Normal, Alabama.

288 *During the series of workshops, Obama administration officials saw just*

how powerful, and how difficult to change, the meat industry had become:
Background interviews by author.

289 *Secretary Vilsack called a meeting:* Background interviews with author.
Accounts of this meeting are based on two individuals who attended
the meeting, both interviewed on background. Secretary Vilsack refused
several requests to comment on the meeting.

290 *After the hearing, the public narrative about the GIPSA rule:* "Hearing
to Review Livestock and Related Programs at USDA in Advance of the
2012 Farm Bill," http://agriculture.house.gov/sites/republicans.agricul-
ture.house.gov/files/testimony/111/111-56.pdf, accessed July 20, 2010

291 *To appease GIPSA's critics, Vilsack extended the public comment period:*
"Proposed Rules," *Federal Register,* Vol. 75, No. 144 (July 28, 2010),
44163, http://www.gpo.gov/fdsys/pkg/FR-2010-07-28/pdf/2010-18458
.pdf; background interviews by author.

291 *To shape the debate, meat company lobbyists used an increasingly common
tactic:* Stewart Doan, "National Chicken Council Organizing Campaign
against USDA's GIPSA Proposal," Agri-Pulse, August 12, 2010, at http://
www.agri-pulse.com/20100812D_NCC_Anti_GIPSA_Campaign.asp.

292 *On October 21, GIPSA got an angry letter from Eunice Richardson:* Letter
from Richardson obtained by author from U.S. Department of Agriculture archive of public comment on GIPSA rules.

292 *Richardson said she sent the letter to GIPSA:* Eunice Richardson, interview by author, 2011.

293 *The public comment from Tyson Foods on the GIPSA rule didn't look like
a letter:* Comment from Tyson Foods, obtained by author from U.S.
Department of Agriculture archive of public comment on GIPSA rules.

294 *The final hearing in the series of USDA/DOJ workshops:* "Workshop on
Agriculture and Antitrust Enforcement Issues in Our 21st Century
Economy," http://www.justice.gov/atr/public/workshops/ag2010/dc-
agworkshop-transcript.pdf, December 8, 2010.

294 *David Murphy arrived at the hearing with some heavy boxes:* David Murphy, interview by author.

295 *During the course of 2011, the meat industry's intensified opposition to the
GIPSA rule began to foster deep divisions:* J. Dudley Butler, interviews by
author; background interviews by author.

295 *To the pragmatists, the GIPSA rule was starting to look like a disaster:* Butler, interviews by author; background interviews by author. Accounts of
meetings are based on the accounts of at least two people who attended

the meetings reported here. Secretary Vilsack refused several requests to comment on the meetings. U.S. Department of Agriculture Public Affairs Director Justin DeJong refused to allow Anne Cannon MacMillan or Krysta Harden to provide comment or responses to the accounts of multiple people who attended meetings with MacMillan and Harden.

297 *On a chilly Thursday morning in October 2011:* "Agriculture Secy: US Having Record Year in Agriculture," MSNBC, *Morning Joe,* aired October 6, 2011.

298 *Inside GIPSA, it became clear that Dudley Butler had lost the fight:* J. Dudley Butler, interviews by author; background interviews by author.

300 *But the so-called "competitive injury" provision had become a political liability:* Remarks by Senator Pat Roberts to the Committee on Agriculture, Nutrition and Forestry, Washington, D.C., June 28, 2011, transcript available at http://www.gpo.gov/fdsys/pkg/CHRG-112shrg71631/html/CHRG-112shrg71631.htm.

301 *The USDA decided it would repropose the "competitive injury" rule:* "USDA Implements Provisions from 2008 Farm Bill to Protect Livestock and Poultry Producers," http://www.usda.gov/wps/portal/usda/usdamediafb?contentid=2011/12/0508.xml&printable=true&contentidonly=true, accessed December 8, 2011.

301 *The House of Representatives passed a spending bill that summer that banned GIPSA from using any money:* Christopher Leonard, "Congress Set to Cut Money for Meat Industry Reform," Associated Press, November 16, 2011.

302 *After the bill was released, meat industry lobbyists gave a special public thanks:* Statement from National Pork Producers Council e-mailed to author.

302 *The Department of Justice released its own small report on the workshops:* "Competition and Agriculture: Voices from the Workshops on Agriculture and Antitrust Enforcement in Our 21st Century Economy and Thoughts on the Way Forward," http://www.justice.gov/atr/public/reports/283291.pdf, May 2012.

303 *Shortly after the GIPSA rule was defeated, Dudley Butler resigned:* Christopher Leonard, "Top Meat Antitrust Regulator Quits," Associated Press, January 19, 2012; J. Dudley Butler, interview by author.

CHAPTER 13: DON'S HORIZON

305 *One of Don Tyson's houses is a palatial estate:* Jim Blair, interview by author.

306 *Don Tyson saw the real opportunity in countries like Brazil, India, and China:* Christopher Leonard, "Don Tyson Says Meat Company Seeks Global Growth," Associated Press, November 3, 2008.

306 *But Don was still surrounded by family:* J.J. Caldwell-Tyson, interview by author, 2011.

307 *When Don was out on the open ocean, he woke up early to go fishing:* J.J. Caldwell-Tyson, interview by author, 2011.

308 *Don and Johnny seemed to overcome whatever hard feelings:* Statement from Tyson Foods, May 2013.

308 *Jim Blair drove down the lonely country roads:* Jim Blair, interview by author.

309 *On Sunday, January 4, 2011, Don Tyson watched:* Jim Blair, interview by author, March 2011; J.J. Caldwell-Tyson, interview by author.

310 *President Bill Clinton was solemn as he walked:* Transcript of remarks by President William Jefferson Clinton at the funeral of Don Tyson, Springdale, Arkansas, January 8, 2011, obtained by author.

310 *Don Tyson left behind a company that reaped $28.4 billion:* Tyson Foods Annual Report 2010, Form 10-K, 17.

311 *On February 4, 2011, Donnie Smith woke up early:* Donnie Smith, CEO Tyson Foods, Earnings Call Transcript discussing Q1 2011 results, February 4, 2011.

311 *The unemployment rate was 9.7 percent:* "Unemployment rate and civilian labor force, January 2008–December 2010," http://www.bls.gov/opub/ted/2011/ted_20110111_data.htm. January 11, 2011.

311 *In the midst of all this, Donnie Smith had some very good news:* Donnie Smith, remarks on Earnings Call, February 4, 2011.

312 *Smith's prediction turned out to be correct:* "Tyson Reports Fourth Quarter and Fiscal Year 2011 Results," November 2011.

313 *After 2011, price hikes and production cuts became central to Tyson's business model:* Analysis by author of Tyson Foods Annual Reports for fiscal years 2007, 2008, 2009, 2010, 2011, 2012.

313 *The operating profit margins of the nation's top four meat companies doubled:* 2011 P&SP Annual Report, Packers and Stockyards Program, March 2012, 32.

313 *By the middle of 2012, the plan was working well:* "News Release, Tyson Reports Second Quarter and Six Months Fiscal 2012 Results," http://ir.tyson.com/phoenix.zhtml?c=65476&p=irol-newsArticle_Print&ID=1692164&highlight=, accessed April 19, 2013.

314 *But it is possible, using government data:* Analysis by the author and Casey Smith, University of Missouri student and IRE database researcher, of county-level income data provided by the U.S. Bureau of Economic Analysis.

317 *Berryville's First National Bank sits on a corner:* Robert West, interview by author, 2011.

318 *Tyson Foods used to recruit new contract farmers:* "Grow with Tyson: A Resource for Independent Growers for Tyson Foods, Inc.," http://www.growwithtyson.com/overview-of-contract-poultry-farming/, accessed April 19, 2013.

INDEX

ABOUT THE AUTHOR

Christopher Leonard was born and raised in Kansas City, Missouri. He is a fellow with The New America Foundation, a nonpartisan public policy institute in Washington, D.C. He is the former national agribusiness reporter for The Associated Press and a graduate of the University of Missouri School of Journalism. He lives outside Washington, D.C., with his family.

FOLLOW CHRISTOPHER LEONARD INSIDE ONE OF THE BIGGEST PRIVATE COMPANIES IN AMERICA...

"*Kochland* is a dazzling feat of investigative reporting and epic narrative writing, a tour de force that takes the reader deep inside the rise of a vastly powerful family corporation that has come to influence American workers, markets, elections, and the very ideas debated in our public square."

—Steve Coll, Pulitzer Prize–winning author of *Private Empire*

Available wherever books are sold or at SimonandSchuster.com

70378